KU-158-105

THE INTERNATIONAL DESIGN YEARBOOK
1989/1990

THE INTERNATIONAL

DESIGN YEARBOOK 1989/1990

EDITOR
OSCAR TUSQUETS BLANCA

GENERAL EDITOR
NONIE NIESEWAND

ASSISTANT EDITOR
CARRIE HAINES

THAMES AND HUDSON

The publisher and editors would like to thank the designers and manufacturers who submitted work for inclusion in this book; Peter and Junko Popham for their help in collecting Japanese contributions; Dragonfly Communications for their translation of Oscar Tusquets Blanca's essay, and the following photographers and copyright holders for use of their material:

Christian Affonso-Storz (3.3, 4); Gil Alkin (3.18); Ron Anderson (1.157); Anthrazit (5.8); Studio Azzurro (3.48, 50–53); Aldo Ballo (2.21; 3.77); Stefaan Beel (4.41–43); John H. Betts, Henry Dreyfuss Assoc. (5.31); Roger Birn (1.28); Bitetto-Chimenti (1.152, 153); Patrick Blake (5.26, 27); Daniele Bormolini (1.128, 139); Burns & Associates (1.124); Santi Caleca (1.24, 26; 2.35; 3.74; 5.3); A. Callari (1.75–78); Kelly Campbell (1.73, 74; 4.17); Carlo Cantini (3.43, 45); Joe Carlson Studio (1.34); Lluis Casals (page 8; 1.37, 85; 4.6–10); Celnick Studios (1.154–156); Centrokappa (1.144); Lisa Charles (3.44, 70); Cesare Colombo/Luciano Svegliado (2.43, 44, 51); Joseph Cosica Jr (1.31); David Crips (3.15, 16, 32); Deltaprint (5.38); Dissing & Weitling AS (5.50); Peter Dudley (1.29); Ego (3.1); Diego Erti (2.48); Maria Espeus (3.6–8; 4.25–27); Peter Fleissig (1.106); Peter Frank (1.9; 3.48); Studio Frei (1.53); John Ganci/Willem Rethmeier (1.112); David Gill (5.44); Decio Grassi (1.51); Alessandro Gui (1.15, 16); Bard Henriksen (1.136); Herlitz AG (5.52); Pete Hill (3.10); Hiroyuki Hirai (1.88; 2.41; 3.75, 76; 5.39, 51); Wilfried Hockmann (3.14); Ikea of Sweden (3.46); Impuls (1.41, 54, 86, 115, 142, 143); Lars Kaae (3.37); Wolfgang Karolinsky (2.34); Kaslov (2.22); Tadayuki Kawahito (5.1, 2); Howard Kingsnorth (1.12, 13); Idris Kolodziej (1.89–94); Shoichi Kondo (1.109–111); Alejandro Leveratto (1.140, 141); Rob Little (5.46, 47); Lorenzo Lucatelli (5.19, 20); Luceblù: Guido Guidi (1.18); Jan Magnussen (2.10); Natalie Mayer (1.11); Chris McElhinny/Antoon Meerman (1.108); Fujitsuka Mitsumasa (3.29, 31; 4.1); Tetsuya Miura (4.56, 63–65); Masahiro Mori (3.21–23); Neotù (1.2, 3); Ian O'Leary (5.18); Osram (2.13); Seppo Pailos (5.25); Hermann Payer (5.24); Tommaso Pellegrini (1.84; 3.24, 25); Studio Pointer (3.42); Louis Poulsen (2.11); Ramazzotti & Stucchi (1.25, 45, 47; 4.21); Gert Reinhardt (5.57); Rieker Studio (1.144); Peter Rose (5.13); Rosenthal AG (3.39, 40, 65, 66); Antoine Rozes (5.4, 5); Studio Schaub (4.18); Studio Hans Schrauwers (1.87); Rainer Schwesig (1.95, 97); Roberto Sellitto (1.72); Luciano Soave (1.123); Kazuo Sugiyama (3.20); A. Sunagawa (5.11); Sunstar Inc. (5.48); Yoshio Takase (2.33); H. Tamura (4.55, 57–61); Christopher Thomas (2.20); Unglee (3.72); Tom Vack (1.1, 8, 10, 43, 44, 61–63, 64; 4.62); Tom Vack/Corinne Pfister (2.15, 16, 20, 24; 3.30, 63); Luis Vells (1.38); Tucker Viemeister (2.17); Gerard Vlaar (2.8, 9); Tsutomu Wakatsuki (3.26, 27); Peter Weidlein (2.31, 32); Lynn Werner (1.57, 82, 83, 107, 118, 120); Wogg AG (1.117); Xylos (1.19); Yamagiwa Corp. (2.42); Zaccaria/Cortinovis (2.25–28); Andrea Zani (2.3).

First published in Great Britain in 1989
by Thames and Hudson Ltd, London

Copyright © 1989 General introduction, chapter introductions and commentaries Nonie Niesewand

Copyright © 1989 All other material John Calmann and King Ltd and Cross River Press Ltd

All rights reserved. No part of this publication may be reproduced or transmitted in any form or by any means, electronic or mechanical, including photocopy, recording or any other information storage and retrieval system, without prior permission in writing from the publisher

This book was produced by
John Calmann and King Ltd, London
Based on an original idea by
Stuart Durant

Designed by Fielding Rowinski, London
Typeset by Composing Operations, Kent
Origination by Toppan, Singapore
Printed in Italy

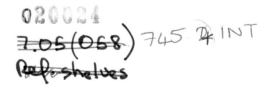

THE LIBRARY
EPSOM SCHOOL OF ART & DESIGN
ASHLEY ROAD
EPSOM, SURREY

020024
7.05(068) 745.2 INT
Ref shelves

CONTENTS

THE RULES OF DESIGN

OSCAR TUSQUETS BLANCA

I never thought I could spend three days opposite the British Museum and resist the temptation to go back and see the Parthenon frieze or the Ashurbanipal hunting lions, and yet it happened. Surrounded by assistants, buried under slides and catalogues, I spent that long London weekend glancing through the office window at the beautiful neo-Greek colonnade that had so moved me even as a child.

The task that prevented me from crossing the road consisted of selecting, out of the several thousand designs submitted, some 450 images; in other words, I was the only member of a jury that could award 450 prizes. I thought it would be easy; but after two and a half days I had only reduced the list to 900 and was still faced with the difficult and sad task of eliminating half of those. No doubt I have made some errors of judgement that history will not be long in laying at my door, but I shall explain the general criteria I applied.

When planning this yearbook, I imagined a film-maker of the 21st century who, wanting to set a film in the late Eighties, would refer to the book to find items that were introduced in that era and exemplified it. I therefore made the decision to exclude products that could not be bought in the marketplace. This *a priori*, which may seem severe and restrictive, requires justification: one feature that distinguishes the art of design from other arts, such as sculpture, is that designs can be repeatedly reproduced by machines or by artisans other than the designer. To continue my film theme, if we were making a film yearbook, we would naturally concentrate on this year's films and would not include scripts for proposed films. Prototypes and one-off pieces are like filmscripts: neither have yet passed the test of fire inherent to their disciplines – production and marketing. Likewise, an architecture yearbook would publish pictures of buildings that had been constructed, not drawings or plans.

I know that my friend and predecessor, Arata Isozaki, applied opposite criteria for *The International Design Yearbook 4*. His theory, surely the same as that of many other respected theoreticians, is that works seemingly unfeasible today often herald the reality of tomorrow. This prediction is an authentic dogma of the avant garde, but I personally feel it to be debatable today, even in the so-called "pure" arts. In the fortunately "contaminated," or applied, arts, it is contradicted every day. I do not see how today's electrifying publicity film spots could have originated in the painfully slow and tedious Video Art experiments of yesterday. Similarly, avant-garde objects and furniture exhibited yearly outside Milan during the Furniture Fair in an "All Night Long Party" seem to me to be repetitive and less exciting than certain items in the fair itself, of which they purport to be the antithesis. I should make clear, however, that although I do not usually find it exciting, such "sculptured" furniture can have its interest, even more so than beautiful design, but it belongs to a different discipline and must be subject to different rules.

Every good rule, of course, must have its exceptions! I have selected the occasional prototype or one-off design when it has seemed to be particularly new or suggestive or has clearly been designed with production in mind. An example is the series of creations developed around an enigmatic school in Berlin (see pages 56–59).

It seems clear to me that nowadays the most creative young designers often ignore the problems of production, usefulness and cost, which should be important aspects of their work. Top producers are more interested in marketing than in the product itself, often regarding it as more important to be on time for the next fair than to work patiently at improving the design. My own compelling need, for example, to revise prototype after prototype in order to achieve something acceptable begins to seem merely quaint and inconvenient. And the fantastic prices asked for furniture make me wonder how much relates to the materials and labour and how much to the advertising, the expensive paper for the useless catalogue, and the prawns for the well-attended cocktail reception.

Oscar Tusquets Blanca
Table, *Alada*
Glass, cast aluminium
H 70 cm (27½ in). W 130 cm
(51⅛ in). D 130 cm (51⅛ in)
Manufacturer: Casas, Spain

The best results are still obtained where a subtle dialogue is sustained between artist and manufacturer. This dialogue is essential; it cannot be improvized and it can easily be downgraded. It is based on mutual respect; on freedom, but with specific requirements; and on formality, but with fun and brightness. Although no one in Italy has emerged to take the place of those brilliant designers who erected a magic bridge between art and industry (Zanuso, Castiglioni, Magistretti . . .), their country is still undoubtedly in the forefront of design because it preserves such a dialogue. This approach does not work solely with Italy's national designers; its results can be seen in the work of guest designers from Japan, France, Czechoslovakia, Germany and Spain.

In the United States, however, design has disappeared because the dialogue has been abandoned in favour of commercial production of pieces at moderate prices. What is left of that distinctive American design that thrived until the Fifties? What has become of the Knoll and Herman Miller catalogues? What happened to Bertola, Eames and Noguchi?

Germany and France, the industrial giants of Europe, have not yet established themselves in this respect. There is the occasional young manufacturer, small and enthusiastic, and a handful of large industries that are just now embarking on tentative experiments in design. The Scandinavians continue with their "clean-cut" style – comfortable, healthy and straightforward, although they are now influenced somewhat by Memphis. Perhaps their only problem is that they are not currently in fashion.

Oscar Tusquets Blanca
Table, *Mesa Metarrigida*
Steel, plastic, glass
H 72 cm (28½ in). W 70 cm (27½ in).
D 70 cm (27½ in)
Manufacturer: BD Ediciones de diseño, Spain

The United Kingdom continues to nurture promising young designers and suggestive prototypes and ideas, but few industrial realities. My good friend, fashion designer Antonio Miró, said some time ago that although new ideas in dress come from England – the "punk" look, for instance – they are never marketed sucessfully there, whereas they are in France, Italy and Japan.

Japan and the East are the great challenge. Several years ago Mirella Clemencigh predicted in a conversation with me the staggering success of Japanese fashion. I was surprised but did not dismiss the possibility. Today I risk nothing in predicting the unstoppable rise of Japanese design; for the drawing together of design and fashion is already undeniable and perhaps irreversible. The Japanese have already produced some important designers; their interior design is original, and their curiosity about design in other countries remains boundless. I have chosen a few pieces of furniture from Japan and, more significantly, the most beautiful and original textiles.

There remains my own country, Spain. From a distance and in the context of worldwide comparison it does indeed appear that something coherent is emerging, not only because of the quality of certain designers, but also because of the almost miraculous conversion of several manufacturers.

I would like to make one final point. In making this selection, the only limits imposed by the publishers were in the number of pictures to be published. I have been greatly assisted by the advice and enthusiasm of the General Editor, Nonie Niesewand, but the sole responsibility for the final selection lies with me.

INTRODUCTION

NONIE NIESEWAND

Guest Editor Oscar Tusquets Blanca wanted this fifth volume of *The International Design Yearbook* to be a stylebook for a 21st-century film-maker. Here are the year's best domestic designs in furniture, lighting, textiles, tableware and products. Mass production is the key to this collection, in a book that serves as a catalogue of popular demands, not a gallery guide or a trend spotter. You can see why. An Agatha Christie thriller set in the Thirties would not have at the dining table the chairs that Salvador Dalí covered in chocolate, although that is when he presented them. The authenticity that Tusquets Blanca seeks calls for furniture that is commercially produced, rather than artworks, part-works or talking points.

Yet *The International Design Yearbook 5* also records the fact that some prototypes and one-offs blueprinted a year ago have made the laborious route into mass production. A sofa by Zaha Hadid, selected by last year's Guest Editor, Arata Isozaki, was a custom-built piece for an interior she had designed. Today her work is mass produced in moulded fibreglass by EDRA in Italy. Ron Arad, who named his London shop One-Off when everything he made was precisely that, now cuts steel to a template to weld in limited batch runs.

Mindful of these spin-offs from original designs, Tusquets Blanca has selected for this volume a few pieces that have obvious production potential. There is Svend Onø's prototype for a stainless steel tea set, as well as the distortions of everyday domesticity from the Berlin underground.

Leafing through this book for ideas, what would "post-Gutenberg man" make of the late 20th century? That the thrust of the aerodynamic age is imprinted upon domestic furniture is immediately obvious. Massimo Iosa Ghini's furniture hovers like spacecraft on landing gear; chairs from Starck put out moon-probe feet; Pallucco and Rivier's weirdly warped geometry twists furniture on its axis. This distinctive look of the decade can be seen in upholstery, too -- elongated and elevated by Zaha Hadid, Jasper Morrison and Dakota Jackson in projectile shapes far removed from the plumped-up, well-rounded, stuffed sofas of the past.

Wood is the favoured material for furniture. It is less crafted than machine-lathed, but has organic shapes that evolve rather than the angularity that results from dovetail jointing. This technology imparts curves that often owe something to Gaudí, as can be seen in Lazzeroni's Catalan collection for Cecotti. The revival of interest in wood – rather than steel, aluminium, lacquer or leather – raises a topical environmental issue addressed by some designers, such as Philippe Starck in his prose poem to plastic (see page 42). Nineteen eighty-eight was the year of weird weather patterns: sunlit winters in the Atlantic, snow in the Sahara, floods in Bangladesh and droughts in the Sudan. Indiscriminate felling of the tropical equatorial rainforest is one of the causes blamed for these disturbances. Environmental groups all over the world now lobby the International Timber Traders' Federation to ensure that any mahogany, teak, sapele, ramin, iroko or utile purchased for furniture is stamped with the declaration that it comes from a sustainable plantation. These are signs and portents of the late 20th century that it would be foolish to ignore.

Nineteen eighty-eight was also the year that Memphis died and, with it, Pop iconoclasm. Some say that the message from its founding father, Ettore Sottsass, became garbled or diluted by his followers, while others claim that its downfall lay in its marketing and price. Memphis is the cult of the decade that made the crossover into public consciousness – never was so little appreciated by so many. It is the look most widely copied today in the packaging of products. Oscar Tusquets Blanca gives it an epitaph that underlines his belief in the disciplines of production and marketing: "My creative processes are far removed from theirs; the way they design objects is similar to the design of clothes. This is what they think – if a sofa costs as much as a suit, why is it acceptable to create suits experimentally, even shockingly, not sofas? Every year they created something new, the fashion on the catwalk. They may have influenced the world, but the amount they've sold is laughable. What I do like about them is the sense of carefree liberty – a breath of fresh air."

To replace Pop packaging, there is a disquieting animal symbolism emerging in furniture and furnishings. The *Ara* light by Philippe Starck for Flos is inspired, he says, by elves' caps. Bulls' horns encircle the sitter on a Bořek Šípek chair for Driade. In Kita and Haring's clone-like light, electro-luminescent panels reveal the outline of a figure – moonwalker, or foetus? Nigel Coates summons up a *Genie* for his stool, while *Scaragoo* by Stefan Lindfors is the insect that glows, the latest species in lights by Ingo Maurer and his team. Branzi's fluorescent green-leaf lamp looks radioactive.

Tableware is also metamorphosing. The fusion between East and West in contemporary cuisine influences the design of cutlery, plates and vessels: Sergio Asti applies a rice-grain pattern in the Chinese manner to porcelain bowls for Ginori in Italy. During this decade, when nouvelle cuisine revolutionized the presentation of food, plate sizes increased inversely to the size of the portions. Big borders were added expansively (as well as expensively) by architects applying ornamentation for the first time. Now, in both pattern and shape, Western tableware owes something to classic Eastern simplicity.

Fabrics look homespun with a textured plainness, like those of the Japanese Junichi Arai, but in reality they are computer-controlled to test both the breaking point and the melting point of metal and plastic thread woven into wool, silk, cotton or synthetics. Even the traditionally screen-printed fabrics have colour and pattern applied in a way that owes more to art than to archives. Graphic illustrations, like those of Javier Mariscal for Marieta in Spain, retain their painterly, freehand quality despite being repeat patterns printed for mass production.

A new species has evolved within the design industry: the editor. VIA, the French equivalent of the UK's Design Council, paid tribute to this newcomer at their stand at the Paris Furniture Fair in 1988, with a collection dedicated to the "editeurs" who had had the pieces commercially produced. The editor finds gaps in the market and commissions creative works to fill them. These designs are produced by small specialist manufacturers, and are launched at commercial prices in a receptive market, but in controlled numbers – anywhere from 200 to 2,000. The assembling of the designs can be a creative process in itself. Manufacturers of hospital beds, for example, can produce tubular steel chair frames; banister turners can make a few thousand chair legs at odd times between their regular orders. Often this is the only way for a talented new designer to get into production; it is how Jasper Morrison began. Some big-name designers actually prefer to work for editors, since industrialists are congratulating themselves on past classics and avoiding new commissions because expensive factory tooling requires huge runs. Caution was the catchword to sum up the manufacturers' attitude in Milan in 1988. The editor can therefore be an important adjunct to the industry. Increasingly, innovative designs rather than safe runs of pedestrian pieces emerge solely because of an editor's confident production techniques and sound marketing practices.

Even in Germany, the most highly industrialized country, there is a breakaway movement of artistic collectives, such as Berliner Zimmer and Designwerkstatt, which now show limited batch productions at the Cologne Furniture Fair. Their designs, as much as their attitude, subvert the old Bauhaus maxims of logicality, construction technique and utilitarian quality. Denmark has traditionally realized contemporary designs in specialist factories on small production runs, which could be why their industry is enjoying something of a revival. Spain, only recently awakened from sleep within Europe, accepts new challenges by commissioning top designers and producing their designs with hand finishes and adaptations. The French designer Marie-Christine Dorner comments on this particular Spanish quality in her work for Scarabat.

Tusquets Blanca is the right synthesis of trained artist, architect and designer to make a selection that ignores furniture as art, or art as interior design. He himself studied art before training as an architect, and his early days of working in the forefront of Catalan design with architects Federico Correa and Alfonsa Milà have left their mark. To design a room without controlling the furniture is not architecture, he believes. In all his work he bears in mind what the interior will be like: "Architecture doesn't go from the outside in. It's a dialectic between the outside and in, the inside and out. All architecture works better from the inside out."

This kind of thinking is needed to confront the fads of fashion that afflict the designer today. The movie *Beetlejuice* played to fuller houses in Milan during the 1988 Furniture Fair than the furniture exhibits. This ghost story, set in a Gothic house in Connecticut, features a done-to-death décor that production designer Bo Welch describes as "embodying the ideas of Richard Meier, Frank Gehry and Philippe Stark, teetering on the brink of caricature." He labels this style Post-Mortemism. This makeover of a homespun couple's old house to modern design is so appalling that it brings back their ghosts to haunt it in protest. In another 1988 film, *Wall Street*, the new designs in a stockbroker's apartment signal excess, not success. The set designer for the film version of Tom Wolfe's bestseller *Bonfire of the Vanities* will face a major challenge from the author's dismissive descriptions of Eighties interior design, New York style.

Once design gave products a competitive advantage. Now it is too often oversold and under-performed, the ephemeral tool of the merely fashion-conscious. In a Spenglerian sense, it has come full circle within a decade, subject to its own cycle of growth and decay. This year's book reflects the period of transition from Memphis to Phoenix. Putting design back into full-scale production, rather than into vignettes, one-offs or sculptures, makes it more commercial and less subject to passing fashion. What lies on the cutting room floor after all this judicious editing, of course, could be the subject of another book.

Abbreviations
Apart from H (height), L (length), W (width),
D (depth) and Di (diameter), the following
abbreviations are used in the book:
ABS acrylo-butyl styrene
LCD liquid crystal display
MDF medium-density fibreboard

FURNITURE 1

Every year the media event in the furniture business, the Furniture Fair in Milan, anticipates the demands of a consumer-hungry society geared to instant fashion. The 1980s end with the clear indication that the industry is unable to cope with these whims. People simply do not change their furnishings as they do their clothes. Only the classics can survive, or else the reasonably priced chair on a big production run, like Starck's *Dr Glob* for Kartell. The big manufacturers – Cassina, B & B Italia, Zanotta – were conspicuous only by their cautiousness in launching new designs for 1989. Self-congratulatory stands evoked the past with pieces that are still in production. Memphis died, the daring cult that spearheaded many an imitation. Experienced designers such as Magistretti, Castiglioni and Bellini returned to their drawing boards to work at buildings rather than products. Only Pallucco and Rivier grabbed the headlines, with four startling designs and their lucrative reproductions of Fortuny lamps and Herbst chairs. It is easy to chart this past decade as one when fashion consumerism moved into the furniture business. It was 1980 when Vico Magistretti introduced his *Sindbad* (after the character in *The Arabian Nights* who could not be unseated) by tossing a cloak over a sofa and chairs for Cassina. This fashion element initiated a long run of imitative, ready-to-seat collections, including loose covers for seasonal changes, until the industry could not sustain any more changes of direction. Though reporters were disappointed at the end of fairs in Milan, Valencia, Paris and Cologne, there is a quiet optimism among retailers, who see the collections as commercial enough to appear in rooms around the world, rather than just museums.

The serious business of turning out commercial furniture is resolved by a crop of this year's designers, who are far removed from the art world. Marie-Christine Dorner, Jasper Morrison and Zaha Hadid show sleek forms marshalling good upholstery, and there is comfort to be found in their pieces. Wood has returned for furniture, always a sure sign of investment. Nigel Coates uses it in his *Genie* stool, a beautifully made piece that combines an 18th-century artifice with a contemporary decadence. Lazzeroni turns to Gaudí's sinuous forms.

Two schools of thought are reconciled: furniture as art, and furniture for a real home. In reality there is not as great a difference between them as might appear. Ron Arad's outrageous one-offs are made available in limited batch production; Vitra encourages workmanlike classics for offices, yet also commissions special editions of furniture by original talents such as Šipek, Mendini and Arad. The German avant garde look to the past, strip it of certain elements, and parade it as something new. Torchlights emblazoned on rough rafters from Brandolini are put into interiors that have a disquieting cosiness, while Designwerkstatt subverts the Bauhaus in tubular steel and leather.

1

Bořek Šípek
Chair, *Ota Otanek*
Wood, steel, copper
H 74 cm (29 in). W 52 cm (20½ in).
D 50 cm (19⅝ in)
Manufacturer: Vitra International,
Switzerland

Bořek Šípek
Table, *Satomi San*
Metal, brass, wood
A small table for games or a stand for
flowers. Limited batch production
H 76 cm (30 in). W 80 cm (31½ in).
L 80 cm (31½ in)
Manufacturer: Neotù, France

2

4

Bořek Šípek
Table, *Ritual*
Black-stained beech and ash, brass,
nickel-plated brass
H 75 cm (29½ in). W 70 cm (27½ in).
L 70 cm (27½ in)
Manufacturer: Leitner Interior Design,
Austria

3

Bořek Šípek
Chair, *Ernst und Guduld*
Ebony, padouk, maple
Limited batch production
H 70 cm (27½ in). W 60 cm (23½ in).
D 45 cm (17¾ in)
Manufacturer: Neotù, France

5

Bořek Šípek
Chair, *Gudrun am Leineufer*
Lacquered beech
H 85.5 cm (33⅝ in). W 69 cm (27⅛ in).
D 37.5 cm (14⅝ in)
Limited batch production
Manufacturer: Leitner Interior Design,
Austria

6

Bořek Šípek
Chair, *Prorok*
Rattan, wood
H 91 cm (35⅞ in). W 85 cm (33½ in).
D 68.5 cm (27 in). Height to seat 44 cm
(17¼ in)
Manufacturer: Driade, Italy

Organic shapes that look handcrafted, yet are factory assembled, are characteristic of the work of Czech-born émigré Bořek Šípek. His ability to weld, upholster, carve, cast metal, throw pots and blow glass shows in the confident design of every material he puts into production. He makes his own models and prototypes, and often personally supervises the tooling-up of the factory. His objects have a life of their own that subverts industrial mechanism. Instead of the rigours of geometry, they display a sinuous line that comes from his assured handling of the material.

To make the furniture for Driade, Šípek went to Manila in the Philippines to learn to plait and weave rattan. Great bulls' horns encircle the sitter, while the feet seem to paw at the ground. "Tradition is important to me," he says. "Not traditional forms, but in the sense of mythology."

Each piece seems to have its own life force. Look at the strange reinterpretation of the conventional button-back Chesterfield sofa. When his triangular tables for the Austrian company Leitner are lined up, they interlock neatly like the teeth of a zip fastener.

"A chair," he believes, "is not an interpretation with your brain on how to use it, but a challenge to your emotions on how to love it. So it's not about ergonomic comfort, but your spirit."

7

Bořek Šípek
Chair, *Helena*
Rattan
H 80 cm (31½ in). W 52 cm (20½ in).
D 55 cm (21½ in). Height to seat 47 cm
(18½ in)
Manufacturer: Driade, Italy

Bořek Šípek
Divan, *Marta*
Cherry heartwood, ebony veneer,
polyurethane foam, quilted leather
H 87.5 cm (34⅜ in). D 92 cm (36 in).
L 200.5 cm (78⅞ in). Height to seat
45 cm (17¾ in)
Manufacturer: Driade, Italy

8

9

Bořek Šípek
Table, *In Eile*
Maple, brass, lacquered MDF
H 72 cm (28½ in). W 75 cm (29½ in).
L 180 cm (70⅝ in)
Manufacturer: Anthologie Quartett,
West Germany

Ron Arad's inventive mind and practical craftsmanship have been put to play in metal, in rubber and now, for the first time, in wood. This collection of pieces, each designed to a different commission, shows his remarkable versatility.

Steel is an industrial material better suited to constructional supports than to these fluid, elegant lines. Arad explains: "In the USSR there is a fable called catching a lion. Well, there aren't too many lions around in the USSR so they say that when you catch a bear, beat it until it becomes a lion." He has tigue-welded stainless steel to mild steel, butted against each other for his *Volumes* collection for Vitra Special Editions. For *Tinker*, red gussets inserted along the edges, and then flame-welded to give the paint a blistered contour, signify a new production method. Although Arad's shop is called One-Off, this way of cutting identical patterns, and then welding in the gussets by hand to give each piece individuality, creates (like haute couture) a limited production line. The aptly named *Crust* chair for Sawaya & Moroni, with rubber sandwiched between steamed plywood sides in a comfortable club chair shape, is intended to be made in quantity.

"In the last five years," according to Arad, "people who have freed themselves from mainstream industry have produced more things. Simultaneously, industry is becoming interested in those designs. Post-Apocalyptic is a label frequently tagged to my work . . . I ask people what it means. To me, Post-Apocalyptic means it should look as though it had been destroyed, whereas my furniture looks as if it has just been created." Although it is true that nothing in Arad's work is made from salvaged materials, his forms are jagged and rent, as if they had gone through some elemental restructuring.

10

Ron Arad
School Chair
Aluminium, rubber
H 97 cm (38¼ in). W 35 cm (13¾ in).
D 50 cm (19⅝ in)
Manufacturer: Vitra International,
Switzerland

11

Ron Arad
Armchair, *Crust*
Plywood, rubber
H 73 cm (28¾ in). W 97 cm (38¼ in).
D 89 cm (35 in)
Manufacturer: Sawaya & Moroni, Italy

Ron Arad
Chair, *Tinker*
Mild steel, stainless steel, panel beaten
Limited batch production
H 95 cm (37½ in). W 50 cm (19⅝ in).
D 80 cm (31½ in)
Manufacturer: One-Off, UK

Ron Arad
Rocking chair, *Big Easy Volume 1*
Mild steel, stainless steel
A hollow structure partly filled with sand
which can be shifted to alter the centre
of gravity; distorted reflections are
emphasized by the chair's movement.
Limited batch production
H 75 cm (29½ in). W 84 cm (33 in).
D 118 cm (46½ in)
Manufacturer: One-Off, UK

Ron Arad
Screen, *Fortuni*
Aluminium, steel
Limited batch production
H 210 cm (82⅝ in). W 80 cm (31½ in).
D 30 cm (11⅞ in)
Manufacturer: One-Off, UK

15

**Perry A. King and Santiago
Miranda**
Desk, from the *Lenikai* collection
Portoro and pink marble
Limited batch production
H 73 cm (28¾ in). W 160 cm (63 in).
D 80 cm (31½ in)
Manufacturer: Lombardi Project, Italy

16

Perry A. King and Santiago
Miranda
Dining table, from the *Lenikai* collection
White Carrara marble
Limited batch production
H 75 cm (29½ in). Di 120 cm (47¼ in)
Manufacturer: Lombardi Project, Italy

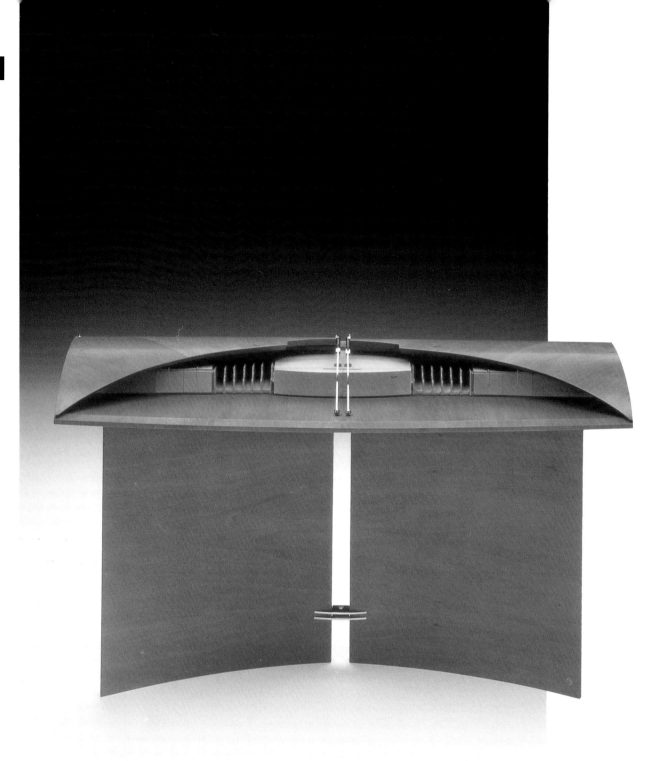

Jaime Tresserra Clapés
Desk, *Carlton House Butterfly*
Walnut, sycamore, nickel-plated metals,
leather details
Limited batch production
H 84 cm (33 in). W 144 cm (56⅝ in).
L 45 cm (17¾ in)
Manufacturer: J. Tresserra Design, Spain

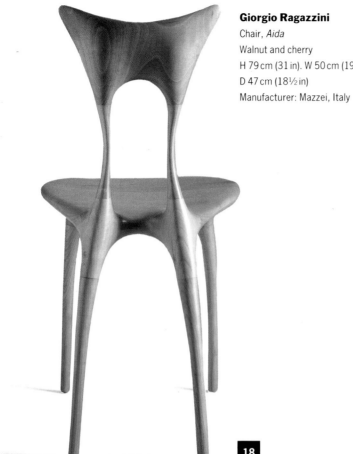

Giorgio Ragazzini
Chair, *Aida*
Walnut and cherry
H 79 cm (31 in). W 50 cm (19⅝ in).
D 47 cm (18½ in)
Manufacturer: Mazzei, Italy

18

Xylos
Low table, *Pomme*
Solid wood and veneer, polyurethane
varnish
Limited batch production
H 27 cm (10½ in). W 97 cm (38¼ in).
L 113 cm (44⅝ in)
Manufacturer: Xylos, France

19

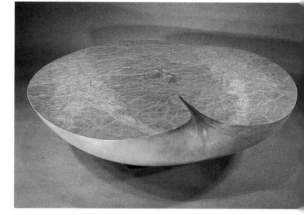

20

Roberto Lazzeroni
Table, *Perro Cansado*
Chair, *Chumbera Primera*
Both from the *Dedos Tenidos* collection
Cherry
Limited batch production
Table: H 75 cm (29½ in). W 191 cm
(75 in). D 93 cm (36½ in)
Chair: H 45 cm (17¾ in). W 40 cm
(15¾ in). D 42 cm (16½ in)
Manufacturer: Ceccotti, Italy

Bold sculptural shapes in fruitwoods attracted a great deal of attention in 1988 as cabinetry came back into fashion. The Italian company Cecotti has introduced this collection designed by Roberto Lazzeroni. Its Art Nouveau table and chair, along with a curvaceous chest of drawers and a spindle-back chair and settee, pay open homage to Catalonia, its seminal architect Antoni Gaudí, and to the Italian Carlo Mollino. Made in solid cherrywood, their organic forms epitomize the new interest in shapeliness and expressionism.

21

Mikael and Elisabeth Goldstein
Desk, *Pamigo*
Padouk, padouk veneer
H 86 cm (33⅞ in). W 86 cm (33⅞ in).
L 135 cm (53¼ in)
Manufacturer: Migoli, Sweden

22

Massimo Morozzi
Cabinet, *Palio*
Black-lacquered acacia
H 191 cm (75 in). W 78 cm (30¾ in).
D 78 cm (30¾ in)
Manufacturer: Giorgetti, Italy

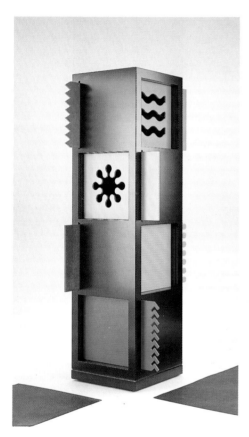

The euthanasia inflicted on the Memphis collection by its founder Ettore Sottsass in the summer of 1988 has passed unmourned. Yet in industrial design and in furniture, the many post-Memphis submissions to this edition of *The International Design Yearbook* bear witness to the collection's continuing influence. Memphis will forever be a chapter in Italian design history. Under Sottsass it became the symbol of culture in a severe design world. These icons of an excessive era took images from Pop – oversized, colourful, playful and irreverent – and produced them at prices few could afford.

23

Massimo Morozzi
Chairs, *Clic*
Plywood
All the parts are held together with a
special Velcro adhesive.
H 70 cm (27½ in). W 42 cm (16½ in).
D 42 cm (16½ in)
Manufacturer: Sedie, Italy

Ettore Sottsass
Dining table, *4 Gopuram*
Pear wood, lacquered wood
Limited batch production
H 74 cm (29 in). W 124 cm (48¾ in).
L 228 cm (89⅝ in)
Manufacturer: Design Gallery, Italy

24

The problem with Memphis lay in the growing difference of view between the master and his followers. At the Design Gallery in the Via Manzoni, Milan, thousands thronged reverentially past the Memphis collection a decade ago. In 1988 it hosted a curious exhibition of Sottsass's *Bharata* furniture and objects: some new limited editions, others from the Golden Eye exhibition at the Cooper-Hewitt Museum in New York. "Bharata" is Sanskrit for India, and in these pieces you can see references to Hindu temple architecture.

Sottsass's superiority, however, does not lie in style (nor lack of it), nor in any other copiable or communicable quality. It consists rather in the expression of a wide knowledge, extracted from many cultures. Now in his 73rd year, he still visits India regularly. His bowls and vessels in bronze and copper were hand-beaten there. The furniture was made in Italy in editions of twelve, to order. He has dedicated the collection to Indian craftsmen, knowing that, as he puts it, "their interminable encyclopedia of rules, knowledge and nostalgia will disappear one day, softly, so softly, goodness knows where." Let us hope that the same fate, or *dharma*, does not happen to the Memphis legacy.

Ettore Sottsass
Corner cupboard, *Porta Nuova*
Plywood, lacquered beech, anodized aluminium, MDF
H 210 cm (82⅝ in). W 105 cm (41½ in).
D 53 cm (20⅞ in)
Manufacturer: Zanotta, Italy

25

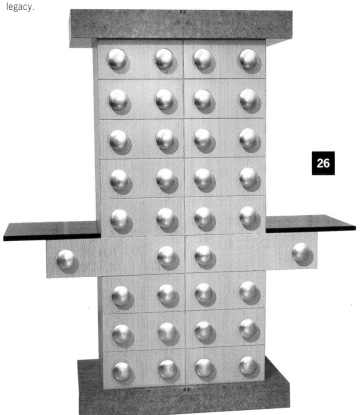

26

27

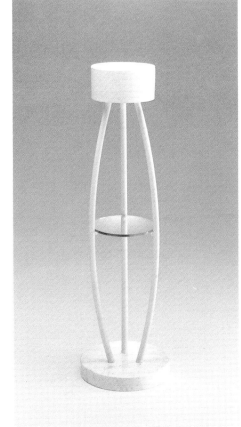

Ettore Sottsass
Cabinet, *Mobile Giallo*
Wood, briar, gilded wooden knobs
H 146 cm (57½ in). W 46 cm (18 in).
L 132 cm (51⅞ in)
Manufacturer: Design Gallery, Italy

Ettore Sottsass
Vase stand, *Ettore*
Carrara marble, stove-enamelled steel,
8 mm glass, ceramic
The intermediate glass top and vase container are removable.
H 131 cm (51½ in). W 39 cm (15⅜ in).
H of vase stand 15 cm (6 in).
Di 30 cm (11⅞ in)
Manufacturer: Zanotta, Italy

John Dunnigan
Chairs, *8616*
Purpleheart, ebonized imbuya, polished
aluminium, handpainted lamous
The hand-painting is by Wahlworks in
collaboration with John Dunnigan.
One-off
H 86.5 cm (34 in). W 58.5 cm (23 in).
L 66 cm (26 in)
Manufacturer: Dunnigan, USA

28

29

Peter S. Dudley
Desk, *Draped Desk*
Mahogany, curly maple, calfskin
Prototype
H 76 cm (30 in). W 79 cm (31 in).
L 165 cm (65 in)
Manufacturer: Peter S. Dudley, USA

30

**Studio Naço: Marcelos Julia
Lagares and Denis Conrady**
Armchair, *Belford*
Wood, leather, polished aluminium
H 82 cm (32¼ in). W 45 cm (17¾ in).
D 45 cm (17¾ in)
Manufacturer: Studio Naço, France

31

Nancy Robbins
Chair, *New York*
Wood, polyurethane foam, polyester
upholstery
H 78 cm (30¾ in). W 68 cm (26¾ in).
D 75 cm (29½ in)
Manufacturer: Cycsa, Spain

32

Nancy Robbins
Chair, *Jazz*
Wood, polyurethane foam, polyester
upholstery
H 84 cm (33 in). W 90 cm (35½ in).
D 88 cm (34⅝ in)
Manufacturer: Cycsa, Spain

33

Christian Ploderer
Armchair, *Altea*
Metal, wood, chrome, leather
H 77 cm (30¼ in). W 84 cm (33 in).
D 73 cm (28¾ in)
Manufacturer: Franz Wittmann, Austria

34

John Caldwell
Chair
Oak
Prototype
H 87 cm (34¼ in). W 55 cm (21½ in).
D 60 cm (23½ in)
Manufacturer: Thonet/Madison, USA

Architetti Associati: Vittorio Gregotti, Lodovico Meneghetti and Giotto Stoppino

Chair, *Cavour*
Tanganyikan walnut laminate, elastic rubber belts, polyurethane foam, calf leather
Originally designed in 1953.
H 85 cm (33½ in). W 56 cm (22 in).
D 56 cm (22 in). Height to seat 48 cm
(18⅞ in)
Manufacturer: Poltrona Frau, Italy

35

36

Hans J. Wegner
Stacking chair, V
Ash, plywood
Prototype
H 80 cm (31½ in). W 56 cm (22 in).
D 56 cm (22 in)
Manufacturer: P.P. Møbler, Denmark

Pete Sans
Armchair, *Sillón Coqueta*
Chromed steel tubing, seat and back of walnut-colour varnished rattan, leather brace
H 92 cm (36 in). W 64 cm (25⅛ in).
D 94 cm (37 in)
Manufacturer: BD Ediciones de diseño, Spain

Jean-Michel Cornu
Table, *French Leg*
Painted iron, wood
H 75.5 cm (29½ in). W 90 cm (35½ in).
D 90 cm (35½ in)
Manufacturer: Santa & Cole, Spain

Pete Sans
Trolley, *Aleta*
Iron, ash
H 56 cm (22 in). W 60 cm (23½ in).
D 90 cm (35½ in). Di 80 cm (31½ in)
Manufacturer: Mobles 114, Spain

40

Joey Mancini
Chair, *Woogie*
Rattan, chrome
H 79 cm (31 in). W 61 cm (24 in). D 73 cm
(28¾ in). Height to seat 43 cm (16⅞ in)
Manufacturer: Pierantonio Bonacina,
Italy

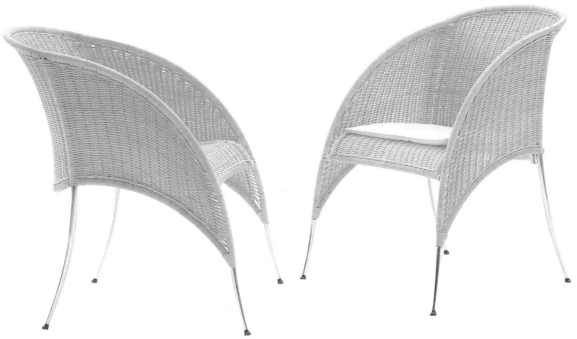

41

Pepe Cortés
Side table, *Zahra T2040*
Teak with natural varnish or black-
lacquered beech, metal
H 50 cm (19⅝ in). W 50 cm (19⅝ in).
D 50 cm (19⅝ in)
Manufacturer: Grupo T, Spain

Oscar Tusquets Blanca
Tilting armchair with writing arm, *Vaivén*
Steel, cast iron, wood, polyurethane
H 110 cm (43¼ in). W 105 cm (41½ in).
D 140 cm (55⅛ in)
Manufacturer: Casas, Spain

42

43

Oscar Tusquets Blanca
Table, *Astrolabio*
Cast iron, galvanized tubular steel with
anti-oxydate protection, brass, glass
A table for interior and exterior use.
H 72 cm (28½ in). Di 54 cm (21¼ in);
90 cm (35½ in) and 116 cm (45¾ in)
Manufacturer: Driade, Italy

44

Oscar Tusquets Blanca
Stacking chair, *Abanica*
Aluminium, iron, rattan
H 87.5 cm (34½ in). W 52 cm (20½ in).
D 55.5 cm (21⅝ in). Height to seat
47.5 cm (18¾ in)
Manufacturer: Driade, Italy

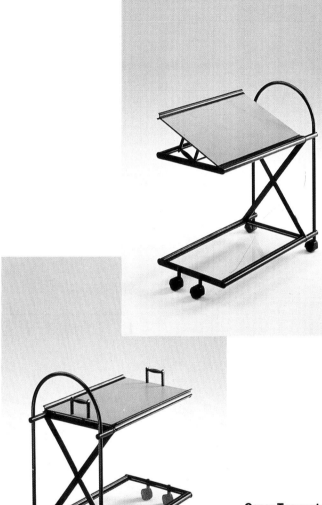

45

Oscar Tusquets Blanca
Trolley/reading stand, *Carrito*
Stove-enamelled steel, laminate, glass
The top tray is removable.
H 84 cm (33 in). D 45 cm (17¾ in).
L 82 cm (32¼ in)
Manufacturer: Zanotta, Italy

Bruno Munari
Chair for very short visits, *Munaria 1*
Walnut frame with inlays, anodized
aluminium seat
Designed in 1945 and now produced in
nine signed and numbered pieces.
H 110 cm (43¼ in). W 35 cm (13¾ in).
D 20 cm (7⅞ in)
Manufacturer: Zanotta, Italy

46

Bruno Munari
Chair, *Munaria 2*
Brass, walnut, velvet upholstery
Designed in 1937 and now produced in
nine signed and numbered pieces.
H 80 cm (31½ in). W 44 cm (17¼ in).
D 57 cm (22⅜ in)
Manufacturer: Zanotta, Italy

47

48

Gemma Bernal and Ramon Isern
Chair, *Fina T-2075*
Metal frame, upholstered
H 85 cm (33½ in). W 40 cm (15¾ in).
D 37 cm (14½ in)
Manufacturer: Grupo T, Spain

**Giulio Cappellini, Rodolfo
Dordoni and Paola Navone**
Chair, *Art.600* from the *Mondo* collection
Stained wood
Re-edition of a chair used in the tea
rooms of Shanghai in the 1930s.
H 85 cm (33½ in). W 35 cm (13¾ in).
D 43 cm (16⅞ in)
Manufacturer: Mondo, Italy

49

The family-owned Italian company Cappellini mixes the work of designers from many different cultures with an authoritative, workmanlike stamp. The company put into full-scale production the wavy S-bend chest of drawers, *Side 1, Side 2*, designed by Shiro Kuramata in 1986, which has come to symbolize the 1980s and is now used to advertise Carlsberg beer with the catchline: "Designed by Kuramata undoubtedly, influenced by Carlsberg Export, possibly?" The persuasive power of good, original design is increasingly used to give cachet to popular products.

The Cappellinis' intention is to make their collection "even more international, and to create pieces that are the productive response to the stimuli of the avant-garde." Home-grown talent Michele Barro has remodelled the classic chair with great delicacy, achieving his desire to combine formality and lightness.

Michele Barro
Chair, *Chiavari*
Metal, aluminium, beech, leather
H 76 cm (30 in). W 78 cm (30¾ in).
D 79 cm (31 in)
Manufacturer: Cappellini, Italy

50

A secondary collection, *Mondo*, was introduced by Cappellini along with their *Déjà-Vu* collection of rattan furniture in 1987. An update of Chinese Chippendale in bold colour, it focusses on comfort and liveability, tapping in to nostalgia but avoiding repro or kitsch; it is the furniture equivalent of the newly fashionable *cuisine grand'mère*.

Giulio Cappellini, Paola Navone and Rodolfo Dordoni set out to trace ideas disconnected from Western design, "to discover and salvage lost or unused craftsmanship and stimulate collective memories." Memories of China are evoked in cross-breeds of pagoda with cupboard, mahjong table with coffee-table, throne with chair, as well as in some bold rugs with signs and symbols of the Orient. There is a kimono-stand redesigned as a suit rack, and a chest of drawers in the form of a staircase from a 1930s Shanhia tea-room. No nails are used, only butterfly joints, and the wood is sanded to bring up the grain, then stained in green and blue, with a matt finish to enhance the wood. The technique has little to do with the decorative Orientalism favoured in Europe at the end of the 19th century. The Mondo team offers, in the end, "a gentle alteration of the original information."

51

**Achille and Pier Giacomo
Castiglioni**
Display unit, *Rampa*
Walnut, glass
Originally designed in 1964.
H 130 cm (51⅛ in). D 90 cm (35½ in).
L 102 cm (40⅜ in)
Manufacturer: Bernini, Italy

52

Mario Bellini
Storage unit, *Onda Quadra* collection
Wood, glass, 18 carat gold-plated brass
A collection of separate furniture
elements which can be free-standing or
positioned against a wall in a variety of
arrangements. Each unit turns
independently through 360 degrees.
H 25.8 cm (10⅛ in) to 55.8 cm (21¾ in).
W 73 cm (28¾ in) to 173.6 cm (68½ in).
D 24 cm (9⅜ in) to 50 cm (19⅝ in)
Manufacturer: Acerbis, Italy

Both innovative and classic, Mario Bellini's designs show a strong concern for tradition, together with what he calls "Western habitative culture." He is as well known for his *Cab* series of leather chairs for Cassina as for his Vitra office collection which includes the *Persona*, *Figura* and *Imago* chairs. Now he has introduced a storage system for the home that harks back to post-war Italian Rationalism, which was concerned with mass production rather than the monumentalism of the Mussolini years.

The *Onda Quadra* system for Acerbis is tooled with traditional cabinetry skills in briarwood, and depends on pivotal engineering to rotate the modular sections. The overall dimensions of the cube compartments on each shelf have been chosen on the basis of the size of books, magazines and objects in daily use. The system is enormously flexible: not only the shelves but even individual cubes swivel, with the option of doors that also turn to reveal either a concave or a convex front. The system can make a workmanlike wall of storage, with just the end pieces turning to house electronic equipment, or it can be a freestanding piece, though Bellini is dismissive of sculptural furniture as art. In an editorial in *Domus* he wrote: "A chair by Le Corbusier is a chair, and to cease to be one it would have to be signed by Duchamp and put on a pedestal like the celebrated bottle rack."

53

Mario Bellini
Chair, *Onda*
Steel, upholstery
Cantilevered chair made stable by
sweeping the form to the floor.
H 86 cm (33⅞ in). W 55 cm (21½ in).
D 47 cm (18½ in)
Manufacturer: Vitra International,
Switzerland

54

55

Jorge Pensi
Chair, *Toledo*
Aluminium
H 76 cm (30 in). W 55 cm (21½ in).
D 54 cm (21¼ in)
Manufacturer: Amat, Spain

Paolo Deganello
Table, *Acubici Uno*
Metal, glass
H 72 cm (28½ in). W 100 cm (39½ in).
L 200 cm (78¾ in)
Manufacturer: Cidue, Italy

56

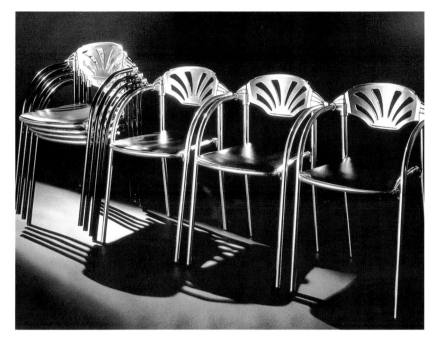

Studio Simonetti
Stacking chair, *Alisea*
Cast aluminium, leather
H 77 cm (30¼ in). W 51 cm (20 in).
D 52 cm (20½ in)
Manufacturer: Bros's, Italy

Martin Ryan
Chair, *Queen Bess*
Mild steel, perforated steel, polyester
coating
For outdoor use.
H 86 cm (33⅞ in). W 50.8 cm (19⅞ in).
D 49.5 cm (19½ in). Seat Di 40 cm
(15¾ in)
Manufacturer: Portfolio, UK

57

58

Jean-Michel Wilmotte
Garden chair, *La Fontaine*
Iron wire
H 74 cm (29 in). W 45 cm (17¾ in).
D 55 cm (21½ in). Di of seat 38 cm (15 in)
Manufacturer: Tebong, France

Philippe Starck had a strong showing worldwide in 1988–89. Apart from the six chairs shown here, he designed cutlery for Sasaki, and the *Arà* light for Flos, which introduced the horn shape (or "elves' cap," as he calls it) that pops up on many of his designs, from firedogs to doorknobs. Starck's chairs still startle with their simplicity and originality, as can be seen in his *Lilla Hunter* for the French company XO, in his new range for Driade, and in his enthusiasm for plastic in the stacking chair for Kartell. His curvaceous *Lola Mundo* chair for Driade does double duty: the back flips down to rest on its studs and the chair becomes a table.

Dr Glob has a steel frame and back legs with a plastic front and seat. Starck maintains that plastic is the only ecological answer to the increasing shortage of wood; a timely statement in view of the depletion of the tropical rainforest. He even wrote a prose poem about it (below).

° **59**

Philippe Starck
Stacking chair, *Lilla Hunter*
Tubular steel, PVC, pearwood
H 72 cm (28½ in). W 51 cm (20 in).
D 52 cm (20½ in)
Manufacturer: XO, France

I dream weird dreams
I dream of chairs
Rather than weep
I have made them my trade
While on a Paris–Tokyo flight
– too long – I dreamt of a small solid chair,
so serviceable and considerate,
she wanted to be plastic
and not kill trees.

60

Philippe Starck
Stacking chair, *Dr Glob*
Polypropylene, steel tubing
H 46 cm (18 in). W 47.5 cm (18¾ in).
D 48 cm (18⅞ in)
Manufacturer: Kartell, Italy

Philippe Starck
Stacking chair, *Romantica*
Anodized moulded and sheet aluminium
A chair suitable for interior or exterior use.
H 85.4 cm (35⅝ in). W 42.7 cm (16⅝ in).
D 62.5 cm (24½ in). Height to seat
44.6 cm (17⅝ in)
Manufacturer: Driade, Italy

61

Philippe Starck
Chair, *44*
Beech, ebony heartwood, wood veneer
H 85.5 cm (33⅝ in). W 47 cm (18½ in).
D 51 cm (20 in). Height to seat 45 cm
(17¾ in)
Manufacturer: Driade, Italy

62

63

Philippe Starck
Dining chair/side table, *Lola Mundo*
Ash, polished aluminium, black chromed
steel, rubber
H 84.5 cm (33⅜ in) or 48.5 cm (19 in).
W 33.5 cm (13½ in). D 53 cm (20⅞ in).
Height to seat 46 cm (18 in)
Manufacturer: Driade, Italy

Alessandro Mendini has been described as a designer who, with every collection, challenges conventional thinking. He pushes against mainstream fashion, sometimes going to outrageous lengths while displaying a very precise knowledge of the architectural orders. His startling pieces look strangely unfamiliar, yet they are destined, by their classicism, to become timeless.

Always critical, this softly spoken architect was the most influential observer of Italian design between 1970 and 1985 when he was editor of *Domus*, *Modo* and *Casabella*. In the wake of Post-Modernism with all its fallen idols and icons, amid fads and fashions that could have come from the theatrical props box, Mendini's individual voice could be heard through the language of his design – exemplified by his *Ollo* collection of furniture and textiles in the Museo Alchemia, Milan.

Mendini's commercialism and sense of colour and fun, combined with functionalism and a formal architectural approach, make his furniture memorable. In this collection for Vitra, which was inspired by travels in Brazil, he partners two sofas and a chair in colour and shape. The conventional three-piece suite is lightened in an exuberant fashion.

Alessandro Mendini

Sofa and armchair, *Maracatu*
Wood, upholstery
H 88 cm (34⅝ in). W 166 cm (65⅜ in).
and 94 cm (37 in). D 80 cm (31½ in)
Manufacturer: Vitra International,
Switzerland

64

Rolf Fehlbaum, Swiss President of Vitra, is a patron of the arts, 1990s style. He sells designs by Charles Eames, George Nelson and Mario Bellini to executive offices worldwide, and uses the profits on a collection of over 500 pieces of modern furniture, housed in the Museum of Modern Design in Switzerland, and on limited editions of artists' and architects' furniture. The choice for the limited editions is his – "design by a committee is a disaster," he remarks. It began in 1988 with Ron Arad, Richard Artschwager, Scott Burton, Paolo Deganello, Frank Gehry, Shiro Kuramata, Gaetano Pesce, Denis Santachiara and Ettore Sottsass. In 1989 he added designs by Mendini and Bořek Šipek, and a table by the German Ginbande group. Each item is dated with the years of conception and production.

Fehlbaum explains his unconventional choice: "The routine production of office furniture leaves little room for experimental design. So we commission a series that does not have to fall in line with an existing product range, nor be fixed to a single design tendency. There are no rules and regulations imposed by marked penetration that lead to barriers against creative experiment." But he stresses that these creative experiments are functional pieces of furniture, not works of art.

Alessandro Mendini

Folding chair, *Margherita*
Epoxy-painted tubular metal frame,
chrome-plated metal
H 82 cm (32¼ in). W 43 cm (16⅞ in).
D 50 cm (19⅝ in)
Manufacturer: Elam Uno, Italy

65

66

Alessandro Mendini

Stacking container stool, *Trick*
ABS, polyurethane
H 44 cm (17¼ in). Di 44 cm (17¼ in)
Manufacturer: Vanini, Italy

The British Architectural Association is a springboard for talent, and some of its 1980s graduates are already achieving international success with their flamboyant designs for buildings – even cities – and furniture.

Zaha Hadid's furniture was originally designed for one of her interiors, but it became a separate collection of four pieces, two of which were featured in *The International Design Yearbook 4*. During 1988, her drawings and schemes formed part of the Deconstructivist Architecture Exhibition at the Museum of Modern Art, New York. The exhibition raised the question: what is Deconstructivism? The prefix suggests destruction, or breaking apart, while Constructivism harks back to the Soviet avant-garde movement of the 1920s, which broke with right-angled, Mondrian-inspired Modernism.

Zaha Hadid
Coffee table, *Constellation*
Glass, forged iron, patinated bronze
H 50 cm (19⅝ in). W 110 cm (43¼ in)
to 190 cm (73⅞ in). L 250 cm (98⅜ in)
to 295 cm (116⅛ in)
Manufacturer: EDRA, Italy

67

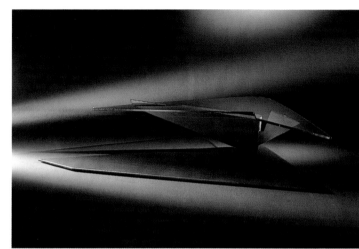

Zaha Hadid
Sofa, *Projection in Red*
Fibreglass
H 40 cm (15¾ in). W 70 cm (27½ in) to
110 cm (43¼ in). L 270 cm (106¼ in)
Manufacturer: EDRA Italy

68

Certainly, Hadid's drawings (already acquiring collectors' price tags) show the diagonal overlapping of rectangular or trapezoidal bars that relate to Malevich and Rodchenko; they stress lines and planes, not space. But her sofa, realized in moulded fibreglass by EDRA in Italy, has little to do with the furniture of El Lissitzky, itself still in production with the German company Tecta. This sofa overturns all conventional thinking on seating, arm and back rests, levels and cantilevers, yet you can still sit or lie on it in comfort. Structural engineers help her tussle with the planes and stresses she incorporates in all her designs, furniture as well as buildings. *Projection in Red* rushes on a curve, then changes direction to swing forwards in an embracing swoop, its high back plunging dramatically. *Constellation* clusters on a fixed axis, then rises up and appears to float in space.

69

El Lissitzky
Table, *M 61*
Ash, steel
Originally designed for the Hygiene
Exhibition, Dresden, in 1930.
H 74 cm (29 in). W 140 cm (55⅛ in).
D 140 cm (55⅛ in)
Manufacturer: Tecta, West Germany

70

El Lissitzky
Chair, *D 61*
Beech plywood
Originally designed for the Hygiene
Exhibition, Dresden, in 1930.
H 73 cm (28¾ in). W 57 cm (22⅜ in).
D 49 cm (19¼ in)
Manufacturer: Tecta, West Germany

Trix and Robert Haussmann
Sideboard, *Stripe*
Synthetic resin panel, tubular steel
columns, glass top
The postforming process allows a
pattern to run seamlessly from one side
to the other. The columns serve as
hinges enabling the four front panels to
turn through 180°. The resin panel is by
Abet-Print, Italy.
H without glass top 80 cm (31½ in).
H with glass top 95 cm (37½ in).
W 50 cm (19⅝ in). L 240 cm (94½ in)
Manufacturer: Wogg, Switzerland

71

72

Mario Botta
Sofa and armchair, *Obliqua*
MDF, expanded polyurethane, fabric or
chamois leather covering
Left to right:
Armchair: H 70 cm (27½ in). W 88 cm
(34⅝ in). D 88 cm (34⅝ in)
Three-seater sofa: H 70 cm (27½ in).
W 212 cm (83½ in). D 88 cm (34⅝ in)
Two-seater sofa: H 70 cm (27½ in).
W 155 cm (61 in). D 88 cm (34⅝ in)
Manufacturer: Alias, Italy

John Hutton/Donghia Design Studio
Club chair, *Luciano*
Hardwood frame, finished wood legs, fabric upholstery
H 92 cm (36 in). W 92 cm (36 in).
D 92 cm (36 in)
Manufacturer: Donghia Furniture and Textiles, USA

73

74

John Hutton
Sofa, *San Marco*
Hardwood frame, hand-tied springs,
fabric upholstery
H 96.5 cm (38 in). W 244 cm (96 in).
D 102 cm (40 in)
Manufacturer: Donghia Furniture and
Textiles, USA

Paolo Pallucco and Mireille Rivier
Sofa and chair, *Le Lamentazioni*
Curved and flat plywood, galvanized
steel, polyurethane foam, fabric covers
Sofa: H 90.1 cm (35⅝ in). W 162 cm
(63¾ in). D 76 cm (30 in)
Chair: H 90.1 cm (35⅝ in). W 71 cm
(28 in). D 61.5 cm (24⅛ in)
Manufacturer: Pallucco, Italy

75

76

Paolo Pallucco and Mireille Rivier
Sideboard, *W II Toro*
Curved and flat plywood, industrial pivot
wheels
H 87.6 cm (34⅝ in). W 43.7 cm (17³⁄₁₆ in).
L 114.6 cm (45⅜ in)
Manufacturer: Pallucco, Italy

Beautiful but warped, this visionary furniture by Paolo Pallucco and Mireille Rivier twists even the parallelepiped for a sideboard, transforms a sofa into a wedge shape on the diagonal, and makes three-legged chairs look balletic in their twirling stance. Consider the complications of the front and back planes of the *W Il Toro* sideboard, which is supported at one end by a pair of castors, or *The Great Drought* sofa, like an elongated triangle, deeper at one end than the other. The launch of this challenging collection was staged outside the Milan Furniture Fair in an abandoned slaughterhouse, with electronic music and copies of Rainer Maria Rilke's poetry on angels handed out in lieu of explanations. But it is angles, not angels, which inspire these designs. Spotlit by Henry Alekan, the lighting director on Wim Wenders' film *Wings of Desire* (also about angels), the shadows from the furniture fall like pinions on the ground.

Paolo Pallucco and Mireille Rivier

77

Sofa, *La Grande Siccità*
Steel, steel rod, polyurethane foam, upholstery, industrial pivot wheels
H 93.5 cm (36⅝ in). W 161.8 cm (63⅝ in). D 99 cm (38½ in)
Manufacturer: Pallucco, Italy

Paolo Pallucco and Mireille Rivier

Chairs, *Merry-go-round*
Tubular steel, curved plywood with epoxy powder finish, sheet steel
H 77.2 cm (30⁵⁄₁₆ in). W 46.6 cm (18⅜ in). D 46 cm (18 in)
Manufacturer: Pallucco, Italy

78

79

Massimo Iosa Ghini
Table, *Momento*
Sheet glass, cut and curved
H 35 cm (13¾ in). W 70 cm (27½ in).
L 155 cm (61 in)
Manufacturer: Fiam, Italy

Danny Lane
Table, *Shell*
Hand-finished curved glass
The base is composed of five L-shaped
legs arranged in a fan, united at one end
by a pivot pin.
H 40 cm (15¾ in). W 125 cm (49¼ in).
L 125 cm (49¼ in)
Manufacturer: Fiam, Italy

Danny Lane moved from the USA to the UK to study stained glass, and later painting. He was tutored in that underestimated school of 20th-century British art known as Neo-Romantic. Thus he draws inspiration from the landscape, and from the mythology and ritual that are part of it. His rough-hewn glass logs rest on metal bolts like rustic benches on a village green; running streams of glass form tables held up on slivers of ice; opalescent twigs support glass discs in pieces as timeless as Stonehenge.

Lane used to be classified as an artist–craftsman, producing sculptural pieces that one could, arguably, use. But Fiam has now put into production two tables, *Atlas* and *Shell*. Seaweed tendrils of glass float beneath a pool of glass in *Shell* with its rococo accents. The solid top of *Atlas* is an ellipse: a pencil placed at the corner will roll gently towards the middle.

Only 40 years ago, sheet glass could be stretched no further than an ordinary window pane. Since then, kilns and techniques have advanced dramatically so that entire skyscrapers can be built with glass façades. Glass remains today a truly innovative material for the designer to conquer. Its transparency annihilates dimension, it suggests great fragility, and it is cold both in expectation and in reality. As a material for furniture, it trades the image of relaxation and comfort for that of caution.

Fiam's achievement in the manufacturing world has been to show that pieces of furniture can be mass-produced in glass, so they are not "ice sculptures" but truly domestic products. Danny Lane's originality in this challenging medium may look casual, but his technical virtuosity is clear: he pushes the material to its limit.

81

80

Danny Lane
Table, *Atlas*
Curved glass surface and sheet glass
legs
H 40 cm (15¾ in). W 70 cm (27½ in).
L 140 cm (55⅛ in)
Manufacturer: Fiam, Italy

Matthew Hilton
Bridge table
Cast aluminium, birch plywood, veneer
H 73 cm (28¾ in). W 94.5 cm (37¼ in).
L 94.5 cm (37¼ in)
Manufacturer: SCP, UK

82

83

Matthew Hilton
Table, *Flipper*
Glass, cast aluminium
H 38 cm (15 in). W 95 cm (37½ in).
L 95 cm (37½ in)
Manufacturer: SCP, UK

**Perry A. King and Santiago
Miranda**
Book shelf system, *Bloom*
Steel
D 33 cm (13 in). L 100 cm (39½ in) or
150 cm (59 in). Uprights: H 200 cm
(78¾ in) to 303 cm (119⅝ in)
Manufacturer: Tisettanta, Italy

84

85

**Lluis Clotet and Oscar Tusquets
Blanca**
Hanging shelf, *Estanteria Cornisa*
White-painted anodized aluminium
The two aluminium profiles are
connected by sliding one on to the other
and are fixed with supports to the wall.
The narrower shelf is fixed directly to
the supports.
L maximum of 300 cm (118½ in).
D 15 cm (6 in) or 30 cm (11⅞ in)
Manufacturer: BD Ediciones de diseño,
Spain

Sergi Devesa Bajet
Coffee table, *Chincheta*
Sheet aluminium painted in epoxy
H 31 cm (12¼ in). Di 100 cm (39½ in)
Manufacturer: Disform, Spain

86

Shiro Kuramata
Bar stool, *BK 86000*
Chromed tubular steel, laminated wood
Limited batch production
H 90 cm (35½ in). W 36 cm (14⅛ in).
D 15 cm (6 in). Di of seat 33 cm (13 in)
Manufacturer: Pastoe, Netherlands

87

Shiro Kuramata
Lounge chair
Mesh metal, steel, glass
Prototype
H 95 cm (37½ in). W 83 cm (32½ in).
D 92 cm (36 in). Height to seat 37 cm
(14½ in). Height to table 50 cm (19⅝ in)
Manufacturer: Cassina Inc., Japan

88

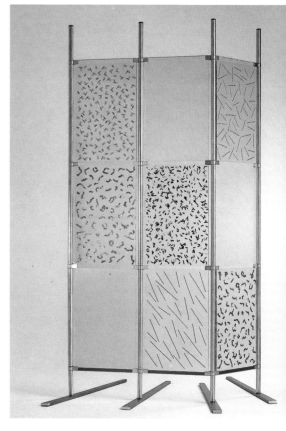

Ad Us Berlin: Manuel Pfahl and Bettina Wiegandt

Screen, *Fish 'n Chips*
Perspex, aluminium, rubber
The metal inserts are iridescent as a
result of heat treatment. Prototype
Screen: H 140 cm (44⅛ in). W 225 cm
(88½ in). D 2.8 cm (1 in). Single panel:
H 40 cm (15¾ in). W 60 cm (23½ in).
D 1 cm (⅖ in)
Manufacturer: Designwerkstatt, West
Germany

90

89

Joachim Stanitzek

Media component holder, *BG 1*
Lacquered steel and wood
The built-in loudspeakers are height-
adjustable. Prototype
H 110 cm (43¼ in). W 49 cm (19¼ in).
L 220 cm (86⅝ in)
Manufacturer: Designwerkstatt, West
Germany

The most interesting development of the decade is the emergence of the Berlin underground, an avant-garde movement that includes some extraordinary talent. Their designs reflect the first major attempt to rebel against the staid correctness of modern German design. The furniture shows obvious distortions of the Bauhaus school, blatantly delineated in tubular steel and leather. There are also some weird perversions of familiar domestic furniture from young sculptors and designers who prefer to call themselves carpenters. This alternative movement began in 1988, during the preparations for the 1989 Cultural City of Europe celebrations. To mark the event in Berlin's calendar, 64 household products from 14 different design groups were commissioned and built under the umbrella of Designwerkstatt. Though the furniture shown here is only in prototype, it can be produced in small or large runs in workshops or by bigger manufacturers.

91

Jörg Hundertpfund and Sylvia Robeck

Writing equipment storage, *Mini*
A ready-made brush with plastic bristles,
plastic wheels attached.
H 13 cm (5⅛ in). W 10 cm (4 in).
L 20 cm (7⅞ in)
Paper holder, *Maxi*
A ready-made broom with plastic
bristles, plastic wheels attached.
H 13 cm (5⅛ in). W 10 cm (4 in).
L 40 cm (15¾ in)
Both prototypes
Manufacturer: Designwerkstatt, West
Germany

Frank Schreiner for Stiletto Studios
Conference chair, *Threeswinger*
Chromed tubular steel and leather
Prototype
H 81.5 cm (32⅛ in). W 57.5 cm (22⅝ in).
D 69 cm (27⅛ in). Height to seat 45.5 cm
(17⅞ in)
Manufacturer: Designwerkstatt, West
Germany

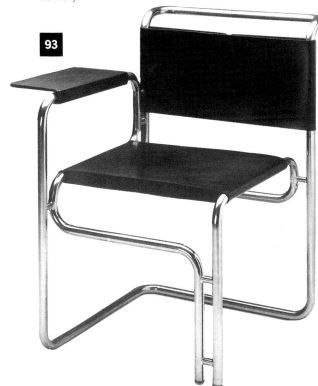

93

Hermann Waldenburg
92
Screen, *Triple Jump*
Nickel-plated steel
H 100 cm (39½ in). L 200 cm (78¾ in)
Side table, *Flat roof*
Anodized aluminium, Perspex
H 66 cm (26 in). W 40 cm (15¾ in)
L 41 cm (16⅛ in)
Dismantlable armchair, *3736*
Nickel-plated steel, shuttering slabs, rod
veneer, upholstered covering
H 89 cm (35 in). W 79 cm (31 in).
D 70 cm (27½ in). Height to arm 40 cm
(15¾ in)
Easily assembled and combined modular
system for various purposes.
Ashtray, *Sacrificial Bowl (Homage to
Joseph B.)*
Corrugated cardboard, nickel-plated and
high-grade steel
H 20 cm (7⅞ in). W 20 cm (7⅞ in).
D 10 cm (4 in)
All prototypes
Manufacturer: Designwerkstatt, West
Germany

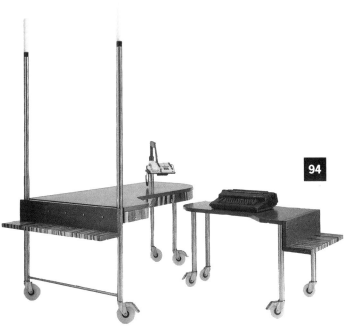

94

Herbert Weinand
Desk, *Karajan 1*
Lacquered chipboard, veneer with silk-
screen print, Nirosta, plastic castors,
fluorescent tubes 40W, built-in radio
H 180 cm (70⅝ in). W 95 cm (37½ in).
L 75 cm (29½ in) and 125 cm (49¼ in)
Typewriter table, *Karajan II*
Lacquered chipboard, veneer with silk-
screen print, Nirosta, plastic castors
H 120 cm (47¼ in). W 65 cm (25½ in).
L 65 cm (25½ in)
Both prototypes
Manufacturer: Designwerkstatt, West
Germany

"Work less, but well; travel widely; enjoy a varied cultural life; and in contrast to technical projects realized aesthetically put those that are resolved in a historic and semantic perspective." This advice, given to students at the University of Decorative Arts in Berlin by their professor, Andreas Brandolini, relates to his own designs. It also sums up the work of the avant garde in Germany today. Working within the studio Berliner Zimmer, Brandolini has led the way in the design of some disturbingly familiar furniture in a new context — cosy sets he calls "family rooms," intended to appeal to the public, not convert them. The lustre of the granite-topped table, the painting on the wall, the sofa and the false parquet rug are quietly domestic, while the blazing lights that emphasize a rough rafter, adding a Wagnerian theatricality to the scene, are replicas of popular Thirties torch lights. The room conveys all the archetypes of traditional living, yet these are subtly perverted. "Design must in some measure be a reflection of the historical, cultural and technological environment, while taking into account the fact that tradition can no longer be considered as a historical continuation, but as a sequence of contradictory events," Brandolini writes. He wants his work to contribute to this crucial debate.

Susanne Neubohn
Stool, *Floh*
Plastic, lacquered steel, rubber
Limited batch production
H 46 cm (18 in). W 50 cm (19⅝ in).
D 40 cm (15¾ in)
Manufacturer: Berliner Zimmer, West
Germany

95

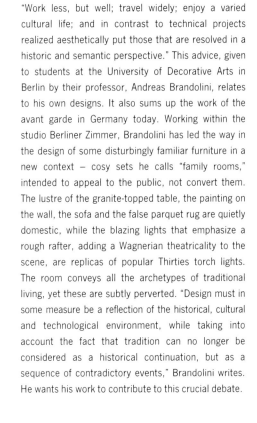

96

Christof Walther
Chair, *No 3*
Steel, mahogany plywood
Limited batch production
H 96 cm (37¾ in). W 38 cm (15 in).
D 45 cm (17¾ in)
Manufacturer: Berliner Zimmer, West
Germany

**Bellefast: Andreas Brandolini,
Joachim Stanitzek**
Table, *Bonanza*
Wood, aluminium, steel, glass
Limited batch production
H 51 cm (20 in). W 70 cm (27½ in).
L 140 cm (55⅛ in)
Manufacturer: Berliner Zimmer, West
Germany

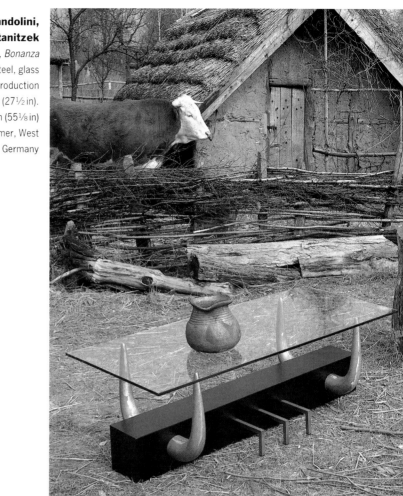

Andreas Brandolini
Kassel Living Room
Armchair: Sandblasted steel, nutwood,
wool upholstery
H 76 cm (30 in). W 100 cm (39½ in).
D 82 cm (32¼ in)
Sofa: Sandblasted steel, nutwood, wool
upholstery
H 76 cm (30 in). W 160 cm (63 in).
D 82 cm (32¼ in)
Table: Chromed steel and granite
H 51 cm (20 in). W 71 cm (28 in).
L 182 cm (71⅜ in)
Rug: Wool
W 300 cm (118⅛ in). L 400 cm (157½ in)
Media unit: H 30 cm (11⅞ in).
W 45 cm (17¾ in). D 38 cm (15 in)
TV furniture: sandblasted steel,
Multiplex, leather
H 80 cm (31½ in). W 60 cm (23½ in) or
90 cm (35½ in). D 55 cm (21½ in)
Limited batch production
Manufacturer: Andreas Brandolini, West
Germany

98

97

99

Andreas Brandolini
Lighting system, *Wiblingen*
Wood, steel, ceramic
The ready-made light fittings take 15W
incandescent bulbs.
Limited batch production
Wall light: H 40 cm (15¾ in). W 20 cm
(7⅞ in). D 10 cm (4 in)
Candelabrum (above): H 40 cm (15¾ in).
W 50 cm (19⅝ in). L 120 cm (47¼ in)
Candelabrum (below): H 40 cm (15¾ in).
W 35 cm (13¾ in). D 35 cm (13¾ in)
Manufacturer: Design Galerie Weinand,
West Germany

Marcel Breuer

Desk/table, *M20*
Black- or white-stained ash, steel
The table top revolves and the steel
base contains a drawer for hanging files.
Originally designed in 1924.
H 74 cm (29 in). W 135 cm (53¼ in).
D 179 cm (70½ in)
Manufacturer: Tecta, West Germany

100

Eckart Muthesius

Dinner-wagon, *Tiwary*
Nickel-plated brass, mirror glass
Originally designed in 1932.
Limited batch production
H 47 cm (18½ in) or 61 cm (24 in).
D 41 cm (16⅛ in) or 50 cm (19⅝ in).
L 120 cm (47¼ in)
Manufacturer: Vereinigte Werkstätten,
West Germany

101

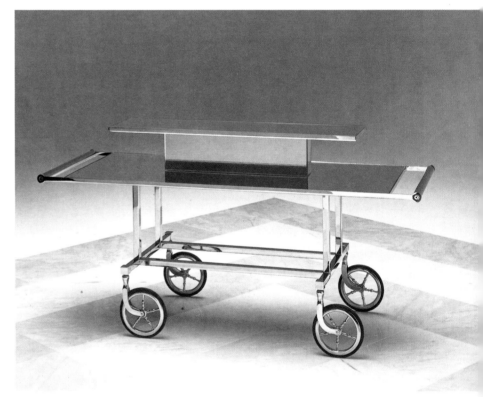

Eckart Muthesius

Armchair, *Roter Sessel*
Wood, nickel-plated brass, leather, two
Dulux EL 7W 220V bulbs, ashtray and
tray for utensils
Designed in 1930–33. Limited batch
production
H 95 cm (37½ in). W 89 cm (35 in).
D 103.5 cm (41 in). Height to seat 41 cm
(16⅛ in)
Manufacturer: Vereinigte Werkstätten,
West Germany

102

Gerrit Rietveld was born in Utrecht on 24 June 1888. His centenary was heralded by the Italian manufacturer Cassina with a reissue based on his original 1935 drawings for the *Utrecht* chair. Typical of all Rietveld chairs, it does not impose itself on its surroundings, since it has no conventional legs to define a rectangular shape. Rather, it sinks precipitately to the ground at the back, kicking away the need for back legs, and suspends the slanted backrest at an agreeable angle for the sitter. Blanket stitching on a fabric or leather cover emphasises the rigorously severe lines.

Rietveld followed a structural code all his own, while being a member of De Stijl, the group that carried to extremes in furniture and architecture the breakdown of composition seen in Cubist paintings. But nobody ever sat in a Cubist painting. It is a surprising fact about Rietveld's chairs that they offer reassurance and comfort, while upending certain norms of ergonomics. Cassina, with exclusive access to his prototypes, drawings and sketches, have faithfully observed the intentions of his original project.

Since 1972, Filippo Alison, "under strict control of the heirs," has been helping Cassina with the enterprise *I Maestri*, carrying out the necessary research to reconstruct the projects accurately. Each piece of furniture in the collection is indelibly numbered, and comes with an individual guarantee. In a decade beleaguered by international copyright wrangles and by cheaper competing copies of classics emerging 50 years after designers' deaths, these reissues are an act of faith by Cassina in the value of the masters' original concepts.

Jean Prouvé
Chair, *B 10*
Tubular steel, leather
Originally designed in 1932.
H 84 cm (33 in). W 42 cm (16½ in).
D 42 cm (16½ in)
Manufacturer: Tecta, West Germany

103

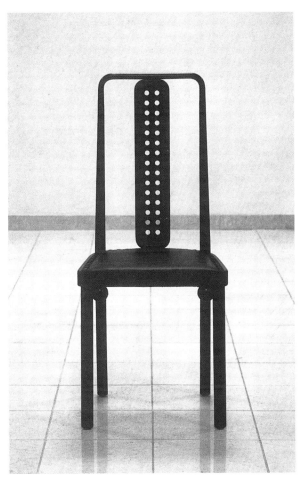

Josef Hoffmann
Dining chair, *Purkersdorf*
Stained beech, leather
Originally designed for the Purkersdorf Sanatorium, Vienna, in 1904.
H 100 cm (39½ in). W 44 cm (17¼ in).
D 45 cm (17¾ in)
Manufacturer: Franz Wittmann, Austria

104

105

Gerrit Rietveld
Armchair, *Utrecht*
Wood, polyurethane foam, polyester padding, fabric upholstery, ABS
Originally designed in 1935.
H 70 cm (27½ in). W 64 cm (25⅛ in).
D 85 cm (33½ in). Height to seat 37 cm (14½ in). Height to elbow rest 49 cm (19¼ in)
Manufacturer: Cassina, Italy

An iconoclastic teacher at the British Architectural Association and theorist of the NATO movement (Narrative Architecture Today), Nigel Coates has been accused of certain Felliniesque excesses. His first furniture, all in wood, is made in Britain by Sheridan Coakley and is as challenging as his architecture.

He crosses historic references with the sublime and the ridiculous. His *Genie* stool with its buttocks' imprint is reminiscent of the Windsor chair, finely tuned in grainy wood. But the central leverage is as disturbing to look at as Coates demonstrating how best to sit on it. Actually, it is comfortable, although Coates maintains, "The notion of a comfortable chair is a myth. Comfort usually goes along in the mainstream of design with the other Ten Commandments. More important is the psychological feeling of relaxation in a chair." His furniture is poised to spring from splayed feet and trim ankles. The *Genie* stool appears to swivel up from the ground. This sense of motion ascribed to inert objects he calls "understated kineticism."

Nigel Coates

Stool, *Genie*
Ash, tubular steel
A carved wooden seat in two parts. Because of the forward tilt of the seat and the saddle effect of the wooden pommel, sitting on it straightens and energizes the spine. One-off
H 66 cm (26 in). W 35 cm (13¾ in).
D 42 cm (16½ in)
Manufacturer: SCP, UK

106

107

Nigel Coates

Armchair, *Noah*
Sandblasted and oiled ash, tubular steel
Limited batch production
H 72 cm (28½ in). W 67 cm (26⅜ in).
D 48 cm (18⅞ in)
Manufacturer: SCP, UK

108

Antoon Meerman
Low table
MDF, Tasmanian myrtle, beech veneer
Limited batch production
H 52.5 cm (20⅝ in). W 136 cm
(53½ in). L 136 cm (53½ in)
Manufacturer: Antoon Meerman,
Australia

Marc Newson
Chair
Steam-bent Tasmanian blackwood
Limited batch production
H 75 cm (29½ in). W 75 cm (29½ in).
D 100 cm (39½ in)
Manufacturer: Idiom, Australia/Idée,
Japan

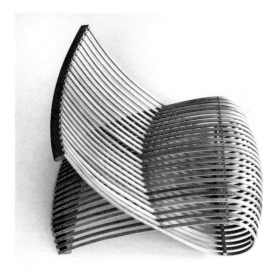

109

Marc Newson
Desk, *Black Hole*
Moulded sheet carbon fibre
Limited batch production
H 70 cm (27½ in). W 90 cm (35½ in).
L 250 cm (98⅜ in)
Manufacturer: Idée, Japan

110

Marc Newson
Chair, *Sine*
Carbon fibre, stainless steel
Limited batch production
H 80 cm (31½ in). W 40 cm (15¾ in).
D 46 cm (18 in)
Manufacturer: Idée, Japan

Rising freight charges worldwide, together with an expensive Australian dollar (known locally as the Pacific Peso), inhibited imports to Australia in 1988. So Australian designers, helped by incentive schemes, were encouraged to begin limited batch production of furniture using indigenous timbers. The New South Wales Crafts Council also promoted a dozen designs by international designers, to be made in Australia by Idiom Furniture. The intention was that some of them would go into production, but schemes that came off the drawing board did not always suit the nature of the indigenous hardwoods, which have traditionally been used for construction (in the building industry or as railway sleepers, for example: the London Underground is underpinned by Western Australian jarrah).

As a promotional exercise, however, it was a great idea, with pieces by Shiro Kuramata, Alessandro Mendini and Andrea Branzi alongside local talent. "An industry/craft experiment," curator Craig Bremner called it, a worthy exercise for the timber industry, since alternatives to traditional woods must now be sought. Young Sydney-born Marc Newson chose to interlace skeins of wood into a tightly woven piece – a symphony of a rocking chair that is as finely tuned as a musical instrument. Newson spent 1987 designing in Tokyo for Idée, commercial producers of his *Charlotte* chair and *Supper Guppy* lamp (see *The International Design Yearbook 4*).

111

112

Shiro Kuramata
Chair, *Sydney*
Brush box, chromed tubular steel
Prototype
H 73 cm (28¾ in). W 82 cm (32¼ in).
D 60 cm (23½ in)
Manufacturer: Idiom, Australia

113

Javier Mariscal
Wheeled chair, *Biscuter*
Metal, fibreglass, upholstery
H 31 cm (12¼ in). W 56.5 cm (22¼ in).
D 77 cm (30¼ in)
Manufacturer: Akaba, Spain

Anna Castelli-Ferrieri
Armchair, *4814*
Technopolymers blend, steel
A new injection moulding process
creates a random spotted material.
H 73 cm (28¾ in). W 65 cm (25½ in).
D 97 cm (38¼ in)
Manufacturer: Kartell, Italy

114

115

Vicente Blasco
Wardrobe, *Eco*
Veneered ash with interior mirrors
H 174 cm (68 in). W 100 cm (39½ in).
D 21 cm (8¼ in)
Manufacturer: Punt Mobles, Spain

116

Ramon Arbos Figueras
Cabinet, *Patós*
Bubinga wood, MDF, steel, steel tubing,
glass
H 160 cm (63 in). D 45 cm (17¾ in).
L 315 cm (124 in)
Manufacturer: Intent, Spain

Masayuki Kurokawa
Desk, *Schrein*
Laminated chipboard
A compact work-space for city life.
Prototype
H 165.2 cm (65¹/₁₆ in). W 120.1 cm
(47³/₈ in). Di 61.8 cm (24¹/₄ in)
Manufacturer: Wogg, Switzerland

117

Jasper Morrison sounds like Milan Kundera when he identifies good design as the "character of an object which exhibits the lightness of being that improves the quality of life around it." Like his philosophy, his furniture deserves further contemplation. Easily underestimated, his pieces are restrained and quietly elegant. Until, that is, you move them into a room where their perfect symmetry is somehow thrown just a bit out, giving them a forceful presence among other, more ordinary, pieces. A 30-year-old postgraduate from the Royal College of Art, London, he spent three months in 1988 on scholarships in Berlin, designing for the European City of Culture programme.

There is something subversive about the way Morrison manipulates geometry, by overlapping corners or folding them in like paper, exaggerating joints, extending armrests and splaying feet. A freeform plywood desk is shaped like a boomerang with a blunt end where it has fallen to earth, and has concealed drawers in the bend. A hatstand's branched antlers at the top exactly duplicate the base.

His sofa is a gentle hillock of plump upholstery rising, peaking, then ending incisively with a bolster at one end and a square cushion at the other to emphasize the angles. The legs do not match either: the front left is angled to kick up the rise in volume, and the right is squarely pegged to the ground to halt the slide.

118

Jasper Morrison
Sofa
Beech, cast aluminium, linen fabric
H 83 cm (32½ in). W 215 cm (84½ in).
D 70 cm (27½ in)
Manufacturer: SCP, UK

119

Jasper Morrison
Chair
Birch plywood, aero-ply seat
A simple chair with or without a solid back. Prototype
H 83 cm (32½ in). W 46 cm (18 in).
D 40 cm (15¾ in)
Manufacturer: Jasper Morrison, UK

120

Jasper Morrison
Dining chair
Beech, steel rod
Limited batch production
H 85.5 cm (33⅝ in). W 39.5 cm (15⅝ in).
D 41.5 cm (16⅜ in)
Manufacturer: SCP, UK

Until his work went into mass production in 1988, Morrison's designs were executed in small workshops throughout Britain, where he took advantage of the specialist services available: "I matched the process to suit the design, or designed to suit the process." This approach is still reflected in the appearance of his chairs which, though mass produced, retain the look of artisanship. His work has been put into production by Sheridan Coakley, along with that of Matthew Hilton and Nigel Coates, and is also manufactured by Cappellini in Italy and Zeev Aram Designs in the UK, along with that of Matthew Hilton and Nigel Coates.

Morrison's intention is to ensure a consistency of purpose, from concept through realization and production to sales, which will allow the initial idea to survive its own processing. He believes any crossover between art, craft and design results in a hybrid, in which art becomes the motive and design the excuse. "I don't believe art has a place in design except as a by-product of refined concept and well-shaped realization, existing as the art of design, nothing more." He argues that, while industry is better equipped than ever to produce ornament in huge runs, the ornament is the same as it has always been, "a decorative surface which covers and confuses the real nature of an object."

121

Marie-Christine Dorner
Pouf, *Fool*
Wood, leather, steel
Prototype
H 50 cm (19⅝ in). W 35 cm (13¾ in).
D 45 cm (17¾ in)
Manufacturer: Mangau, France

122

Marie-Christine Dorner
Table, *Teena*
Beech with black varnish, sandblasted
plated metal
H 73 cm (28¾ in). W 120 cm (47¼ in).
L 120 cm (47¼ in)
Manufacturer: Scarabat, Spain

The work of this 29-year-old is still changing – progressing, she calls it, with the many commissions she receives for furniture and interior designs. She trained with Jean-Michel Wilmotte, and her first furniture collection was commissioned by Idée in Japan two years ago. The angular pieces in that collection look as if they are based on origami paper-pleating techniques. A hint of this approach remains in her current collection, but it unfolds gently in more curvaceous, and capacious, furniture. She explains: "Maybe that relates a little to the disciplined professionalism in Japan where the manufacturing approach is harder, more rigorous than the free form still available in Spain where Scarabat, for whom I design, are generous with their time, their talent and their handcrafting. But more and more, I like design for mass production."

One of her ambitions is to make the stolid four legs on tables and chairs virtually disappear. "My aim is to design furniture without legs," she says, "floating above the ground." Tables, therefore, have a cantilever or a substantial trim to the top, below which the legs taper away, like those on the *Teena* table, which heralded a new collection for Scarabat. Her *Fool* pouf, prototyped for the *Avant Première* collection at the Victoria and Albert Museum in London in 1988, is like a punctuation mark, a comma in leather, with a neat zipper down the back ending in a full stop at ground level. It is good from all angles.

During 1988, she worked at the 18th-century, 35-room Hotel Villa in St Germain des Prés, Paris, designing everything from the linen to the furniture. Strong colours – saffron, purple and claret – now give a public building a sense of identity.

123

Vico Magistretti
Chair, *Raffles*
Wood, expanded polyurethane, Dacron and goose down upholstery, cotton covers
H 83 cm (32½ in). W 80 cm (31½ in).
D 103 cm (40½ in). Height to seat 45 cm (17¾ in)
Manufacturer: Edizioni de Padova, Italy

124

Robert Arko
Chair, *Arena*
Hardwood, hardwood ply, post-catalyzed lacquer, nylon, polyurethane foam upholstery
H 76 cm (30 in). W 63.5 cm (25 in).
D 61 cm (24 in)
Manufacturer: Metropolitan Furniture Corporation, USA

125

Gae Aulenti
Sofa, *Minuetto*
Beech, steel tubing, rubberized horsehair, down cushions, calfskin
H 90 cm (35½ in). W 174 cm (68½ in).
D 85 cm (33½ in). Height to seat 47 cm (18½ in)
Manufacturer: Poltrona Frau, Italy

Andrée Putman   126

Sideboard, *Project Alpha*
Multi-layer high-density chipboard, glass
H 72 cm (28½ in). D 45 cm (17¾ in).
L 160 cm (63 in)
Manufacturer: deSede Projects,
Switzerland

Top French designer Andrée Putman bridges the gap between home and office with her customary discretion. Her designs look as good at the hearth as at the heart of a multi-million dollar office complex. Her chair for deSede is simple, with a faint echo of Art Deco. It is colourful in a subtle way since she uses colour only for accents, adding melon, aquamarine or cobalt to her basic taupe, cream, grey and black design, "like spices in cooking." The range depends on a single piece – say, the desk – upon which she pegs accessories such as a sofa or coffee table.

Factory-produced faux finishes replicating stone or marble interest her. "Why use craft and hand-finishes when technology permits so many effects?" she asks. She acquired what she calls "underground training" by visiting factories to learn how different processes work. "I think I'm a Modernist," she claims. "Less *is* more. Style is an elusive quality which, when sought, vanishes. To develop style, you have to kill that paralysing respect for it, for period, and for all images of wealth. But we need a moral idea to reconcile ourselves with the things that are too simple." Putman's clients include Yves St Laurent and Karl Lagerfeld, yet she remains committed to accessible style. Her company, Ecart International, reissues classics by Robert Mallet Stevens and Eileen Gray. As an *editeur*, she commissions new designs to put into production.

127

Andrée Putman

Armchair, *Project Alpha*
Multi-layer high-density chipboard,
leather
H 72 cm (28½ in). W 79 cm (31 in).
D 84 cm (33 in). Height to seat 43 cm
(16⅞ in)
Manufacturer: deSede Projects,
Switzerland

128

William Sawaya

Armchair, *Iki-Oko*
Metal, polyurethane foam and fibre,
fabric covering, lacquered metal
accessories
H 86 cm (38⅞ in). W 100 cm (39½ in)
D 80 cm (31½ in)
Manufacturer: Sawaya & Moroni, Italy

"Discreetly and limpidly elegant," is how William Sawaya describes his *Iki-Oko* armchair and its matching two- and three-seater sofas. The comforting proportions of a club chair are plumply upheld, yet the distinctive wedge back, separated from the seat, creates a tension that is purely modern. This free-wheeling manipulation of space is intriguing and pragmatic since it allows for the insertion of small invisible fittings which can alter the angle of the wedge. The classic wing chair takes off into the space age.

Josep Lluscà
Multifunctional chair, *BCN*
Steel, polyester, fibreglass
H 80 cm (31½ in). W 57 cm (22⅜ in).
D 56 cm (22 in)
Manufacturer: Enea, Spain

Leo Aerts and Ingrid Wijnen
Table, *Meta*
Black-lacquered wood, plate glass,
varnished steel
A low table with a rotating higher shelf.
Base: H 40 cm (15¾ in). W 150 cm
(59 in). D 40 cm (15¾ in)
Top: H 50 cm (19⅝ in). W 150 cm (59 in).
D 60 cm (23½ in)
Manufacturer: B & B Italia, Italy

129

130

The value of this table system lies, simply, in its ability
to complement B & B Italia's spectacularly successful
modular furniture *Sity*, designed by Antonio Citterio.
That particular grand piano of a system with its
detachable back, armrests and bolsters was launched
in 1987 together with a competition to find other
furnishing elements to fit in with it. Since *Sity* is the
most flexible system to wrap itself around any space, it
was clear that entrants would have to create dual-
purpose designs. This is the winner, by two young
Belgians, Leo Aerts and Ingrid Wijnen.

Alex Locadia
Sofa, *Slice*
Wood, steel, glass, leather
Limited batch production
H 63.5 cm (25 in). W 244 cm (96 in).
D 58.5 cm (23 in)
Manufacturer: Art et Industrie, USA

131

Fabrizio Ballardini and Fulvio Forbicini
Sofa, *Ribalta*
Metal frame, cast iron base,
polyurethane foam upholstery
Each angle can be modified to six
different positions.
H 80 cm (31½ in). W 118 cm (46½ in).
L 162 cm (63¾ in). Height to seat 41 cm
(16⅛ in)
Manufacturer: Arflex, Italy

132

Rud Thygesen and Johnny Sørensen
Chair, *Dark Horse*
Steel
H 70 cm (27½ in). W 58 cm (22⅞ in).
D 46 cm (18 in). H to seat 44 cm (17¼ in)
Manufacturer: Botium, Denmark

133

Rud Thygesen and Johnny Sørensen
Chair, *Mobile*
Laminated beech
H 65 cm (25½ in). W 55 cm (21½ in).
L 170 cm (67 in)
Manufacturer: Magnus Olesen, Denmark

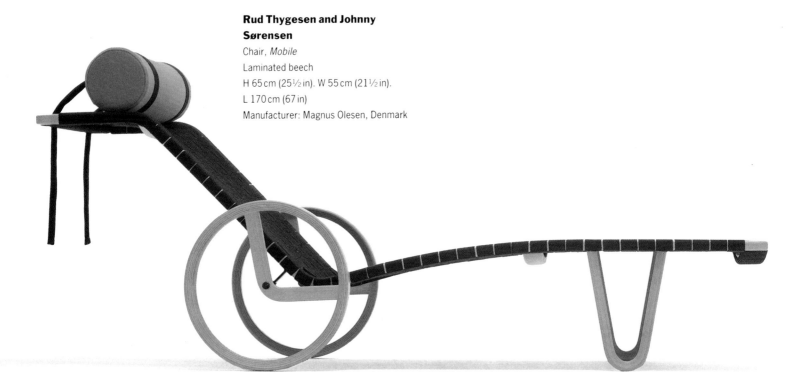

Stefan Wewerka
Table, *M 5*
Ash
Dining table for eight, with storage space
in the base. The decoration, "Ariadne", is
by Maximilian Seitz.
H 73 cm (28¾ in). W 151 cm (59½ in).
D 98 cm (38½ in)
Manufacturer: Tecta, West Germany

135

136

Torben Skov
One-legged stacking chair
Stainless steel, laminated beech
H 84 cm (33 in). W 48 cm (18⅞ in).
D 56 cm (22 in)
Manufacturer: Fritz Hansen, Denmark

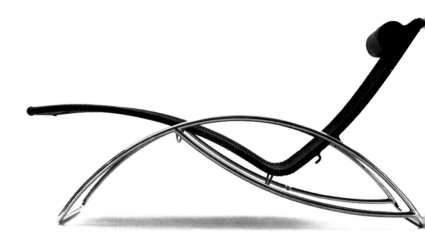

137

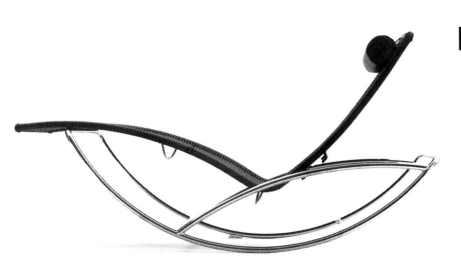

Torben Skov
Chaise longue, *Still-Leben*
Chromed steel, synthetic wickerwork
A recliner or a rocking chair.
H 94 cm (37 in). W 61 cm (24 in).
L 158 cm (62⅛ in) or 180 cm (70⅝ in)
Manufacturer: Gebrüder Thonet,
Denmark

Riccardo Dalisi
Table, *Pulcinella*
Tin or silver with a removable tray and
die-cast mask
H 91 cm (34⅞ in). Base Di 40 cm
(15¾ in). Tray Di 36.8 cm (14⅜ in)
Manufacturer: Vanini, Italy

138

Sawaya & Moroni, the Milan-based duo of interior designers, began producing their own finely made furniture four years ago. Their aim was to make "a kind of register which is sensitive to the trends of each year's designs." That sense of fashion and fun is injected into an idiosyncratic annual collection which attracts big-name artists and architects, and has launched new design talents such as Bořek Šipek. Charles Jencks, Michael Graves, Luigi Serafini and Kazuo Shinohara have designed pieces for them.

The young Italian architect Marco Mencacci, who has designed fabrics for Paris couturiers, made the front page of the design section of the *New York Times* with this chair, his first piece of furniture. Called *Tatlim*, it sets a delicately pierced plywood back on a severe metal spine. The name is Turkish for sweet, and the back – in bold contrast to the base – suggests the paper lace doily lining of a box of Turkish Delight.

139

Marco Mencacci
Chair, *Tatlim*
Wood stained blue or prune, plywood
back, nickel-plated steel joint
H 91 cm (35⅞ in). W 36 cm (14⅛ in).
D 37 cm (14½ in)
Manufacturer: Sawaya & Moroni, Italy

Ricardo Blanco
Armchair, *Toneta*
Laminated wood
H 77 cm (30¼ in). W 69 cm (27⅛ in).
Seat Di 45 cm (17¾ in)
Manufacturer: Tacu, Argentina

140

141

Ricardo Blanco
Chair, *Madrid*
Laminated wood
Can be dismantled.
H 82 cm (32¼ in). W 40 cm (15¾ in).
D 40 cm (15¾ in)
Manufacturer: Tacu, Argentina

Pedro Miralles

Nest of tables, *Andrews Sisters*

Bubinga wood laminate

Big table: H 50 cm (19⅝ in). W 62 cm
(24⅜ in). D 54 cm (21¼ in)

Medium table: H 46 cm (18 in). W 62 cm
(24⅜ in). D 42 cm (16½ in)

Small table: H 42 cm (16½ in). W 62 cm
(24⅜ in). D 30 cm (11⅞ in)

Manufacturer: Punt Mobles, Spain

Pedro Miralles

Trolleys, *Camarera Veloz*

Beech panels laminated with oak,
chromed metal frame

Back left: H 73.5 cm (28⅞ in). W 50 cm
(19⅝ in). L 100 cm (39½ in)

Back right: H 49.4 cm (19½ in). W 50 cm
(19⅝ in). L 122 cm (48 in)

Front: H 73.5 cm (28⅞ in). W 50 cm
(19⅝ in). L 100 cm (39½ in)

Manufacturer: Punt Mobles, Spain

Pedro Miralles received international acclaim for his designs in fashion, furnishings, interiors and exhibitions before he had completed his architectural studies in Madrid in 1980. In 1987 he graduated from the Domus Academy in Milan, and in 1989 he released a great many designs into the mass market, like these stacking tables in three sizes for Punt Mobles which he calls *The Andrews Sisters*. "Each piece of furniture represents a different problem," he says. "Labels depend on the final reference to which they allude. I understand the creative process as a grouping of ideas put at the service of an aim. More than innovation, therefore, I am interested in reinvention and recording objects." In Spain, where he believes Italian designers are imitated too much, his original talent shines through. One of his best known pieces is the *Egypte* light, now in production with Santa & Cole, which has two arms astride a long pole, like those fan-waving figures on Egyptian friezes. But his work also alludes to the Spanish landscape, with the fishpond from the Alhambra Gardens reproduced as a rug for BD Ediciones, and to Fifties-style furniture, to which he gives a curiously Eighties poise and line. He lives in Madrid in a small loft, constructed for industrial use in the Fifties, which has "great beams of steel visible in a façade of Rationalist influence, divided into beige squares and rectangles with white, assymetric stripes." Miralles likes to link architectural and design ideas with literature, for he claims: "Only literature is capable of evoking the same emotional response – that of transportation into a different world – that is produced by the spatial positioning of a building or of furniture." A certain mannerist irony emerges in his work – the result, perhaps, of the influence of his favourite authors: Henry James, Jane Austen, Edith Wharton and Gertrude Stein.

144

George Nelson
Chair, *Coconut*
Tubular steel, plastic, leather
Originally designed in 1956.
H 80 cm (31½ in). W 100 cm (39½ in).
D 80 cm (31½ in)
Manufacturer: Vitra International,
Switzerland

**Jane Dillon, Peter Wheeler
and Floris Van Den Broecke**
Seating system, *Vis-à-Vis*
Rigid and flexible polyurethane foam
The backs of the seats (in two sizes) are
independent from the bases so that they
can be placed at a number of points
around the base units (in three sizes).
H 71 cm (28 in). W 73 cm (28¾ in),
135 cm (53¼ in) or 195 cm (76⅞ in).
D 80 cm (31½ in)
Manufacturer: Perobell, Spain

145

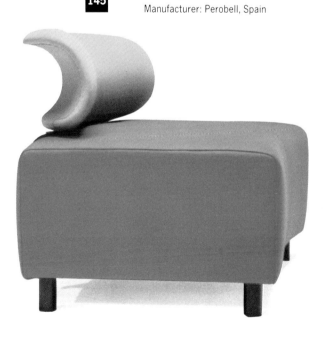

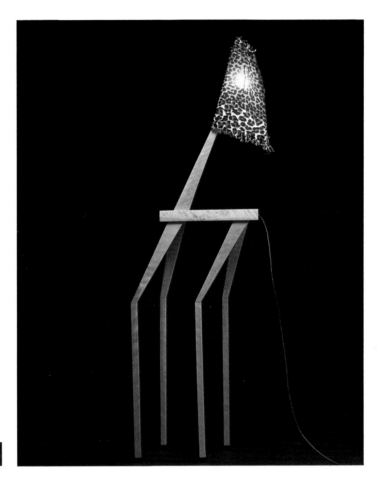

146

Steven Lombardi
Bedside table, *Madonna*
Birch, ebony
The light fitting takes one 60W 120V
bulb. Limited batch production
H 165 cm (65 in). W 23 cm (9 in).
L 40.5 cm (16 in)
Manufacturer: Lombardi, USA

**Isao Hosoe in collaboration with
Masaya Hashimoto, Ann Marinelli
and Alessio Pozzoli**
Tables, *Bio*
Wood, aluminium
This design enables a limitless number of
shapes to be formed from a number of
basic elements. The tables come with
standard legs and 26 different shaped
tops, which can be put together in any
combination. The configuration shown
here comprises three tables.
H 70 cm (27½ in). W 126 cm (49¾ in).
L 150 cm (59 in)
H 70 cm (27½ in). W 105 cm (41½ in).
L 105 cm (41½ in)
H 70 cm (27½ in). W 119 cm (47 in).
L 210 cm (82⅝ in)
Manufacturer: Itoki, Japan

147

**Isao Hosoe in collaboration with
Masaya Hashimoto, Ann Marinelli
and Alessio Pozzoli**
Table, *Bio*
Wood, aluminium
H 70 cm (27½ in). W 99 cm (39 in).
L 150 cm (59 in)
Manufacturer: Itoki, Japan

148

Michele De Lucchi
Folding table, *Clack*
Anodized aluminium
Suitable for outdoor use.
H 73 cm (28¾ in). W 64 cm (25⅛ in).
D 64 cm (25⅛ in)
Manufacturer: Bieffe, Italy

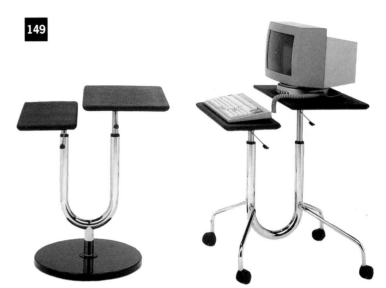

149

Toshiyuki Kita
Chaise longue, *Ara*
Steel frame, leather upholstery
H 61 cm (24 in). W 190 cm (74⅞ in).
D 78 cm (30¾ in)
Manufacturer: Interprofil, West Germany

Toshiyuki Kita
Table and matching trolley,
Step 2, Step 1
Metal, polyurethane
The two shelves are individually
adjustable in height and the castors are
provided with a braking system.
H 60 cm (23½ in) to 73 cm (28¾ in).
D 53 cm (20⅞ in). W of lower shelf 25 cm
(9⅞ in). W of upper shelf 36 cm (14⅛ in)
Manufacturer: Airon, Italy

150

151

Toshiyuki Kita
Chair, *Nice*
Wood, padded cloth
H 70 cm (27½ in). W 65 cm (25½ in).
D 56 cm (22 in)
Manufacturer: Accademia, Italy

Maurizio Peregalli

Bench, *Canapé*
Epoxy-painted iron rod, stainless steel
H 81 cm (31¾ in). W 120 cm (47¼ in).
D 48 cm (18⅞ in)
Manufacturer: Noto, Italy

152

153

Maurizio Peregalli

Stool, *Platform*
Epoxy-painted steel, birch plywood
H 74 cm (29 in). W 31 cm (12¼ in).
D 40 cm (15¾ in)
Manufacturer: Noto, Italy

154

Dakota Jackson
Chaise, *K3-'Zü*
Laminated plywood frame, leather
H 81.25 cm (32 in). W 61 cm (24 in).
L 193 cm (76 in)
Manufacturer: Dakota Jackson, USA

155

Dakota Jackson's *Deco Echoes* highlight the essential difference between the Art Deco revival in Europe and that in the US. European Art Deco has come to symbolize the comfortable and capacious cruiseliner look of the *Normandie* or the Savoy stateroom. It evolved differently in the States, introduced about the time that Prohibition was lifted and the Jazz Age began: it was more streamlined, more movie-house and – in the case of Miami's famed Art Deco quarter – more kitsch.

Deco is boldly redrawn in the *K3-'Zü* upholstered collection, which includes a chaise, a club chair, an ottoman, a love-seat, a sofa and a dining chair – all ready for work, rather than cruising or lounging. Showing appreciation for the 1930s master-craftsman Emile-Jacques Ruhlmann, the armchair has an irony to its flapper legs which is pure Charleston, and a sharp line to the arms and back which is rather Calvin Klein.

Dakota Jackson
Armchair, *K3-'Zü*
Hardwood frame, ebonized mahogany
front legs, leather
H 85 cm (33¼ in). W 67.5 cm (26½ in).
D 63.5 cm (25 in)
Manufacturer: Dakota Jackson, USA

156

Dakota Jackson
Club chair and ottoman, *K3-'Zü*
Hardwood frame, leather
Chair: H 78 cm (30¾ in).
W 85 cm (33½ in). D 87.5 cm (34½ in)
Ottoman: H 45 cm (17¾ in). W 60.5 cm
(23¾ in). D 60.5 cm (23¾ in)
Manufacturer: Dakota Jackson, USA

Phillip Schroeder

Sofa, *Car's The Star '59 Cadillac "DeVille Divan"*
Original 1959 Cadillac rear-end with cassette player concealed behind the licence plate and power antenna and telephone in the armrest. The tail-lights take 110V bulbs. Prototype
H 92 cm (36 in). W 213 cm (84 in).
D 106.5 cm (42 in)
Manufacturer: 50's AutoArt, USA

157

Setting up home in the back seat of an old Cadillac is possible with Phillip Schroeder's AutoArt. His custom-built furniture takes its lead in design from the Detroit style engineers of the Fifties and Sixties who stretched the chromium fin so far that it eventually went into oblivion.

Chairs, love-seats, tables, desks, bars and sculptures are created from parts of obsolete big-finned American cars, such as Cadillacs and Chevrolets. "Elvis, rock 'n roll and pink Cadillacs are the true icons of the Fifties in America," he says. "We're trying to create furniture that is fun and has a sense of humour." Lined in fake suede, ocelot or zebra, the lightweight fibreglass bodies get their high-gloss glitter with 20 hand-rubbed lacquer coats. Like the cars, the claims made for them are extravagant. "Neo-Retro is the new way to look back," says Freda Schroeder, owner of the company, 50's AutoArt.

Lamps like fishbones, insects, birds, leaves and elves' caps? Whatever happened to High Tech? In lighting, the 1989/90 collection is more literal than ever. Now that engineers have so effectively harnessed light sources on a small scale, designers experiment less with the source and instead explore shape. The result is less a light show of dazzling theatrical effects than a collection of honest, functional objects. Even spotlights by Gregotti Associati or the Sottsass Design Team look exactly like spotlights of the Sixties. While Krohn and Viemeister pick clean the carcass of a floor lamp with their *Sardine*, Branzi's glowing green leaf represents the last area of design to display Memphis's distinctive freedom — form rather than function.

Post-Tech is the label for this transformation of aesthetic notions, but in reality the friendly lights in this section hold a bank of technology. Ingo Maurer's production of Stefan Lindfors' glowing insect may look sci-fi, but it is touch-sensitive and brings light to

LIGHTING

your fingertips. Guen Bertheau-Suzuki's lotus lamp opens and closes like a flower in true organic fashion, using an innovative metal

2

alloy that repeatedly returns to its "remembered" shape. Collaboration between art and science can also be observed in the experiment by the industrial designer Kita and the artist Haring. Their lamp outlines a figure floating in space in an electroluminescent panel, which is attached by an umbilical cord to its ground control, a rock.

This preoccupation by designers with the cord that contains the wiring is evident in several pieces. It becomes the spinal cord of the *Sardine*, and is looped like a tether to Ingo Maurer's floor lamp. Ingo Maurer and his team pioneered the lamp that did away with cords, substituting trapeze wires upon which the fittings travelled. Now they work on the vertical plane.

Achille Castiglioni harnesses the emotive quality of light in his new pendant for Flos, which could easily be a symbol of corporate power. It is an interesting statement from a designer who is most proud of a 30-year-old design for a modest little lightswitch, still found on table lamps and marketed around the world without any credit to its designer. King and Miranda explore light's reflective quality with shades and shutters on *RAI*. Mario Botta works on similar lines in a seesaw drum of a lamp for Artemide that filters light through a mesh.

Not since Art Deco have designers so favoured chrome, though there is no echo of Deco in their forms. Philippe Starck's lamp for Flos, named *Arà* after his daughter, is shaped like a horn, while Jorge Pensi's *Olympia* is a projectile missile. The industry is refreshingly free this year of special lenses and theatrical props. Alongside this simplicity comes a freedom of shape, rooted in nature or in mythology.

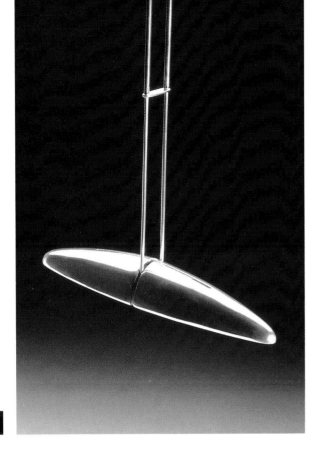

1

Jorge Pensi
Ceiling lamp, *Olympia*
Aluminium, stainless steel, glass
Takes two 150W halogen bulbs.
H 260 cm (102⅜ in). W 47 cm (18½ in)
Manufacturer: Belux, Spain

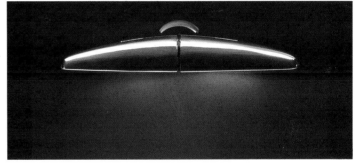

2

Jorge Pensi
Wall lamp, *Olympia*
Aluminium, stainless steel, glass
Takes two 150W halogen bulbs.
W 47 cm (18½ in). Overhang 15 cm
(5⅞ in)
Manufacturer: Belux, Spain

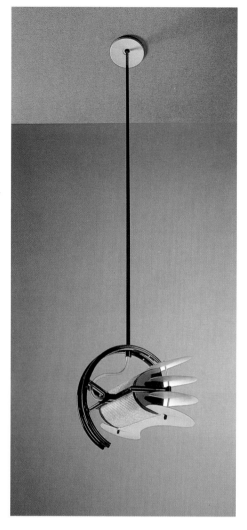

3

It is hard to pinpoint the quality that makes King and Miranda's lights bestsellers in an extremely competitive business. Their spot-track *Expanded Light System* for Marcatrè, and their pendant light shaded by a cobalt-blue glass disc for Flos, are both classics, but it is more than just a track system or shade that illuminates their understated designs. They make elegant lights that are flexible, permitting the user to control the source. At a time when lights are either general or directional, and you need a textbook – or a stepladder – to focus them, King and Miranda design lights that pivot or swivel and are shaded with metal wings or adjustable shutters. They make easy work of sophisticated technology, and the result is an accessible collection.

**Perry A. King and Santiago
Miranda**
Spotlight, *RAI*
Aluminium, steel
Can be ceiling or track-mounted.
Takes one 200/300W 220/240V halogen bulb.
H 18.7 cm (7²⁄₅ in). W 31 cm (12¼ in).
D 18.3 cm (7¹⁄₆ in)
Manufacturer: Arteluce Flos, Italy

Since they address the design problems so openly, it is interesting that they have called their latest light *RAI*, the initials of the main Italian radio and television network. "It looks like a microphone," says Perry King amiably. Like the microphone, it is finely tuned to shift position, to track the slightest change, and also to give a high-quality light over a set area. The source can be fitted with louvres, as shown here, or with directional shades, glass diffusers or coloured filters. *RAI* is the first of a range of three spotlights, intended to be mounted in either the *Expanded Light System* or on the ceiling at home. It was designed for the new Marcatrè office equipment showroom, which opened in Paris in 1989.

Angelo Mangiarotti
Floor lamp, *Techne*
Extruded aluminium, reflector of
chromed lamella
Takes one 250W halogen bulb.
H 189 cm (74⅛ in). Base Di 39 cm
(15⅜ in). Reflector Di 28 cm (11 in)
Manufacturer: Pollux Group Skipper,
Italy

Angelo Mangiarotti
Table lamp, *Etrusca*
Alabaster, metal
Takes one 50W halogen bulb.
H 28 cm (11 in). W 27 cm (10½ in).
D 23 cm (9 in)
Manufacturer: Pollux Group Skipper,
Italy

6

Josep Lluscà
Table lamp, *Bolonia*
Chromium-plated iron, brass, glass
The adjustable shade has a matt
opalescent glass diffuser.
Takes one 20W 12V halogen bulb.
H 40 cm (15¾ in). Base Di 14 cm (5½ in)
Manufacturer: Metalarte, Spain

7

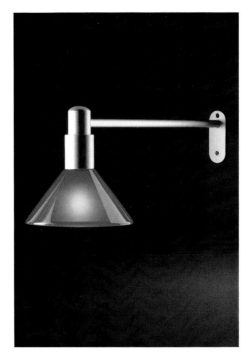

Gregotti Associati
Wall lamp, *Nuova Segno Quattro*
Metal, finished in black, grey or pale
grey, white or blue glass shade
Takes one 100W E17 halogen bulb.
H 16 cm (6¼ in). L 16 cm (6¼ in).
Di 25 cm (9⅞ in) or 40 cm (15¾ in)
Manufacturer: Fontana Arte, Italy

Lumiance Design Team   8
Spotlight, *Primostar Conic Cool 50*
Aluminium
Should be connected to the ceiling plug
with a separate transformer.
Takes one 50W 12V coolbeam bulb.
H 6.2 cm (2½ in), 28 cm (11 in), 50 cm
(19⅝ in). Cone Di 8.5 cm (3⅜ in)
Manufacturer: Lumiance, Netherlands

Lumiance Design Team   9
Spotlight, *Primostar Basic Cool 50*
Aluminium
Should be connected to the ceiling plug
with a separate transformer.
Takes one 50W 12V coolbeam bulb.
H 6.2 cm (2½ in), 28 cm (11 in), 50 cm
(19⅝ in). Cone Di 2.5 cm (1 in)
Manufacturer: Lumiance, Netherlands

Alfred Homann
Table lamp, *AH*
ABS
An asymmetric lamp for terminals,
keyboards, workstations or to be used as
a traditional table lamp. Three moulded
parts plus a reflector form the lamp; the
transformer is in the base.
Takes one 12V tungsten halogen (quartz)
bulb without reflector.
H 46 cm (18 in). W 7 cm (2¾ in)
Manufacturer: Louis Poulsen, Denmark

10

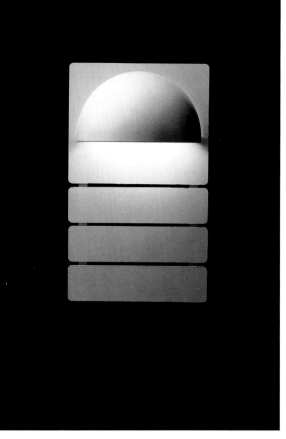

Alfred Homann
Wall lamp, *Homann*
Moulded siluminum, an alloy of
aluminium and silicon
Incandescent lamp with a candelabra
base.
Takes one 40W 120V or 220V half pearl
bulb.
H 20 cm (7⅞ in). W 24 cm (9⅜ in)
Manufacturer: Louis Poulsen, Denmark

11

12

Daniela Puppa and Franco Raggi
Wall or ceiling lamp, *Altair Plafoniera*
Die-cast aluminium, glass
Takes three spherical milky-white 40W
incandescent bulbs.
D 18 cm (7 in). Di 40 cm (15¾ in)
Manufacturer: Fontana Arte, Italy

Dieter Witte
Ceiling lamp, *Dulux-Pendell*
Plastic
Takes one Dulux EL 20W bulb,
equivalent to one 100W incandescent
bulb.
H 29 cm (11⅜ in). Di 15 cm (6 in)
Manufacturer: Osram, West Germany

13

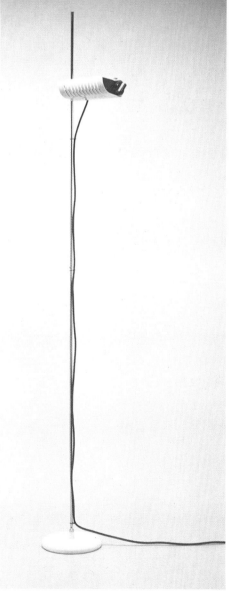

14

Joe Colombo
Floor lamp, *626*
Chromium-plated and lacquered steel
Originally designed in 1972.
Takes one 500W halogen bulb,
adjustable with a dimmer switch.
H 210 cm (82⅝ in). Base Di 24 cm
(9⅜ in)
Manufacturer: Oluce, Italy

Joe Colombo, who was born in Milan in 1930 and died in 1971, was the designer of the Sixties whose work, influenced by American culture and the Pop idiom, took on a space-age line. His interest in plastics and Perspex freed his designs from the timber technology prevalent at the time, with sinuous results. There are his spaceship swivel armchair, the *Elda* for Confort, and Oluce's reissue of rounded, Perspex lights. In a tribute to Colombo, Oluce held an exhibition of his designs in their new Milan showroom during the Furniture Fair of 1988. Many of the lamps he designed are still in production, from model *281* – the famous curved Perspex light of 1962, which won the gold medal at the Thirteenth Triennale in 1964 – to model *626*, the halogen lamp which appeared on the market in 1972, shown here. Colombo's understanding of new technology inspired his designs, which were so far ahead of their time that they remain contemporary to this day.

When Ingo Maurer saw this chrysalis-like light in Finland, the brainchild of 26-year-old Stefan Lindfors, he decided to put it into production. Its jointed aluminium, steel and plastic carcase is more science fiction than the real world, more alien than anthropomorphic. Ingo Maurer's explanation of it is far removed from most manufacturers' instructions, illustrating the playful quality he brings to high technology: "*Scaragoo* is a far cry from the monotony of black and white and simple shapes. It is fantastic and mysterious, a great gold insect on frail legs. It is waiting for you, but be careful when you touch it. *Scaragoo* moves and lights up, providing as strong or muted light as you wish."

Stefan Lindfors for the Ingo Maurer Team
Floor lamp, *Scaragoo*
Aluminium, steel, plastic
Takes one 50W 12V halogen bulb.
H 53 cm (20⅞ in) to 79 cm (31 in).
W 33 cm (13 in). L 46 cm (18 in)
Manufacturer: Design M Ingo Maurer, West Germany

15

Martine Bedin
Table or desk lamp, *Swing*
Aluminium, brass
Takes one 12V low tension halogen bulb.
H 61 cm (24 in). W 14 cm (5½ in).
L 28 cm (11 in)
Manufacturer: Memphis, Italy

16

Tucker Viemeister and Lisa Krohn
Ceiling lamp, *Sardine Light*
Metal spring, lead, paper shade
Uses any voltage with a matching bulb;
this one is a standard 110V with a 40W
chandelier bulb. Prototype
H 12.5 cm (5 in). W 5 cm (2 in).
L 46 cm (18 in)
Manufacturer: Gallery 91, USA

17

Andrea Branzi
Wall lamp, *Foglia*
Electro-luminescent glass
The electrical current of this low-voltage
lamp is generated through the "veins" of
the leaf.
W 25 cm (9⅞ in). L 45 cm (17¾ in)
Manufacturer: Memphis, Italy

18

A lamp called *Sardine Light* lays bare its bones. The flex is controlled within a metal spring vertebra on an adjustable fulcrum. The fish head is luminous. First shown at the Furniture and Counterparts Exhibition at Gallery 91 in New York, it is a collaboration between Lisa Krohn, a Cranbrook Academy graduate, and Tucker Viemeister, a principal of the Smart Design group; a former collaboration won them the 1987 plastics design competition in Finland (see *The International Design Yearbook 4*). Smart Design is committed to what Viemeister calls "democratic design, available to everyone."

Viemeister and Krohn are typical of the new breed of industrial designers whose counter-offensive to European design began in the Fifties with cars and office equipment, and re-emerged in the Nineties as the antithesis of corporate design. They not only reflect society, but help to shape it. The qualities they value, which can be clearly seen in this light, are visual, tactile, funny and functional.

Reacting against the harsh purity of Modernism, devoid of colour and ornament, Andrea Branzi's work has a distinctive charm and energy that goes beyond Mannerism. He was invited to participate in the last Memphis collection, presented in the summer of 1988. The collection of lights by 23 international designers underwrites the group's epitaph. The fallen-leaf light from Branzi, aglow in fluorescent green, is the best example of the Memphis design aesthetic, where function no longer dictates form. Essential structural elements act as ornaments. Underlining Branzi's lack of interest in formal lighting, this frivolous approach makes rigorous "good taste" look a little tired.

19

This light, with the brutal visual assault of subway graffiti, is the result of an unusual collaboration between an industrial designer, Toshiyuki Kita, and an artist, Keith Haring. Organic is perhaps too explicit a label to tag on to the result. Electro-luminescent panels have an industrial application, which Toshiyuki Kita has used for the first time in the home to send light through a normal current. He works as an industrial designer in Japan and Italy, while the American Haring describes his artistry as "video clones, specta-colour billboards, rain dance, Live Aid and Pop shop in both New York and Tokyo."

Toshiyuki Kita and Keith Haring
Table lamp, left: *On Taro*
right: *On Giro*
Natural stone, glass
The electro-luminescent fixture can be plugged into 110V or 220V. The consumption is minimal, about 4W, and the lifetime is over 10,000 hours.
H 52 cm (20½ in). W 29 cm (11⅜ in).
D 15 cm (6 in)
Manufacturer: Kreon, Belgium

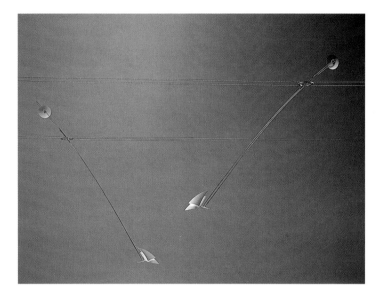

20

Bernhard Dessecker, Bernd Axel Kluge, Franz Ringelhan for Ingo Maurer and Team
Ceiling lamps, *Tijuca*
Metal, plastic
The four halogen lighting elements of 50W 12V each can be moved horizontally and vertically by means of counterweights, and are adjustable through 360 degrees.
H up to 6 metres (19 ft 8 in). W 12 cm (4¾ in)
Manufacturer: Design M Ingo Maurer, West Germany

Light in motion is the novel idea of Ingo Maurer and his team. At every exhibition, Ingo Maurer's stand is a real crowd-puller. The concept of freeing light from its socket and moving it along visible wires brilliantly unmasks the technology. The idea began with the *YaYahoho* low-voltage halogen light on a trapeze, which Ingo Maurer designed in the mid-Eighties. Each year a further development on the theme produces a new species of light with more adjustable or hanging elements, as well as refinements such as high-quality dimmer circuits, adjustability, and touch-sensitive controls and switches. Ingo Maurer explains his latest design: "My idea was to create a jungle of light that flies like a bird in the jungle of Tijuca. A light that dances, glides, tilts, balances and rotates and, above all, provides a clear and precise light by which to work, read or dream. I regard it as a straightforward piece of functional industrial design." Maurer's vision is translated into these precise terms by his team, without whom he refuses to be credited.

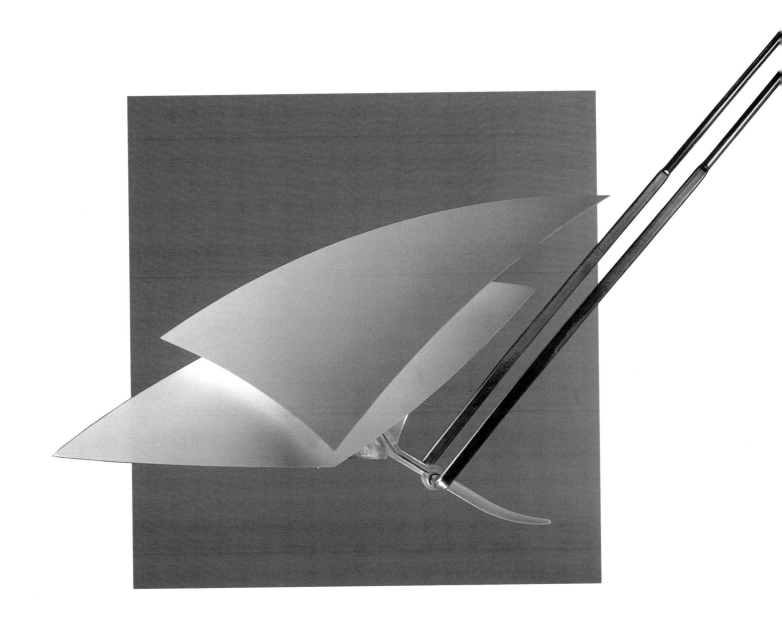

Steven Lombardi
Outdoor wall lamp, *Filicudara*
Anodized aluminium, polyester
Takes one 100W incandescent bulb or a
candle.
H 44 cm (17¼ in). W 30.5 cm (12 in).
D 23.5 cm (9½ in)
Manufacturer: Artemide, Italy

21

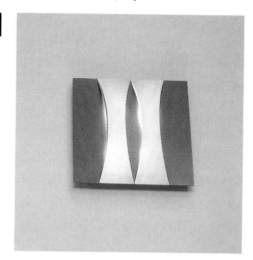

Torben Holmbäck
Floor lamp, *A3*
Sheet aluminium
A "folded" lamp inspired by standard
paper formats.
Bulbs from 40W to 75W may be used,
although the construction of the lamp is
such that reflection of light is optimal
and 40W is therefore ample.
H 49 cm (19¼ in). W 33 cm (13 in).
D 33 cm (13 in)
Manufacturer: B.J. Metal, Denmark

22

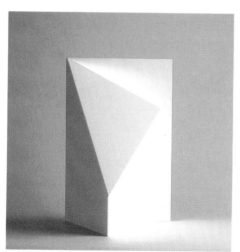

23

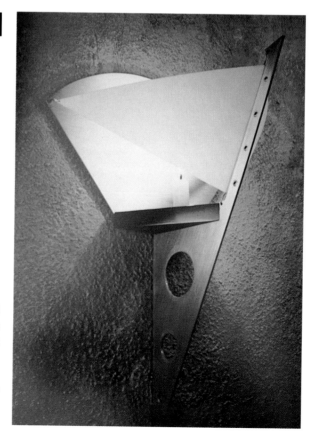

Arata Isozaki
Wall lamp, *Eye*
Steel, aluminium
Takes four 25W 100V halogen bulbs.
H 36 cm (14⅛ in). W 36 cm (14⅛ in).
D 8 cm (3⅛ in)
Manufacturer: Yamagiwa Corporation,
Japan

24

**Bernhard Dessecker, Bernd Axel
Kluge, Franz Ringelhan for Ingo
Maurer and Team**
Ceiling lamp, *Little Black Nothing*
Metal, plastic, glass
Adjustable in height. The lamp swivels
180 degrees at ceiling point and the
reflector rotates 360 degrees. The
electronic transformer–sensor–dimmer
is manually controlled or can be used in
conjunction with a standard 12V built-in
transformer.
Takes one 50W 12V halogen bulb.
H 180 cm max (70⅝ in). W 20 cm (7⅞ in)
Manufacturer: Design M Ingo Maurer,
West Germany

Gianfranco Frattini
Floor lamp, *Acheo*
Painted metal, glass
A wall lamp with a diffuser balanced
by tension wires.
Takes one 300W halogen bulb.
H 181 cm (71⅜ in). W 39 cm (15⅜ in)
Diffuser: L 23.5 cm (9½ in)
Manufacturer: Artemide, Italy

Gianfranco Frattini
Wall lamp, *Acheo Parete*
Painted metal, glass
A floor lamp with a diffuser balanced by
tension wires.
Takes one 300W halogen bulb.
H 21 cm (8¼ in). W 23.5 cm (9½ in)
Manufacturer: Artemide, Italy

25

26

Mario Botta

Ceiling lamp, *Zefiro*
Metal, perforated plate
A suspension lamp with a white-painted
perforated plate diffuser.
Takes one 300W halogen lamp.
H 100 cm (39½ in) to 130 cm (51⅛ in).
W 92 cm (36 in)
Manufacturer: Artemide, Italy

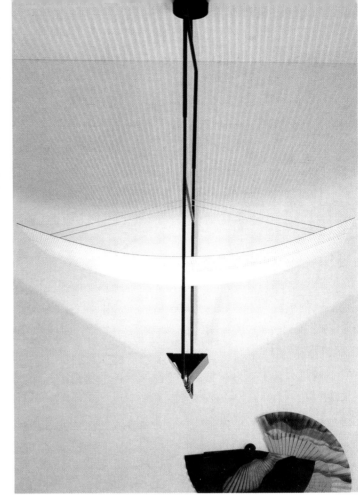

27

Ernesto Gismondi

Outdoor lamp, *Giasole T.S.*
Painted metal, sandblasted glass
Takes one 100W E27 incandescent
bulb or one 18W PL fluorescent bulb.
H 33 cm (13 in). W 16 cm (6¼ in).
D 12 cm (4¾ in)
Manufacturer: Artemide, Italy

Swiss-born architect Mario Botta has landed the prize
commission to design the new San Francisco Museum
of Modern Art, a $70 million project, due to be built by
about 1993. In art galleries, the harnessing of natural
and artificial light is of primary importance. Botta's
energetic and inventive control of light and shade has
produced here the most illuminating scheme for
Artemide. The shades created from perforated mesh
are simple in form yet throw elaborate patterns of
light on wall, floor or ceiling surfaces, depending on
the fitting. He uses light both for ornamental effect
and to define space, to break mass and to accent with
shadow. His design work does not fiercely reject the
mantle of Modernism. Botta emphasizes, in a prosely-
tizing manner: "I believe that there can in fact
be no creative activity without the intention on one
hand and the convention on the other. I believe there
is always, at once, a newness of the old and an
archaeology of the new."

28

29

Christian Hvidt

Outdoor wall lamp, *Chr. 4. Mini*
Die-cast and extruded aluminium,
fibreglass-armed polyester,
polycarbonate shade
Takes one 125W quicksilver or 70W
sodium bulb.
H 36 cm (14⅛ in). Di 42 cm (16½ in)
Manufacturer: Solar Belysning, Denmark

30

Christian Hvidt

Outdoor lamp, *Chr. 4. Maxi*
Die-cast and extruded aluminium,
fibreglass-armed polyester,
polycarbonate shade
Takes one 125W quicksilver or 70W
sodium bulb.
H 48 cm (18⅞ in). Di 62 cm (24⅜ in)
Manufacturer: Solar Belysning, Denmark

31

Andrzej Duljas
Floor lamp, *Tria F-5184*
Aluminium, blue glass
Takes one 500W halogen bulb,
adjustable with a dimmer switch.
H 177.5 cm (74 in). Base W 23 cm (9 in).
Shade W 20.5 cm (8 in). Shade D 7.5 cm
(3 in)
Manufacturer: Koch & Lowy, USA

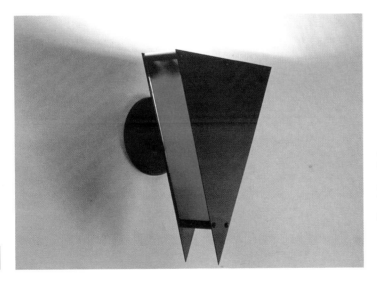

32

Andrzej Duljas
Wall lamp, *Tria P/W-84*
Aluminium, blue glass
Takes one 300W halogen bulb,
adjustable with a dimmer switch.
H 30.5 cm (12 in). W 20.5 cm (8 in)
D 15 cm (6 in)
Manufacturer: Koch & Lowy, USA

In this lotus flower of a light, petals conceal the latest technology that makes it open and close. At the base are six springs on a coil, each made from a remarkable substance called Shape Memory Alloy. This is a metal that has a memory and responds to heat. For example, a horseshoe shape made from the alloy can be crumpled up into a corkscrew; as it is warmed, it will return to its original shape. In *Spring Greetings*, as the light heats up, the alloy coils gradually unfurl the petals that shade the bulb. When it is switched off, a second set of normal steel coils, which flank the Shape Memory Alloy ones, take over and close the light petals over the low-halogen bulb in a tight bud. It is a brilliant example of something functional being given a beautiful form; until now, the alloy has been used for prosaic pieces, from orthodontics to car bumpers, where its memory bank has more obvious advantages.

33

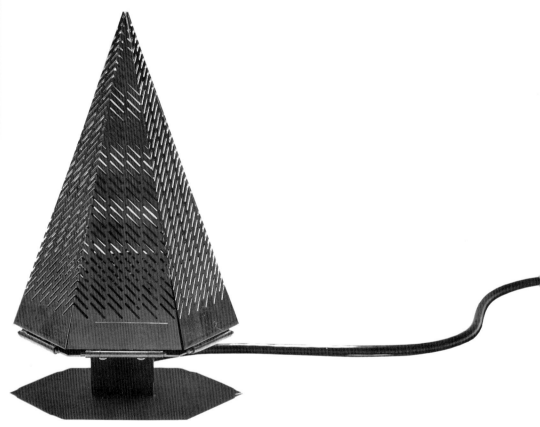

Guen Bertheau-Suzuki
Table lamp, *Spring Greetings*
Perforated aluminium, Shape Memory
Alloy, steel, glass, brass
The petals open with the bulb's heat
within three minutes and close when the
lamp is switched off.
Takes one 50W 12V halogen bulb.
Limited batch production
H 25 cm (9⅞ in). D 14 cm (5½ in)
Manufacturer: Ishimaru, Japan

34

Joerg Wurmitzer
Table lamp, *Triaglight*
Wood, brass, parchment
Takes three 50W 24V halogen bulbs.
Limited batch production
H 40 cm (15¾ in). W 34 cm (13⅜ in).
D 15 cm (6 in)
Manufacturer: Woka Lamps Vienna,
Austria

35

Ettore Sottsass
Floor lamp, *Traliccio*
Painted metal, brass
A floor lamp with a diffuser.
Takes one 500W halogen bulb.
H 195 cm (76⅞ in). Base W 25 cm
(9⅞ in). Base D 25 cm (9⅞ in)
Manufacturer: Memphis, Italy

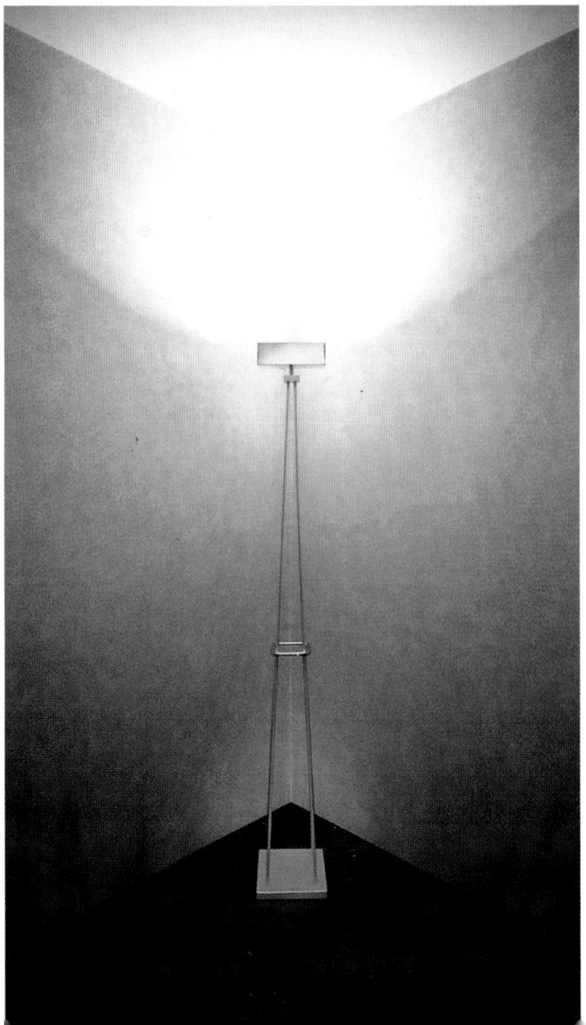

Sottsass Associati
Lighting system, *Halo-Click 1, Halo-Click
2, Halo-Click 3, Halo-Click Track*
Plastic, metal
The series is characterized by a
360-degrees articulation which enables
the optic unit to rotate completely on
the two axes.
Left to right:
Table lamp: Takes one 20W 12V halogen
bulb.
H 39.5 cm (15⅝ in). Base H 8.5 cm
(3⅜ in). Base D 12 cm (4¾ in) Shade
W 6.4 cm (2½ in). Shade D 7.7 cm (3 in)
Wall lamp with transformer and switch:
Takes one 20W 12V halogen bulb.
H 15 cm (6 in). Base H 7.5 cm (3 in). Base
W 7.5 cm (3 in). Shade W 6.4 cm (2½ in).
Shade D 7.7 cm (3 in)
Track lighting: Takes one 50W 12V
halogen bulb.
Stem H 23.5 cm (9½ in). Shade W 6.4 cm
(2½ in). Shade D 7.7 cm (3 in)
Floor lamp with switch and transformer:
Takes one 50W 12V halogen bulb.
H 150 cm (59 in). Base H 12 cm (4¾ in).
Base W 20 cm (7⅞ in). Shade W 6.5 cm
(2½ in). Shade D 7.8 cm (3⅛ in)
Manufacturer: Philips Lighting, Italy

36

37

Gaspar Glusberg
Ceiling lamp, *X140/C*
Enamelled metal, opalescent glass
The base has a built-in mechanical
transformer.
Takes one 50W 12V halogen bulb.
H 67 cm (26⅜ in). Shade H 17.5 cm
(6⅞ in). Shade W 17.5 cm (6⅞ in)
Manufacturer: Modulor, Argentina

38

Gaspar Glusberg
Ceiling lamp, *X160 "SUS"*
Enamelled metal
Adjustable lamp with a recessed
transformer.
Takes one 50W 12V halogen bulb.
H 7 cm (2¾ in). W 12 cm (4¾ in)
Manufacturer: Modulor, Argentina

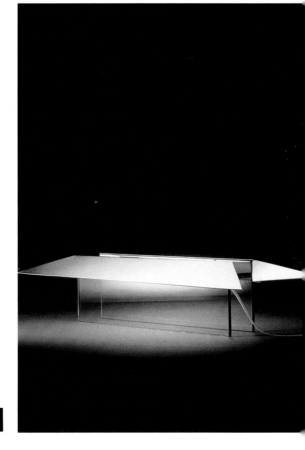

40

39

Elisabeth Garouste and Mattia Bonetti

Candleholder, *Tripod*
Mild steel, terracotta
Limited batch production
H 15 cm (6 in). Di 11.5 cm (4½ in)
Manufacturer: ceramic by M. Bonetti;
ironwork by La Ferronerie d'art, France

Gae Aulenti and Piero Castiglioni

Table lamp, *Pietra*
Glass, Pyrex, nickel-plated brass
Takes 18 10W 12V incandescent bulbs
in two tubes (9 bulbs in each).
H 16 cm (6¼ in). W 29 cm (11⅜ in).
L 69 cm (27⅛ in)
Manufacturer: Fontana Arte, Italy

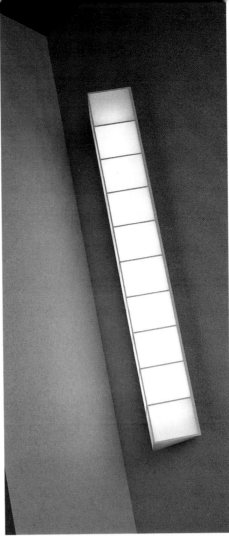

41

Masayuki Kurokawa
Table lamp, *Lavinia*
Aluminium
Takes one 50W 12V halogen bulb.
H 40 cm (15¾ in). W 56 cm (22 in).
D 66 cm (26 in)
Manufacturer: Artemide, Italy

Masayuki Kurokawa
Ceiling lamp, *Albore*
Steel, Japanese paper
Takes one 40W 100V bulb.
H 16 cm (6¼ in). W 13 cm (5⅛ in).
L 24 cm (9⅜ in)
Manufacturer: Yamagiwa Corporation,
Japan

42

Afra and Tobia Scarpa
Floor lamp, *Vol-au-Vent*
Aluminized fibreglass, metal
One or two further lighting fixtures can
be fitted to the stem by a simple
mechanical attachment. The diffuser
rotates 360 degrees.
Takes one 500W halogen bulb.
Prototype
H 220 cm (86⅞ in). W 32 cm (12½ in).
W of diffuser 56 cm (22 in). Base Di
44 cm (17¼ in)
Manufacturer: Flos, Italy

43

44

Achille Castiglioni

Ceiling lamp, *Taraxacum '88*

Aluminium

An icosahedron with an equilateral triangle holding a variable number of bulbs up to a maximum of 200. The structure consists of 20 hinged, bright aluminium triangles, each holding 3, 6 or 10 25/40W Globolux clear bulbs.

Di 76 cm (30 in) for 60 bulb configuration

Di 105 cm (41⅝ in) for 120 bulb configuration

Di 130 cm (51⅛ in) for 200 bulb configuration

Manufacturer: Flos, Italy

45

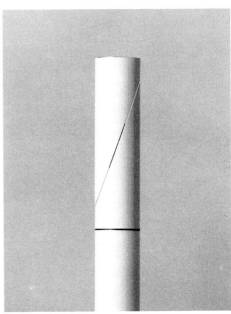

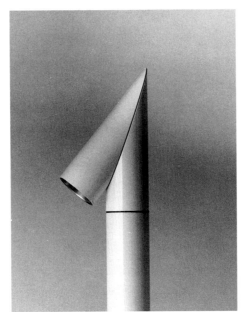

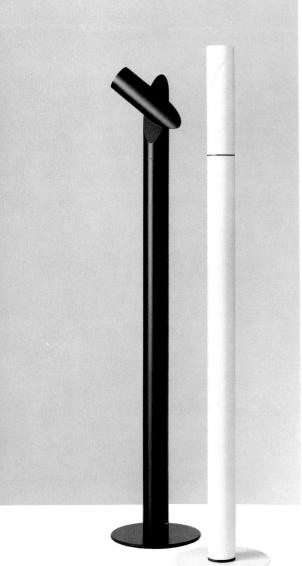

**Herbert Schultes, for
Schlagheck & Schultes Design**
Floor lamp, *Orion*
Aluminium, steel
A floor lamp with a swivelling top and
dimmer switch.
Takes one 250W halogen bulb.
H 190 cm (74⅞ in). Base Di 39 cm
(15⅜ in)
Manufacturer: Vereinigte Werkstätten,
West Germany

46

Robert Sonneman
Wall lamp, *Diamond*
Plate aluminium
Takes one 100W 110V halogen bulb.
H 21.5 cm (8½ in). W 43.5 cm (17 in).
D 10 cm (4 in)
Manufacturer: George Kovacs Lighting,
USA

47

48

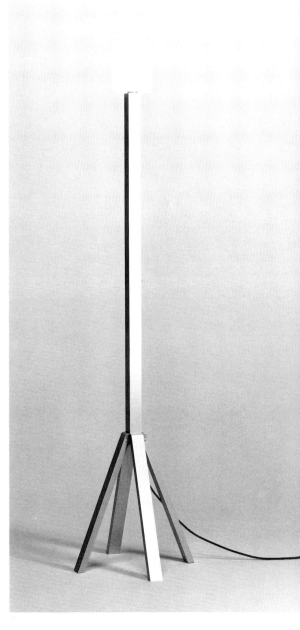

Robert Sonneman
Floor lamp, *Motto Yubi*
Cast, extruded and plate aluminium
Has a full range dimmer.
Takes one 300W 110V (11.7 cm/4½ in)
halogen bulb.
H 175.5 cm (69 in). Base H 25.5 cm
(10 in). Base W 15 cm (6 in). Shade
H 10 cm (4 in). Shade W 46 cm (18 in)
Manufacturer: George Kovacs Lighting,
USA

Michele De Lucchi
Floor lamp, *Click*
Anodized aluminium, sanded opalescent
glass diffuser
Takes one 250W 220V candle-shaped
halogen bulb.
H 200 cm (78¾ in). Base Di 50 cm
(19⅝ in)
Manufacturer: Bieffe, Italy

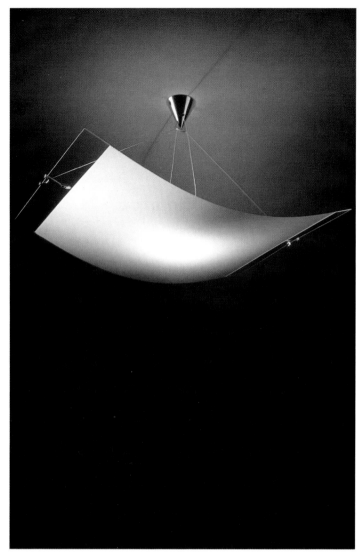

49

Franco Raggi
Ceiling lamp, *Velo*
Brushed die-cast aluminium, steel, glass,
Pyrex glass
Takes one 300W halogen bulb.
H 50 cm (19⅝ in), 70 cm (27½ in), 90 cm
(35½ in), 110 cm (43¼ in) or 130 cm
(51⅛ in). W 77 cm (30¼ in). D 60 cm
(23½ in)
Manufacturer: Fontana Arte, Italy

50

Alfredo Pizzo Greco
Floor lamp, *Arpa*
Black-enamelled aluminium, white
Carrara marble
Originally designed in 1965.
Takes one incandescent bulb, 40W to
100W.
H 133 cm (52⅜ in). W 35 cm (13¾ in)
Manufacturer: Zanotta, Italy

51

Philippe Starck describes himself as a "creative junkie" who spends his holidays doing what he does every day of his life – designing. Of all the products to which he turns his prolific pen, he most enjoys designing lights, since there is the added magic of light. "Even if it is right for a lamp to give out light – its functional aspect – there are always thousands of lamps and ways to solve the problem. Objects must change with each generation. After the functionalism of the industrial period, and the age of the beautifully designed object, designers now have to bring them to life. This lamp, in particular, is similar to a little person, a charming elf just like the ones you read about in tales all over the world." He called it *Arà* after his daughter. The integrity of this lamp comes from the material as well – chrome-plated cast aluminium, which has not undergone any treatment that degrades its natural quality. "It's a purely modern material, lightness and unalterability being the expression of this modernity."

Philippe Starck
Table lamp, *Arà*
Chrome-plated cast aluminium
Adjustable lamp which is switched on
and off by turning the shade.
Takes one 35W 12V halogen bulb.
H 55 cm (21½ in). Shade W 27 cm
(10½ in)
Manufacturer: Flos, Italy

In an age of conspicuous consumption, tableware designed by architects and artists gets star billing. While all this activity might have made them household names, the tribute should really go to the manufacturers and promoters who turned designer china into a status symbol. But despite the famous collection of 11 architects' tea sets from the Italian manufacturer Alberto Alessi, and the architects' tableware by the American duo Swid Powell, the design of tableware did not actually change much beyond a decorative border or finish – until now. This volume records an interesting development driven by changes in the popular taste in food. Tableware and cutlery are becoming suitable for both Western and Eastern cuisines. Implements capable of scooping, cutting and lifting replace regular place settings, like Philippe Starck's new cutlery for Sasaki. Hosak-Robb's *Göffel* is a cross between a spoon and a fork destined for fast canteen food (whether it will introduce a new etiquette remains to be seen). Bowls can be used for drinking or for soup, and desserts are moved on to small plates that can double as side plates. Kawabe's stacking orange pagoda of plates, *Kan Kan*, is practical and multifunctional.

Flower vases also show this cross-pollination of Occident and Orient. Japanese, French, German, Spanish and Italian designers have all come up with individual designs that control the direction and placing of each flower. Their discipline owes a great deal to the Japanese art of flower arranging, *ikebana*. Komatsu's half-moon in stainless steel, *Arch*, lines up flowers in a swoop like a high-rise building; Starck's precise vessels for Daum, shaped like horns in coloured glass, discourage armfuls of flowers; and Müller, Deganello and Tusquets Blanca all concentrate on single flower supports.

TABLEWARE 3

Metal and marble are materials that are hard to work – springy, tense and dense compared with malleable clay. Particular forms in these uncompromising materials are radiant and strong and surprising. Martine Bedin stacks black and white bands of marble off balance, like the Leaning Tower of Pisa, in a vessel that is precise yet at the same time adrift in a disconcerting reassessment of the rules. There are some lovely examples of Venetian glass, so imaginative in its form: decanters sprouting fantastical stoppers, and stems with twists that are never repeated twice – mass produced, yes, but not machine-turned.

To underline Oscar Tusquets Blanca's firmly held belief that only mainline production pieces should be shown, students' designs are represented only if a major manufacturer has taken them up or, as opposite, they have clear potential for mass production. *In the Spirit of the USA*, a competition sponsored by Villeroy & Boch with the Viennese Academy of Applied Arts, is interesting less for its playful shapes (which hardly meet the dictum of form and function) than for the attitudes expressed by the students towards American culture.

This coffee and tea set by Svend Onø is a perfect example of a design that stems from traditions of metal-working rather than porcelain. Stainless steel sheets are first pressed under heat to shape the pieces around moulds and templates. Usually, the materials left over along the edges are cut away for resmelting, just as fabric remnants are trimmed away from garments. But Svend Onø has made that edge an intrinsic feature of this innovative design by bolting the pieces together, a visual nicety that also works actively to support the long spout. Traditionally, a long spout, well away from the body, is best for pouring, but it is always the weak part on a steel pot since it has to be soldered on. Onø's design avoids this potential flaw in much the same way as Oscar Tusquets Blanca did when he designed his tea and coffee set for the Italian company Alessi five years ago. He, too, made the object in two parts, keeping the spout on one side, and the handle on the other, then soldering them across the diagonal. Tusquets Blanca unreservedly admires this prototype by Onø which, he believes, was designed for mass production. As steel is a malleable metal, the design meets technological requirements and is ready to go into standard production.

Svend Onø
Coffee and tea set
Stainless steel, brass, silicone rubber, mahogany plywood
Prototype
Coffee pot: H 34 cm (13⅜ in). W 17 cm (6⅝ in). Di 12 cm (4¾ in).
Tea pot: H 28 cm (11 in). W 18 cm (7 in). Di 13 cm (5⅛ in)
Milk jug: H 15 cm (6 in). W 8 cm (3⅛ in). Di 6 cm (2⅜ in)
Sugar bowl: H 12.5 cm (5 in). W 11.5 cm (4½ in). Di 9.5 cm (3¾ in)
Tray: H 2.5 cm (1 in). W 40 cm (15¾ in). L 54.5 cm (21⅜ in)
Manufacturer: Svend Onø, Denmark

1

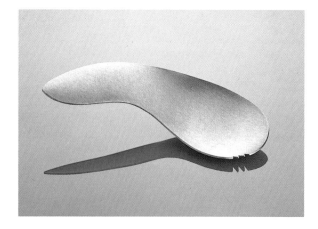

Bibs Hosak-Robb
Eating utensil, *Göffel*
Stainless steel
W 6 cm (2⅜ in). L 14 cm (5½ in)
Manufacturer: Carl Mertens Solingen,
West Germany

2

Bibs Hosak-Robb
Bench for restaurants and cafés
Galvanized steel, stainless steel, rubber,
plastic
This bench comes with a tray, *Fripsl*;
different sized cones for food; a deep
cone for drinks, *Trinktute*; and an eating
implement combining the functions of a
spoon and a fork, *Göffel* ("Spork").
Bench: H 100 cm (39½ in). W 80 cm
(31½ in). L 200 cm (78¾ in)
Tray: D 30 cm (11⅞ in). L 59 cm (23¼ in)
Food cone: H 4 cm (1½ in). Di 12 cm
(4¾ in)
Drinks cone: H 20 cm (7⅞ in). Di 9 cm
(3½ in)
Manufacturer: Carl Mertens Solingen,
West Germany

This bench represents new implements for eating which rest on a tray that, in turn, rests on a corrugated work bench. The galvanized steel benches are shaped to hold the geometric configurations of the take-away trays, each of which contains shallow cones for food, deeper ones for drinks, and urns for ices. The different depths of these vessels are absorbed by the trenches in the table top below, allowing a flat surface. They are a smart line for cafeterias and fast food restaurants. There is also the *Göffel*, a mix of spoon and fork, which Hosak-Robb, its inventor, simply calls an "eating utensil."

3

Lino Sabattini
Whisky bottle with double chamber and cup
Heavily silver-plated brass alloy
One-off
Bottle: H 26 cm (10¼ in). Di 16.5 cm (6½ in)
Cup: H 5 cm (2 in). Di 8.5 cm (3⅜ in)
Manufacturer: Sabattini Argenteria, Italy

4

5

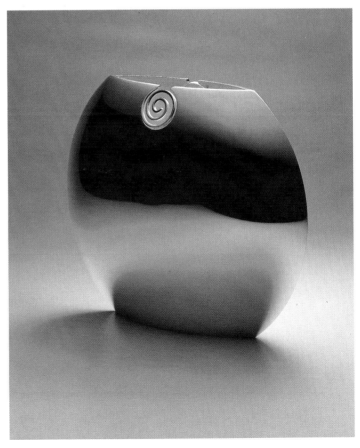

Lino Sabattini
Vase, *B/336 Caprice*
Silver-plated brass alloy
H 23 cm (9 in). Di 29 cm (11⅜ in)
Manufacturer: Sabattini Argenteria, Italy

6

Javier Mariscal
Vase, *Olé*
White or coloured porcelain
H 34.5 cm (13½ in). W 23 cm (9 in)
Manufacturer: Porcelanas del Bidasoa,
Spain

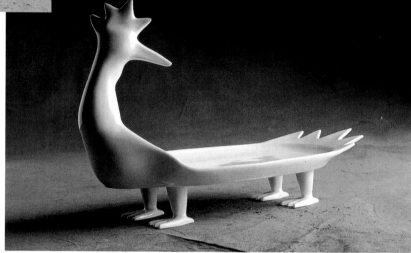

7

Javier Mariscal
Serving platter, *Bird Platter*
White, green or brown porcelain
H 26.8 cm (10⅝ in). W 7 cm (2¾ in).
L 41.2 cm (16³⁄₁₆ in)
Manufacturer: Porcelanas del Bidasoa,
Spain

8

Javier Mariscal
Pot/vase
White, black or copper porcelain
H 25 cm (9⅞ in). W 26.3 cm (10⁵⁄₁₆ in)
Manufacturer: Porcelanas del Bidasoa,
Spain

9

Brancusi's sculptural influence is evident in all the work of American designer Ward Bennett. It is not that his designs embody fish and fowl, but that he imposes fluid organic shapes on hard-edged metal-work. Ward Bennett was on the road at 13, his travels taking him to Europe, East Asia, Egypt, Japan, the USSR, Cambodia and Mexico, where he designed a jewellery collection that is now in the Museum of Modern Art, Mexico City. He worked as a dress designer, sketcher, and window-display designer before training as an artist. He studied in Florence at the Porot Romano School, in Paris with Brancusi, and in New York with painter Hans Hoffman. It is Ward Bennett's metalwork that stands out from his prolific output as the best example of innovative design – tactile and functional. Sasaki USA put this cutlery into their collection. In 1963 and 1971, Ward Bennett was retained by Tiffany and Co. to design china, glassware and silver. His third cutlery collection, *Trylon*, is on permanent display at the Museum of Modern Art, New York, and also at the Cooper-Hewitt Museum, New York, alongside his *Metro* and *Summit* patterns.

Ward Bennett
Cutlery
18/8 stainless steel
Spoon: W 4.8 cm (1⅜ in).
L 18.5 cm (7¼ in).
Knife: W 1.5 cm (¾ in).
L 21 cm (8¼ in)
Fork: W 2.8 cm (1 in).
L 19 cm (7½ in)
Manufacturer: Sasaki, USA

Spoons, forks and knives were defined in form in the 18th century, their function established in the age of formal five-course meals. As eating habits changed and the Modernist movement challenged shapes, forms evolved which eliminated all that was superfluous. Canteens of silver-plated cutlery were exchanged for dishwasher-proof stainless-steel sets. But these new forms were not always suitable for eating – spoons were too shallow for soups, forks let food slip off, knives had no cutting edge.

David Mellor's new *Savoy* silver-plate cutlery, manufactured in his factory in Derbyshire, is a modern design classic. Following the outline of traditional cutlery, David Mellor gives his utensils a contemporary edge, without sacrificing their usefulness. Handles are slender, yet weighty and perfectly balanced, with the knife's handle in black or ivory. The long-pronged fork is designed for stabbing, not baby-food shovelling, while the spoon is for sipping. "I'm puritan in the sense that I wouldn't want a kettle or a knife and fork for ornamental purposes. That's bogus. I like utilitarian, workmanlike classics that are nothing to do with a fancy handle," Mellor says. "I'm also intensely at odds with the wave of nostalgia Britain is gripped by. I don't like things because they're old, I like them because they work. This yearning for the past is very sad."

10

David Mellor
Cutlery, *Savoy*
Silver plate, plastic
The knife handles are available in black or ivory. The design is a reinterpretation of a traditional English theme.
Knife: W 2 cm (¾ in). L 22 cm (8⅔ in)
Fork: W 2 cm (¾ in). L 19 cm (7½ in)
Dessertspoon: W 4 cm (1½ in).
L 18 cm (7 in)
Teaspoon: W 3 cm (1½ in). L 13 cm (5⅛ in)
Manufacturer: David Mellor Design, UK

Sergio Asti
Tea cup
Porcelain
Made using the rice technique.
H 6 cm (2⅜ in). Di 11 cm (4⅜ in)
Manufacturer: Richard Ginori, Italy

11

Sergio Asti
Tea pot, cup and saucer
Porcelain
Teapot: H 14 cm (5½ in)
Cup: H 6 cm (2⅜ in). Di 11 cm (4⅜ in)
Saucer: Di 14 cm (5½ in)
Manufacturer: Richard Ginori, Italy

With its Oriental dual purpose as a bowl or cup, and the use of an ancient technique for its monochrome pattern, this plain white porcelain by Sergio Asti for Richard Ginori looks to the future. Rice is set in the wet clay before firing in the kiln, which turns it translucent and makes a pattern of light. The shape of the porcelain is purely Occidental. Richard Ginori, in Tuscany, is the tableware manufacturer.

Sergio Asti
Flat plate and soup plate
Porcelain
Flat plate: Di 26.5 cm (10⅜ in)
Soup plate: Di 24 cm (9⅜ in)
Manufacturer: Richard Ginori, Italy

12

13

Sergio Asti
Display or multi-purpose plate
Porcelain
Di 31 cm (12 in)
Manufacturer: Richard Ginori, Italy

14

**Antonio Citterio with Rainer
Krause**
Tableware, *Milano*
Porcelain
Left to right:
Creamer: H 6 cm (2⅜ in). Di 8.5 cm
(3⅜ in)
Sugar bowl: H 8.5 cm (3⅜ in). Di 8.5 cm
(3⅜ in)
Cup: H 6 cm (2⅜ in. Di 8.5 cm (3⅜ in)
Saucer: D 1.7 cm (¾ in). Di 15 cm (6 in)
Manufacturer: Anthologie, Quartett,
West Germany

15

Christopher Williams
Vase, *Face*
Glass
The body is hand-blown into a metal
mould and the top finished when cold.
Limited batch production
H 33 cm (13 in). W 14 cm (5½ in).
L 11 cm (4⅜ in)
Manufacturer: The Glasshouse, UK

Christopher Williams
Jug/vase
Glass
The body is hand-blown into a mould and
the rim finished when cold. The surface
is sandblasted. Limited batch production
H 28 cm (11 in). W 11.5 cm (4½ in)
L 16 cm (6¼ in)
Manufacturer: The Glasshouse, UK

16

Carsten Jørgensen
Salt and pepper mills, *Dragonfly*
Brass, polypropylene, aluminium,
acrylic, silver or gold plate
The design of the base retains any loose
salt and pepper.
H 12.3 cm (4⁷⁄₈ in) or 22.5 cm (8⁷⁄₁₆ in).
Di 5.2 cm (2¹⁄₁₆ in) or 11 cm (4³⁄₈ in)
Manufacturer: Bodum, Switzerland

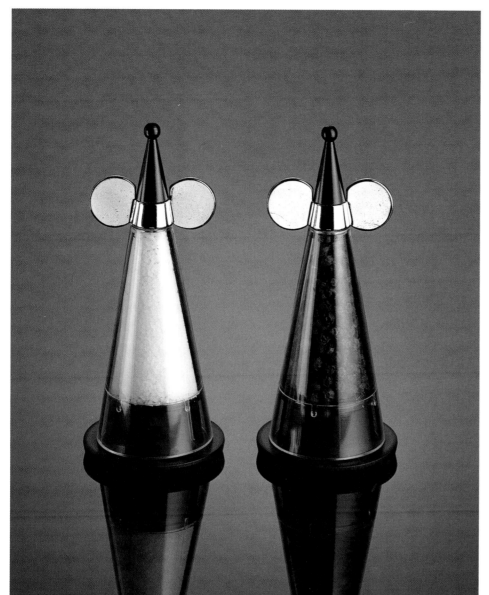

17

18

Max Leser
Coffee or tea server
Lathe-blown Pyrex
The lines are sandblasted on the surface.
The server can be kept warm on a gas
burner or electric element. Limited
batch production
H 27 cm (10½ in). Di 7.5 cm (3 in)
Manufacturer: Leser Design, Canada

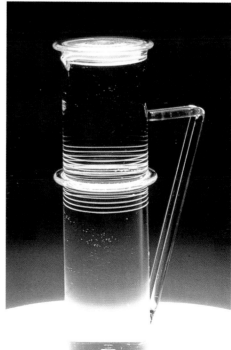

Soichiro Sasakura

Tableware, *San Marino*

Glass

Left to right:

Black goblet: H 16 cm (6¼ in). Di 8.4 cm
(3¼ in)

Clear goblet: H 16 cm (6¼ in). Di 8.4 cm
(3¼ in)

Black decanter: H 19 cm (7½ in).
Di 11.2 cm (4½ in)

Black jug: H 16 cm (6¼ in). Di 11 cm
(4⅜ in)

Manufacturer: Sasaki Glass Co., Japan

19

20

Minoru Sugahara

Tableware, *Indigo and Clear Frost*

Limited batch production

Left to right:

Plates: W 12 cm (4¾ in). L 12 cm (4¾ in)

W 18 cm (7 in). L 18 cm (7 in)

W 24 cm (9⅜ in). L 24 cm (9⅜ in)

Vases: H 18 cm (7 in). Di 4 cm (1½ in)

H 20 cm (7⅞ in). Di 5 cm (2 in)

Flowers: L 25 cm (9⅞ in) to 35 cm
(13¾ in)

Manufacturer: Sugahara Glass

Corporation, Japan

21

Masahiro Mori
Cups, *Sake-III*
White porcelain with underglaze
decoration
H 5.5 cm (2⅛ in). Di 6 cm (2⅜ in)
Manufacturer: Hakusan Porcelain Co.,
Japan

Masahiro Mori
Bottle and cups, *Sake-II*
White porcelain with turquoise blue
decoration
Bottle: H 12.5 cm (5 in). Di 14 cm (5½ in)
Cup: H 5.5 cm (2⅛ in). Di 6 cm (2⅜ in)
Manufacturer: Hakusan Porcelain Co.,
Japan

22

23

Masahiro Mori
Bottle and cups, *Sake-I*
White porcelain with unglazed grey body
and silver leaf decoration
Bottle: H 14.5 cm (5¾ in). Di 9 cm (3½ in)
Cup: H 5.5 cm (2⅛ in). Di 6 cm (2⅜ in)
Manufacturer: Hakusan Porcelain Co.,
Japan

24

Perry A. King and Santiago Miranda
Vase, *Antiochia*
Satin or polished opalescent cut glass
Limited batch production
H 43 cm (16⅞ in). Di 18 cm (7 in)
Manufacturer: Veart, Italy

25

Perry A. King and Santiago Miranda
Bowl, *Bergamo*
Transparent and coloured glass with
Murino glass supports
Limited batch production
H 12 cm (4¾ in). Di 35 cm (13¾ in)
Manufacturer: Veart, Italy

26

Sachiko Kawabe
Tableware, *Kan Kan*
Set of raised plates
Lacquered wood
Made using the traditional lacquerware
method of Urushi.
H 8.6 cm (3⅜ in). Di 24.5 cm (9⅔ in
H 7.5 cm (3 in). Di 18 cm (7 in)
H 6.5 cm (2½ in. Di 16 cm (6¼ in)
Manufacturer: Yamada-Heiando, Japan

27

Sachiko Kawabe
Tableware, *Kan Kan*
Twelve-cornered plates
Lacquered wood
Made using the traditional lacquerware
method of Urushi.
Di 67 cm (26⅜ in) and 48.5 cm (19 in)
Manufacturer: Yamada-Heiando, Japan

Paolo Deganello
Vase, *Prosthesis*
Glass, polished stainless steel
Limited batch production
Base: H 10 cm (4 in). Di 7 cm (2¾ in)
Steel structure: H 16 cm (6¼ in)
Vase: H 6 cm (2⅜ in)
Manufacturer: Venini, Italy

28

29

Makoto Komatsu
Vase, *Arch*
Black or grey polished stainless steel
H 20 cm (7⅞ in) or 10 cm (4 in).
W 14 cm (5½ in). D 7.5 cm (3 in)
Manufacturer: G11, Japan

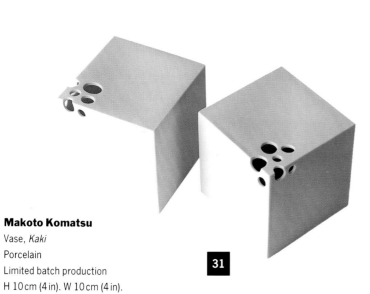

Makoto Komatsu
Vase, *Kaki*
Porcelain
Limited batch production
H 10 cm (4 in). W 10 cm (4 in).
D 10 cm (4 in)
Manufacturer: Product M, Japan

31

30

Christophe Pillet
Candlestick
Silver plate
H 28 cm (11 in). Base H 1 cm (⅖ in).
W 6.2 cm (2½ in)
Manufacturer: Algorithme, France

32

Annabel Newham
Vase
Glass
A hand-blown body with pre-cast
moulded and ground feet reheated and
attached when hot. Limited batch
production.
H 30.5 cm (12 in). Di 16.5 cm (6½ in)
Manufacturer: The Glasshouse, UK

Oscar Tusquets Blanca
Vase, *Nippon*
Porcelain
H 12.5 cm (5 in). Di 26.8 cm (9⅗ in)
Manufacturer: Porcelanas del Bidasoa,
Spain

33

34

Thomas Müller
Vase, *Onerose*
Pressed steel
The finishes include chrome, nickel,
plate or lacquer. Limited batch
production
H 30 cm (11⅞ in). W 8.5 cm (3⅜ in).
D 11 cm (4⅜ in)
Manufacturer: Thomas Müller, West
Germany

When Alessandro Mendini began thinking about designing this range of vases for Venini, he was awestruck by glass – "that intangible and privileged substance or, should I say, form of light." He carefully studied the company's collections, past and present, even peering at glass in the making in the furnace. "I hoped to discover the secret of archetypes that have created such an enduring individual style and then to offer it my own interpretation." Eventually, he established a *mélange* of inventive form with certain colours. "I sought to immerse myself in this tradition and within these boundaries, and I hope that I have been absorbed by them." In these vases, his imagination bows to the permanence and skill of a specific style of craftsmanship, which is the starting point for each and every one of these items.

Alessandro Mendini
Vases, *Arado*
Glass
Hand-blown glass made of alternating multicoloured rods.
H 38 cm (15 in). Di 14 cm (5½ in)
Manufacturer: Venini, Italy

35

Alessandro Mendini
Bottles, *Berito*
Glass
Hand-blown glass with a round, white, opalescent glass neck and a vertical pattern of transparent rods.
Left to right:
H 26 cm (10¼ in). Di 19 cm (7½ in)
H 37 cm (14½ in). Di 12 cm (4¾ in)
H 31 cm (12¼ in). Di 15 cm (6 in)
Manufacturer: Venini, Italy

36

Darryle Hinz
Bowl
Blown cased glass, joined when hot, cut and polished
H 12 cm (4¾ in). W 20 cm (7⅞ in).
L 25 cm (9⅞ in)
Manufacturer: Kjaer & Hinz
Glasvaerkstedet, Denmark

37

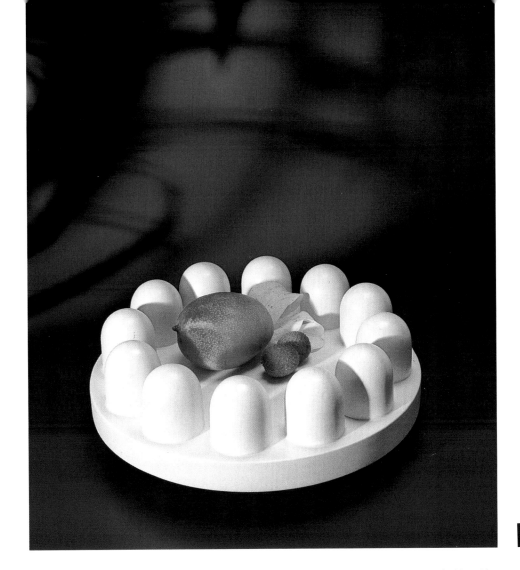

38

Ettore Sottsass upturned the conventional table and tea tray with a collection of tea pots, jugs and bowls for fruit and sugar, originally drawn in the Seventies and inspired by his memories of India. Launched at the Antonia Janone Gallery in Milan in 1987, the collection was distributed worldwide the following year by Anthologie Quartett. Great jelly moulds of china form fruit bowls more in the spirit of the days of the Raj than of contemporary Europe. Coloured by Sottsass in sand, turquoise, coral and indigo, this collection is both familiar and disturbing, cumbersome yet fragile – full of the contradictions he introduces into everyday items.

Ettore Sottsass
Fruit bowl, *The Indian Memory*
Ceramic
H 9.5 cm (3¾ in). Di 31 cm (12¼ in)
Manufacturer: Anthologie Quartett, West
Germany

Michael Boehm 39

Glasses, *Papillon*
Range of 11 drinking glasses.
Left to right:
Sherry flute: H 22.5 cm (8⅘ in)
Sweet wine: H 22.3 cm (8⅗ in)
Beer: H 22.9 cm (8⁹⁄₁₀ in)
Champagne bowl: H 22.5 cm (8⅘ in)
White wine ouvert: H 24.2 cm (9½ in)
Water: H 26.6 cm (10⅗ in)
Champagne flute: H 27.4 cm (10⅖ in)
Liqueur: H 15.8 cm (6⅘ in)
Red wine bouquet: H 28.9 cm (11⁹⁄₁₀ in)
Red wine bouquet: H 26.7 cm (10⁷⁄₁₀ in)
White wine bouquet: H 25.2 cm (9⅕ in)
Manufacturer: Rosenthal, West Germany

40

Rosenthal Studio Line Collection

Champagne flutes
Hand-made and signed by the artists.
Left to right:
A. Bayliss, *Serpenta*
H 30 cm (11⅞ in)
M. Boehm, *Amulett*
H 30.5 cm (12 in)
M. Boehm, *Carnival*
H 24 cm (9⅜ in)
A. Bayliss, *Paradiso*
H 35 cm (13¾ in)
M. Boehm, *Capriole*
H 35 cm (13¾ in)
A. Bayliss, *Helix*
H 35 cm (13¾ in)
N.S. McKinney, *Black Corona*
H 35 cm (13¾ in)
N.S. McKinney, *Network*
H 35 cm (13¾ in)
Manufacturer: Rosenthal, West Germany

Luciano Gaspari
Bottles, *Primavere*
Glass
Clear blown glass with bands in bright
colours applied when the glass is still
hot. The stoppers are in the shape of
flowers.
Left to right:
H 17 cm (6⅝ in). Di 12 cm (4¾ in)
H 30 cm (11⅞ in). Di 14 cm (5½ in)
H 25 cm (9⅞ in). Di 17 cm (6⅝ in)
Manufacturer: Salviati, Italy

41

42

Luciano Gaspari
Bottle, *Colonne*
Glass
Solid hand-blown glass, with multicoloured
bands and spots.
H 25 cm (9⅞ in). Di 15 cm (6 in)
Manufacturer: Salviati, Italy

43

David Palterer
Glasses, *Idra*
Left to right:
H 24 cm (9⅜ in). Di 12.6 cm (5 in)
H 28 cm (11 in). Di 6.6 cm (2½ in)
H 23.5 cm (9½ in). Di 11.9 cm (4⅝ in)
Manufacturer: Nuova Vilca, Italy

44

David Palterer
Candlestick
Silver-plated brass
H 30.5 cm (12 in). Di 10 cm (4 in)
Manufacturer: Swid Powell, USA

45

David Palterer
Glasses
Left to right:
Grifone: H 17 cm (6⅝ in). Di 9 cm (3½ in)
Cariddi: H 25 cm (9⅞ in). Di 7 cm (2¾ in)
Arpia: H 18 cm (7 in). Di 8.5 cm (3⅜ in)
Manufacturer: Nuova Vilca, Italy

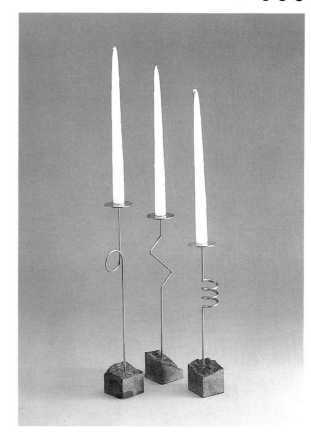

46

Paolo Portoghesi
Candlesticks, *Achphat and Tlemcen*
Electro-plated brass
Left to right:
H 10.5 cm (4⅛ in). Di 12.2 cm (4¾ in)
H 25.5 cm (10 in). Di 10 cm (4 in)
Manufacturer: Alessi, Italy

Ehlen Johansson
Candlesticks
Stone, steel, brass
Left to right:
H 45 cm (17¾ in)
H 40 cm (15¾ in)
H 35 cm (13¾ in)
Manufacturer: Ikea, Sweden

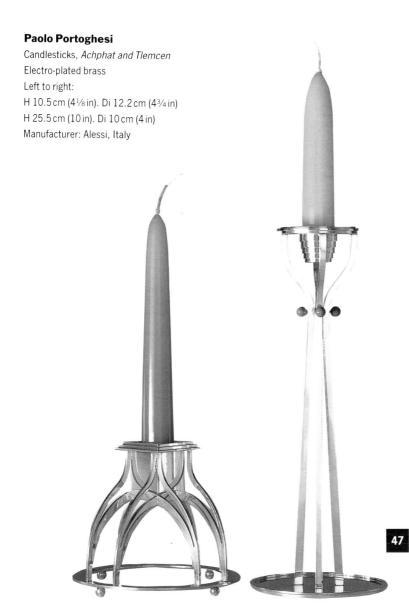

47

Matteo Thun
Vases, *Castelli in Fiore*
Ceramic
Five different vases in a range of colours
and finishes.
Far left: *Castel Fondo*
H 76 cm (30 in). Di 15 cm (6 in)
Second from left: *Castel Altaguardia*
H 106 cm (41¾ in). Di 30 cm (11⅞ in)
Third from left: *Castel Thun*
H 94 cm (37 in). Di 20 cm (7⅞ in)
Sixth from left: *Castel Brughier*
H 97 cm (38¼ in). Di 26 cm (9 in)
Eighth from left: *Castel Cagno*
H 72 cm (28½ in). Di 23 cm (9 in)
Manufacturer: Anthologie Quartett, West
Germany

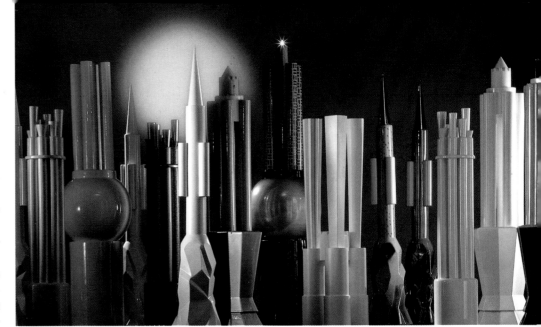

48

49

Matteo Thun
Cocktail shaker, *Campari*
Stainless steel, glass, silicon rubber
H 27.7 cm (10⅞ in). Di 10.5 cm (4⅛ in)
Manufacturer: Alessi, Italy

Matteo Thun
Vases, *Urban Signals: Andy*
Ceramic
H 71 cm (28 in). Di 28 cm (11 in)
Manufacturer: Anthologie Quartett, West
Germany

50

Matteo Thun
Vases, *Urban Signals: Jasper*
Ceramic
H 69 cm (27⅛ in). Di 11 cm (4⅜ in)
Manufacturer: Anthologie Quartett, West
Germany

51

52

Matteo Thun
Vase, *Urban Signals: Frank*
Ceramic
H 69 cm (27⅛ in). Di 11 cm (4⅜ in)
Manufacturer: Anthologie Quartett, West
Germany

53

Matteo Thun
Vase, *Urban Signals: Roy*
Ceramic
H 69 cm (27⅛ in). Di 11 cm (4⅜ in)
Manufacturer: Anthologie Quartett, West
Germany

Margit Denz

Tableware, *Bronx*

Earthenware

Limited batch production

Sugar bowl: H 10 cm (4 in). W 8 cm
(3⅛ in). D 5 cm (2 in)

Coffee pot: H 18.5 cm (7⅛ in). W 14.5 cm
(5¾ in). D 6.5 cm (2½ in)

Cup: H 6 cm (2⅜ in). W 10 cm (4 in).
D 8 cm (3⅛ in)

Saucer: Di 12 cm (4¾ in)

Manufacturer: Villeroy & Boch, West
Germany

The tea and coffee sets on these and the following pages, *In the Spirit of the USA*, were winners in a competition held at the Vienna Academy of Applied Arts for students working under the tutorship of Matteo Thun. When Villeroy & Boch put each set into limited production of 50 editions, they accomplished a great technical feat. In many ways, the designs typify European attitudes towards American achievements this century. Predictably, there is a Coke bottle (supplied with a funnel for filling it), the Stars and Stripes, an American football player, a Thanksgiving turkey and, the most powerful symbol of the States, the Statue of Liberty. They are all transformed in witty ways to make functional pourers. Sometimes the effect is bizarre, like the egg-head football hero in Johanna Schmeiser's tea pot, his arm extended beneath padded shoulders into a spout for pouring, rather than scoring.

Some unusual interpretations provide more interesting insights into modern America. In Margit Denz's *Bronx*, rigorous corrugations in porcelain are reminiscent of the iron sheds that line the poorer parts of the Bronx. Ali Scherhaufer's *Fifties* has Hollywood sunspec shapes like cats' eyes, patterned with a comic book blow-up screen image. In Maria Wiala's *Catch the Line*, the uncompromising glitz of Wall Street is reflected in a skyscraper façade.

55

Margit Denz
Tableware, *Liberty I, II and III*
Earthenware
Limited batch production
Cup: H 9 cm (3½ in). W 10 cm (4 in).
D 6.5 cm (2½ in)
Saucer: W 12 cm (4¾ in). L 12 cm (4¾ in)
Plate: W 19 cm (7½ in). L 19 cm (7½ in)
Coffee pot: H 33 cm (13 in). W 17 cm
(6⅝ in). D 9.5 cm (3¾ in)
Milk jug: H 21 cm (8¼ in). W 12 cm
(4¾ in). D 7 cm (2¾ in)
Sugar bowl: H 13.5 cm (5⅖ in). W 8 cm
(3⅛ in). D 8 cm (3⅛ in)
Manufacturer: Villeroy & Boch, West
Germany

56

Renate Hattinger
Tableware, *Turkey*
Earthenware
Limited batch production
Milk jug: H 9.5 cm (3¾ in). W 13.5 cm
(5⅖ in). D 8.5 cm (3⅜ in)
Egg cup: H 10 cm (4 in). Di 5 cm (2 in)
Plate: Di 21 cm (8¼ in)
Coffee pot: H 29.5 cm (11⅝ in).
W 19.5 cm (7⅗ in). D 15 cm (6 in)
Cup: H 7.5 cm (3 in). W 12.5 cm (5 in).
D 8.5 cm (3⅜ in)
Saucer: Di 14.5 cm (5¾ in)
Manufacturer: Villeroy & Boch, West
Germany

Maria Wiala
Tableware, *Catch the Line*
Earthenware
Limited batch production
Big plate: W 25.5 cm (10 in). L 25.5 cm
(10 in)
Small plate: W 21 cm (8¼ in). L 21 cm
(8¼ in)
Saucer: W 12.5 cm (5 in). L 12.5 cm (5 in)
Cup: H 7.5 cm (3 in). W 9 cm (3½ in).
D 6 cm (2⅜) in)
Coffee pot: H 29.5 cm (11⅝ in).
W 18.5 cm (7½ in). D 6.5 cm (2½ in)
Sugar bowl: H 12.5 cm (5 in). W 8.5 cm
(3⅜ in). D 8.5 cm (3⅜ in)
Manufacturer: Villeroy & Boch, West
Germany

57

58

Ali Scherhaufer
Tableware, *The Fifties*
Earthenware
Limited batch production
Cup: H 10 cm (4 in). W 15 cm (6 in).
D 9.5 cm (3¾ in)
Saucer: Di 16.5 cm (6½ in)
Milk jug: H 10 cm (4 in). W 10.5 cm
(4⅛ in). D 9.5 cm (3¾ in)
Coffee pot: H 23 cm (9 in). W 19 cm
(7½ in). D 15 cm (6 in)
Sugar bowl: H 10 cm (4 in). Di 9.5 cm
(3¾ in)
Plate: Di 21 cm (8¼ in)
Manufacturer: Villeroy & Boch, West
Germany

Michaela Lange
Tableware, *Fly High*
Earthenware
Limited batch production
Sugar bowl: H 13 cm (5⅛ in). Di 8.5 cm
(3⅜ in)
Milk jug: H 9.5 cm (3¾ in). W 10.5 cm
(4⅛ in). D 6.5 cm (2½ in)
Big plate: Di 25.5 cm (10 in)
Astronaut sugar shaker: H 17 cm (6⅝ in).
W 10 cm (4 in). D 9 cm (3½ in)
Salt cellar: H 9.5 cm (3¾ in)
Small plate: Di 21 cm (8¼ in)
Coffee pot: H 30.5 cm (12 in). W 19 cm
(7½ in). D 9 cm (3½ in)
Cup/mug: H 8 cm (3⅛ in). Di 6.5 cm
(2½ in)
Manufacturer: Villeroy & Boch, West
Germany

59

Klara Obereder
Tableware, *Coca Cola*
Earthenware
Limited batch production
Milk jug: H 18 cm (7 in). W 8 cm (3⅛ in).
D 5 cm (2 in)
Coffee pot: H 30 cm (11⅞ in). Di 9 cm
(3½ in)
Cup/mug: H 11 cm (4⅜ in). Di 6 cm
(2⅜ in)
Plate: Di 21 cm (8¼ in)
Hamburger sugar bowl: H 9 cm (3½ in).
Di 9 cm (3½ in)
Funnel: H 12 cm (4¾ in). Di 10 cm (4 in)
Manufacturer: Villeroy & Boch, West
Germany

60

Ingrid Smolle
Tableware, *Blue Magic*
Earthenware
Limited batch production
Sugar bowl: H 8.5 cm (3⅜ in). Di 10 cm
(4 in)
Plate: Di 21 cm (8¼ in)
Coffee pot: H 17 cm (6⅝ in). W 27 cm
(10½ in). D 14.5 cm (5¾ in)
Milk jug: H 7.5 cm (3 in). W 12 cm (4¾ in).
D 6.5 cm (2½ in)
Cup: H 7 cm (2¾ in). W 12 cm (4¾ in).
D 7.5 cm (3 in)
Manufacturer: Villeroy & Boch, West
Germany

61

62

Johanna Schmeiser
Tableware, *American Football*
Earthenware
Limited batch production
Cereal bowl: H 7 cm (2¾ in). W 15.5 cm
(6⅛ in). D 13 cm (5⅛ in)
Tea pot: H 25 cm (9⅞ in). W 33 cm (13 in).
D 11 cm (4⅜ in)
Sugar bowl: H 9 cm (3½ in). W 8.5 cm
(3⅜ in). L 9 cm (3½ in)
Mugs: H 9 cm (3½ in) and 14 cm (5½ in).
W 4.5 cm (1¾ in) and 8.5 cm (3⅜ in).
L 8.5 cm (3⅜ in) and 9.5 cm (3¾ in)
Plate: W 19 cm (7½ in). L 21.5 cm (8½ in)
Manufacturer: Villeroy & Boch, West
Germany

63

Martine Bedin
Salt and pepper holders
Silver-plated metal
H 7 cm (2¾ in). W 6 cm (2⅜ in). D 1.5 cm
(⅔ in)
Manufacturer: Algorithme, France

Martine Bedin
Vase, *Piotr*
White, green and black marble
H 30 cm (11⅞ in). Di 22 cm (8⅔ in)
Manufacturer: Up & Up, Italy

64

Marcello Morandini
Tableware, *Alphabet*
Porcelain
Monogrammed place or wall plates with
seven optional colours on the rim.
Di 30 cm (11⅞ in)
Manufacturer: Rosenthal, West Germany

65

66

Mario Bellini
Dinner service, *Cupola*
Porcelain, glass, stainless steel
Addition to tea service, 1987.
Sauce boat: H 13 cm (5⅛ in). W 12 cm
(4¾ in). L 23.5 cm (9½ in)
Stainless steel plate: Di 31 cm (12¼ in)
Soup bowl: Di 13 cm (5⅛ in)
Glass: H 19 cm (7½ in). Di 6.5 cm (2½ in)
Salt and pepper: H 7 cm (2¾ in). Di 4 cm
(1½ in)
Tureen: H 26 cm (10¼ in). Di 24 cm
(9⅜ in)
Glass bowl: Di 12 cm (4¾ in)
Manufacturer: Rosenthal, West Germany

67

Michael Graves
Sugar bowl with spoon
18/10 stainless steel, polyamide
handles and knob
Bowl: H 8 cm (3⅛ in). Di 10.5 cm (4⅛ in)
Spoon: L 10 cm (4 in)
Manufacturer: Alessi, Italy

68

Michael Graves
Creamer
18/10 stainless steel, polyamide handle
H 4.5 cm (1¾ in). Di 10.5 cm (4⅛ in)
Manufacturer: Alessi, Italy

69

Michael Graves
Pepper mill
18/10 stainless steel, polyamide fins
H 13.2 cm (5⅛ in). Di 6.3 cm (2½ in)
Manufacturer: Alessi, Italy

70

Michael Graves
Tableware, *Delos*
Porcelain
Left to right:
Buffet plate: Di 30.5 cm (12 in)
Luncheon plate: Di 23 cm (9 in)
Saucer: Di 15 cm (6 in)
Cup: H 5.7 cm (2⅜ in). Di 8.25 cm (3¼ in)
Manufacturer: Swid Powell, USA

71

Michael Graves, America's most notorious architect, has become a media event. This phenomenon was brought about largely by his product designs which, he believes, make him more accessible than his buildings, and give people a chance to own affordable art. Graves, who used to call product design "my expensive hobby," now devotes 25 per cent of his time to it. It was Alessi, the stainless steel manufacturers in Italy, that raised everyday design-consciousness by choosing some of the world's top architects to design household equipment. Michael Graves was one of them, and his *Whistling Bird* kettle took off: Alessi sold 150,000 worldwide in three years. Royalties from just four of Graves's products made up 10 per cent of the cost of running his architectural practice in 1988.

        At first glance, this mild-mannered Princeton professor and one-time controversial exponent of Post-Modernism is an unlikely candidate for such intensive publicity. Now he keeps an etcher in his studio so that he can stamp his signature on kettles when he's asked to autograph them. In 1988 he added this pepper mill with Mickey Mouse ears, and the stainless steel creamer and sugar bowl, to the *Whistling Bird* series.

Marianne Brandt
Cocktail shaker
Stainless steel
Designed in 1932.
H 18 cm (7 in). Di 13.8 cm (5⅖ in)
Manufacturer: Alessi, Italy

Nemo
Cheese tray and knife
Polyethylene, chromed nickel-plated
brass, stainless steel
Tray: Di 30 cm (11⅞ in)
Knife: L 18.5 cm (7⅕ in)
Manufacturer: Algorithme, France

72

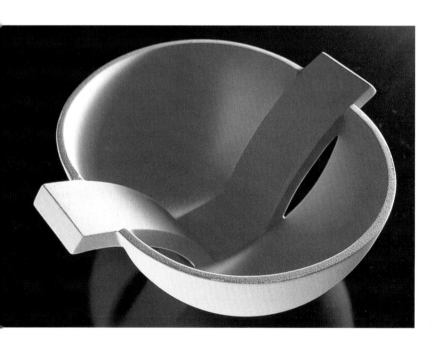

Nicholas Bewick
Fruit bowl
Terracotta
H 15 cm (6 in). Di 30 cm (11⅞ in)
Manufacturer: Solid, Italy

73

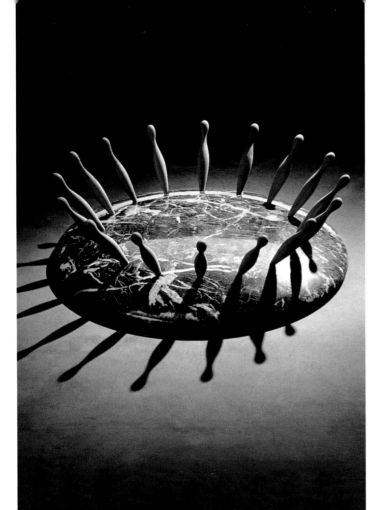

74

Marco Zanuso Jr
Bowl, *Riccio*
Marble, wood
Limited batch production
H 12 cm (4¾ in). Di 38 cm (15 in)
Manufacturer: Ultima Edizione, Italy

Each year there is a wealth of entries to *The International Design Yearbook* for one particular type of object, which has, for no apparent reason, been given the full designer treatment. This year's flashlights may be followed by door handles or bathroom taps. Familiar, useful and accepted without question, these everyday tools suddenly appear in new guises. Though it is tempting to dismiss their transformation as merely clever packaging, a good design goes deeper than that. This year, in tableware, it is the turn of cheese boards and fruit bowls. From the intimidating spikes with which Kuramata encircles his fruit bowl to the simple design of Nick Bewick which nonetheless masks a disciplined approach, these sculptural shapes are entirely functional in purpose.

Shiro Kuramata
Fruit bowl
Wood, metal
Prototype
H 18.5 cm (7⅜ in). Di 36.2 cm (14⅛ in)
Manufacturer: Central Market, Japan

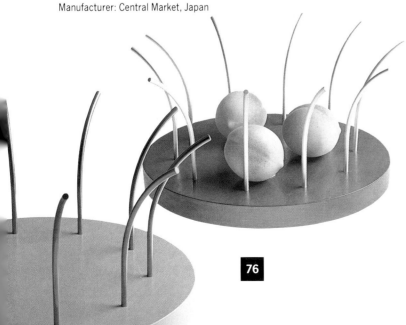

76

75

Shiro Kuramata
Fruit bowl
Wood, metal
Prototype
H 12.5 cm (5 in). Di 33.2 cm (13 in)
Manufacturer: Central Market, Japan

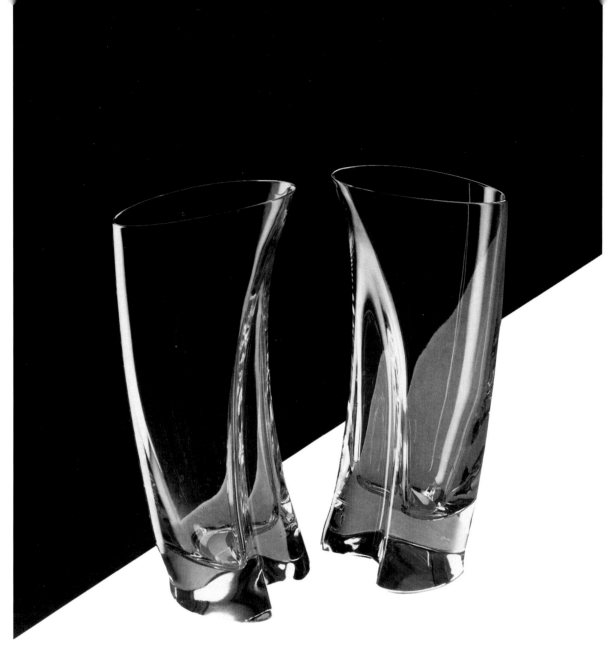

77

Angelo Mangiarotti
Glass, *First Glass*
H 14.5 cm (5¾ in). Di 7 cm (2¾ in)
Manufacturer: Colle, Italy

Philippe Starck
Cutlery, *Objects Pointus 1*
Stainless steel
Sticks: L 24.5 cm (9⅔ in)
Teaspoon: H 15.5 cm (6⅛ in)
Dessertspoon: H 22 cm (8⅔ in)
Fork: L 22.5 cm (8⅞ in)
Knife: L 25 cm (9⅞ in)
Manufacturer: Owo, France/
Sasaki, Japan

78

In this impatient age of swift changes in fads and fashions, Philippe Starck seeks to design products he calls *juste*, or honest to their function. He always has an original approach. This collection of cutlery was not designed for a specific restaurant but created on an intuition that future eating habits will be based on a mixture of Eastern and Western cuisines. The pieces were finally made in Japan and sold in the USA. The design for Starck's latest office complex in Tokyo, the Nani Nani (No Name) building, took him two hours to conceive and two days to elaborate; this cutlery for Sasaki, however, took him a year and a half. "The design of the knife blade alone, just the point on the cutting edge, took two days."

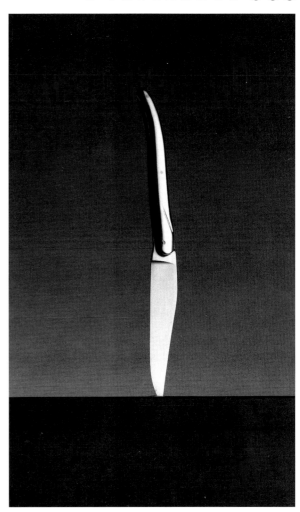

79

Philippe Starck
Knife, *Laguiole*
Aluminium, stainless steel
L 17 cm (6⅝ in) to 21 cm (8¼ in)
Blade: L 9 cm (3½ in) to 11 cm (4⅜ in)
Manufacturer: Owo, France

80

Philippe Starck
Place-name holder, *Berta Youssouf*
Aluminium
H 5.5 cm (2⅛ in)
Manufacturer: Owo, France

82

81

83

Philippe Starck

Vase, *3 Etrangetes sous un mur*
Glass
H 46 cm (18 in). W 40 cm (15¾ in).
L 50 cm (19⅝ in)
Manufacturer: Daum, France

Philippe Starck

Vase, *4 Etrangetes contre un mur*
Glass
H 60 cm (23½ in). W 46 cm (18 in).
L 50 cm (19⅝ in)
Manufacturer: Daum, France

Philippe Starck

Vase, *Une Etrangete sous un mur*
Glass
H 55 cm (21½ in). D 2 cm (¾ in).
Vase H 50 cm (19⅝ in)
Manufacturer: Daum, France

One would think that the vase is commonplace and well established, with nothing new to add. It interested Philippe Starck for precisely that reason. His extraordinary series of vases for the French company Daum makes one look at the vase's function and aesthetics in a new way. What is a vase? It is a little morbid to regard it as a coffin for dead flowers for at the same time it should be a reminder of the living flower, as well as being that most humble of vessels, a container for water. With Starck's design, one can view the flowers from different angles – on the diagonal or from a horizontal plane. Flowers spill from the vessels, yet they never spill water. "Function," Starck says, "isn't the water, the flower or the vase, but the uncertain momentary look, subjective and contemporary, which unites all these elements."

Philippe Starck

Vase, *4 Etrangetes sous un mur*

Glass

H 46 cm (18 in). W 55 cm (21½ in).

L 60 cm (23½ in)

Manufacturer: Daum, France

84

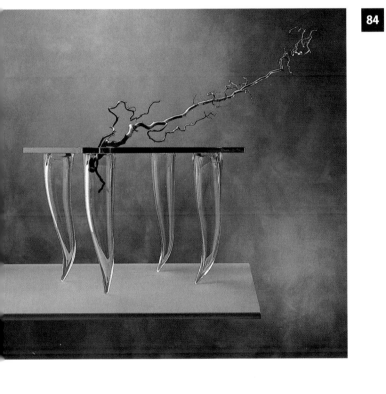

85

Philippe Starck

Vase, *L'Etrangete*

Glass

H 13.5 cm (5¼ in). L 55 cm (21½ in)

Manufacturer: Daum, France

86

Philippe Starck

Vase, *Une Etrangete contre un mur*

Glass

H 70 cm (27½ in). D 2 cm (¾ in).

Vase H 38 cm (15 in)

Manufacturer: Daum, France

85

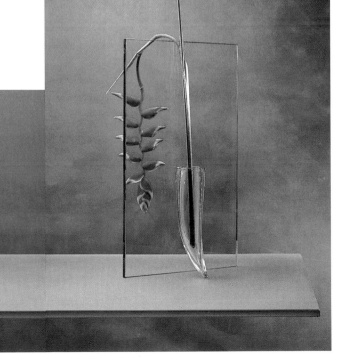

At the end of a decade starved of colour and richness, these lively textiles awaken an interest in interior design. Architectural sobriety determines plain backgrounds, with blinds rather than curtains, and rugs in shades of grey. Perhaps that is why textiles, more than any other field of design, are dominated by patterns of the past. New designs are few and far between. Fields of flowers on chintz, unchanged for centuries, are still mass produced today.

Computer-age innovation, combined with an ageless aesthetic discipline, are revealed in the textiles from Japan that dominate this section. Rings on bark, frothing foam, cloven wings of cloud, pinnacles and peaks – these fabrics are literally land-scaped. There are no nostalgic depictions of flowers and bees, but grand vistas in chiaroscuro, representations of nature in terms of light and shade. Ishimoto's textiles depict bamboo sprouts, watery backgrounds and prisms of light. Awatsuji prints out rippling dunes, falling water and full-blown peonies in fine-line graphs. Junichi Arai's textiles are far from plain, yet they have little surface pattern apart from bands of colour. Like a scientist, he charts the progress of his mixtures of materials – cotton, wool, metal and plastic – until he finds the exact formula that leaves nothing to chance.

Spain takes the lead in translating graphic designs into repeat patterns, with a freedom that makes them more vigorous than the over-worked emblems in other countries. Javier Mariscal draws confident scrolls and irregular outlines on his fabrics; even his borders on bed-linen are irregular, reducing coronets and crests into deceptively simple jottings. This freehand quality is not seen in any other submission. Marcello Morandini's artistry in rugs for a Swiss company presents precise geometric patterns and allows the owner the final say in how to arrange them. A new carpet series from Vorwerk presents a highly original concept: whereas elaborate patterning in carpets usually requires hand-knotting, they have used broadloom manufacturing techniques to mass produce the diverse designs of artists and architects. As well as offering the widest variety of yarn, including synthetics, broadloom provides the best opportunity to change direction and pattern during the process. They have reduced and enlarged artists' designs to make repeat patterns. Wall-to-wall Roy Lichtenstein in striking, diagonal bands is better suited to large spaces such as airport lounges or hotel foyers, but the squiggle of Californian sunshine colour in David Hockney's inimitable style suits both the public and domestic markets.

TEXTILES 4

1

Hiroshi Awatsuji
Fabric, *Sou*
Silk-screen printed cotton
W 137 cm (54 in)
Manufacturer: Hiroshi Awatsuji Design,
Japan

Hiroshi Awatsuji
Fabric, *Hana*
Silk-screen printed cotton
W 137 cm (54 in)
Manufacturer: Hiroshi Awatsuji Design,
Japan

2

Hiroshi Awatsuji
Fabric, *Hibiki*
Silk-screen printed cotton
W 137 cm (54 in)
Manufacturer: Hiroshi Awatsuji Design,
Japan

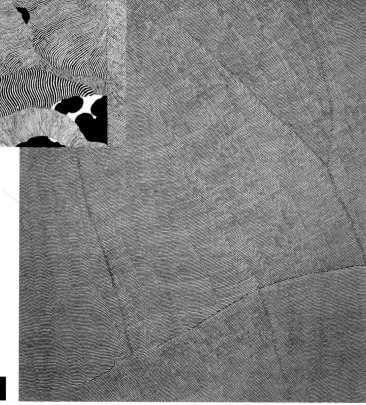

3

4

Hiroshi Awatsuji
Fabric, *Seki*
Silk-screen printed cotton
W 137 cm (54 in)
Manufacturer: Hiroshi Awatsuji Design,
Japan

When Hiroshi Awatsuji says, "For me, textiles are wrapping," there are resonances of the artist Christo who climbs skyscrapers and clifftops to hang his parachute material. But Hiroshi's fabrics are designed for furnishing. His awareness of the environment brings a beautiful pattern to his textiles: they are ringed like bark, dappled like moss, veined like leaves. *Hibiki* depicts the cosmic ripple effect of echoes, *Kazu* a mass of bubbles, *Hana* a large flower, and *Sou* (see page 159) an outsized leaf. These representations of nature do not have the botanical authenticity that so often dulls the effect of natural studies printed on fabrics. Rather, the pattern lives vividly in a series that interior designer Shigara Uchida believes is approaching philosophy. Uchida comments, "His work deals with spiritual concerns through the medium of pattern."

5

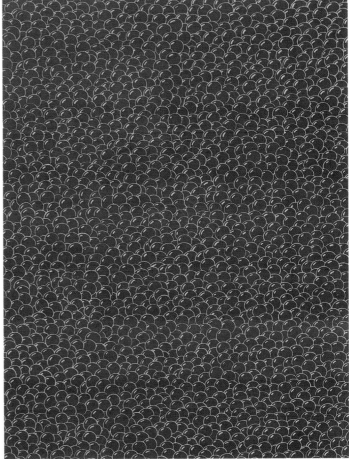

Hiroshi Awatsuji
Fabric, *Kazu*
Silk-screen printed cotton
W 137 cm (54 in)
Manufacturer: Hiroshi Awatsuji Design,
Japan

Pedro Miralles

Rug, *Calzada en Primavera*

Wool

A hand-knotted rug made in Turkish knot.

Limited batch production

W 170 cm (67 in). L 240 cm (94½ in)

Manufacturer: BD Ediciones de diseño,

Spain

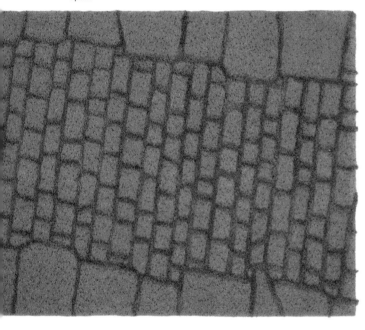

Pedro Miralles

Rug, *Alfombra Cármenes*

Wool

A hand-knotted rug made in Turkish knot.
The design is based on the gardens of
the Alhambra Palace. Limited batch
production

W 170 cm (67 in). L 240 cm (94½ in)

Manufacturer: BD Ediciones de diseño,

Spain

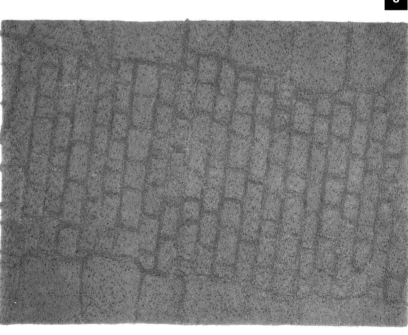

Pedro Miralles

Rug, *Calzada en Otoño*

Wool

A hand-knotted rug made in Turkish knot.

Limited batch production

W 170 cm (67 in). L 240 cm (94½ in)

Manufacturer: BD Ediciones de diseño,

Spain

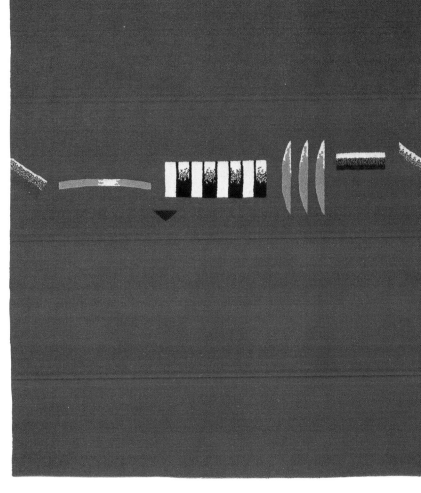

Martine Bedin
Rug, *Pxock*
Wool
A hand-knotted rug made in Turkish knot.
Limited batch production
W 170 cm (67 in). L 240 cm (94½ in)
Manufacturer: BD Ediciones de diseño,
Spain

Martine Bedin
Rug, *Lótż*
Wool
A hand-knotted rug made in Turkish knot.
Limited batch production
W 170 cm (67 in). L 240 cm (94½ in)
Manufacturer: BD Ediciones de diseño,
Spain

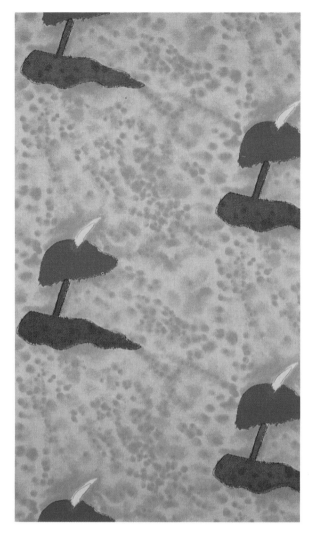

11

Angel Jové
Fabric, *Kampala*
Printed cotton
W 160 cm (63 in)
Manufacturer: Transtam, Spain

12

Antoni Llena
Fabric, *Caras*
Printed cotton
W 160 cm (63 in)
Manufacturer: Transtam, Spain

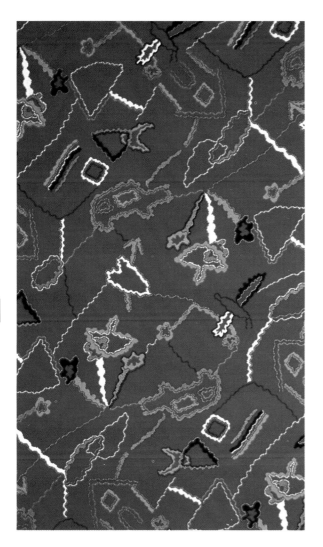

13

Silvia Gubern
Fabric, *Yukatan*
Cotton
W 160 cm (63 in)
Manufacturer: Transtam, Spain

14

Silvia Gubern
Fabric, *Clorofila*
Cotton
W 160 cm (63 in)
Manufacturer: Transtam, Spain

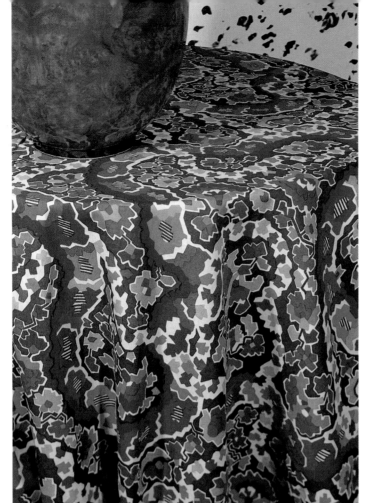

15

Javier Mariscal
Fabric, *Llea*
Cotton
W 160 cm (63 in)
Manufacturer: Marieta Textil, Spain

16

Gaston & Daniela Design Team
Fabric, *Bosforo*
Cotton
W 140 cm (55⅛ in). Repeat 68 cm (26¾ in)
Manufacturer: Gaston & Daniela, Spain

**Glenn Peckman for Donghia
Design Studio**
Fabric, *Arras*
94% cotton, 6% viscose
W 130 cm (51 in). Repeat 40.5 cm (16 in)
Manufacturer: Donghia Furniture &
Textiles, USA

17

18

Manufacturer Ranbir Singh of the enterprising company Equator Productions commissioned a number of
artists to paint canvases for two by three metre rugs,
which would be used and trampled underfoot rather
than hung on the wall. With designs by Georg Dokoupil,
Rosemarie Trockel, Rob Scholte, Donald Baechler
and Andreas Schultze, as well as this example by
Walter Dahn, the rugs were hand-made in India in
limited editions of up to 15. The freehand, graphic
quality of Dahn's original work has not been lost. "The
great thing about seeing the designs in production
was that each artist had transformed his or her very
individual vision into a usable object," says Ranbir
Singh. "Not only to be stared at, but to be used . . . with
a spirit much larger than it appears. Here are
depicted optimism and adventure, subversion and
mystery, love and pain, playfulness and youth, intelli-
gence and beauty, life and chance."

Walter Dahn
Rug, *Spiral*
Wool, cotton
Hand-knotted in India. Limited batch
production, series of ten
W 250 cm (98⅜ in). L 250 cm (98⅜ in)
Manufacturer: Equator Productions,
West Germany

Christian Duc
Rug, *Carré d'As*
Wool
W 180 cm (70⅝ in). L 270 cm
(106¼ in)
Manufacturer: Toulemonde Bochart,
France

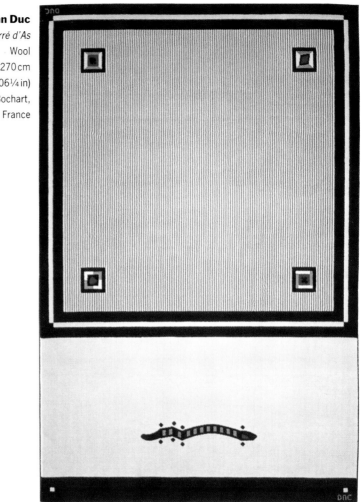

19

"Là Bas" literally means "over there," and the designer of *Là Bas*, Marie-Christine Dorner, elegantly gestures towards her rug as she says so. "The pattern is inspired by the sense of two people walking together. Romantic? Maybe." Draw back a little and the outline suggests their shadows. Move closer and it is like the emblem of the dove of peace. Marie-Christine Dorner found this rug difficult to design. "For me it was a new experience. You find a direction, or you don't give any. It is easier for me to work in 3D than it is to create an artwork. This is more like a painting." She considers the frame important but dislikes the conventional border on rugs, which is similar to a picture frame. This one has been created by varying the pile depth; a fine, irregular groove has been etched into the surface. As always, Dorner's colours are original: saffron and coral, and the inter-mingling of two warm greys. More than in her pre-vious work, she now seems to favour bright colours, perhaps inspired by her recent travels in Rajasthan.

A French gambling term, *Carré d'As*, refers to rare good fortune at the gaming table. Christian Duc's rug for Toulemonde Bochart has one tiny card suit in each corner and an anorexic squiggly dragon to represent luck in the year of the dragon (1988). There are two discernible themes in his work: yin and yang, which balance in perfect symmetry the two halves of any design; and light and shade. Duc's rugs are always printed in two versions, one with a black background to represent night, and the other with a white back-ground. Sometimes he makes minute changes to a design to record the passage of time from night into day, or winter into summer. Christian Duc observes that, "In French, *desseins* [schemes] and *dessins* [designs] are two words loaded with meaning, with just a vowel separating them."

At the furniture show in Paris 1989, Christian Duc was awarded the best designer prize by VIA, the French promotional design council, for his new pressed aluminium chairs and pogo-stick swivel bar-stool for the Parc des Villettes in northern Paris.

20

Marie-Christine Dorner
Rug, *Là Bas*
Wool
Limited batch production
W 180 cm (70⅝ in). L 230 cm (90½ in)
Manufacturer: Elisée Editions, France

Gillo Dorfles
Rug, *Giardino*
Wool
A hand-knotted rug made in Turkish knot.
Limited batch production
W 140 cm (55⅛ in). L 200 cm (78¾ in)
Manufacturer: Edizioni Tessili, Italy

21

22

Sergio Asti
Rug, *Homage to Gertrude Stein*
Wool
W 170 cm (67 in). L 240 cm (94½ in)
Manufacturer: Sisal, Italy

23

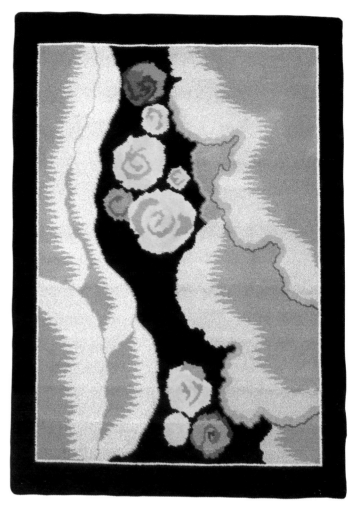

Sergio Asti
Rug, *Homage to Oscar Wilde*
Wool
W 170 cm (67 in). L 240 cm (94½ in)
Manufacturer: Sisal, Italy

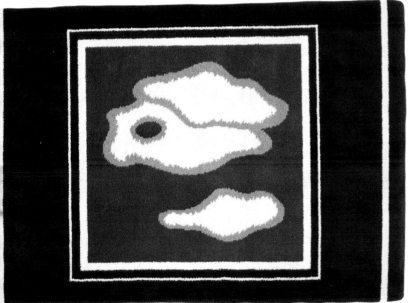

24

Sergio Asti
Rug, *Homage to René Magritte*
Wool
W 140 cm (55⅛ in). L 200 cm (78¾ in)
Manufacturer: Sisal, Italy

25

Perico Pastor
Fabric, *Malta*
Cotton
W 160 cm (63 in)
Manufacturer: Marieta Textil, Spain

26

Perico Pastor
Rug, *Rigoletto*
Wool
W 170 cm (67 in). L 240 cm (94½ in)
Manufacturer: Marieta Textil, Spain

Maarten Vrolijk
Fabric, *Roses*
Cotton
W 160 cm (63 in)
Manufacturer: Marieta Textil, Spain

27

28

Javier Mariscal
Fabric, *Peacock*
Printed cotton
W 180 cm (70⅝ in) or 270 cm (106¼ in).
L 270 cm (106¼ in)
Manufacturer: Bures Industries, Spain

29

Roy Lichtenstein
Carpet, from the *Dialog* collection
Polyamide
W 400 cm (157½ in). Repeat W 50 cm
(19⅝ in), L 47 cm (18½ in)
Manufacturer: Vorwerk, West Germany

The most exciting collection of wall-to-wall carpeting for a decade has been launched by the West German carpet manufacturer Vorwerk. Using the designs of big-name artists and architects, commissioned by Peter Littmann, Vorwerk's affordable, mass-produced broadloom carpets have challenged the outdated concept of selecting a carpet simply to match the curtains and wallcovering. With *Dialog* the dramatic carpet has set the scene with 24 new designs by 11 artists and architects. The artists are David Hockney, Sol LeWitt, Roy Lichtenstein, Sam Francis and Gerhard Richter. The architects are Norman Foster, Arata Isozaki, Michael Graves, Matteo Thun, Oswald Mathias Ungers and Hans-Ullrich Bitsch.

Representing a technical breakthrough, the carpets closely resemble the original artwork in colour, line, brushstroke effects and subtlety of shading. There are Californian pool ripples from David Hockney, while Roy Lichtenstein contributes grid lines in a dramatic repeat pattern. The Californian painter Sam Francis has trailed fine splatters that look like blood on a white background. Representing the architects (see the following pages), Matteo Thun's great crescents of colour in turquoise and purple, on white or red, make vivid colour accents. Michael Graves's gilded columns support acanthus or ivy leaves, while Arata Isozaki has designed a complicated repeat pattern like a pointillist painting, with starbursts of broken colour scattered across a night sky. Hans-Ullrich Bitsch, the Düsseldorf architect, has clusters of cubes, constellations in a starry sky reflecting a satellite view of the world. The art-form broadloom carpeting uses velour in ICI timbrelle fibres, rated as heavy contract wear.

30

Sam Francis
Carpet, from the *Dialog* collection
Polyamide
W 400 cm (157½ in). Repeat W 200 cm
(78¾ in), L 92.5 cm (36¼ in)
Manufacturer: Vorwerk, West Germany

David Hockney
Carpets, from the *Dialog* collection
Polyamide
W 400 cm (157½ in). Repeat W 100 cm
(39½ in), L 92.5 cm (36¼ in)
Manufacturer: Vorwerk, West Germany

31

32

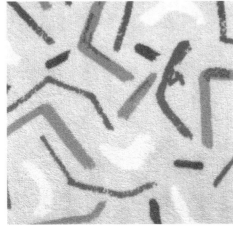

33

34

Michael Graves
Carpets, from the *Dialog* collection
Polyamide
W 400 cm (157½ in). Repeat W 50 cm
(19⅝ in), L 92.5 cm (36¼ in)
Manufacturer: Vorwerk, West Germany

35

36
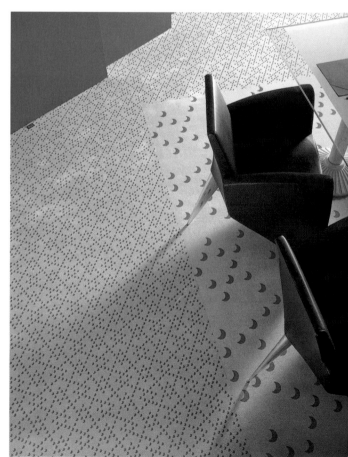

Matteo Thun
Carpet, from the *Dialog* collection
Polyamide
W 400 cm (157½ in). Repeat W 20.5 cm
(8 in), L 19 cm (7½ in)
Manufacturer: Vorwerk, West Germany

37

Arata Isozaki
Carpets, from the *Dialog* collection
Polyamide
W 400 cm (157½ in). Repeat W 50 cm
(19⅝ in), L 31.5 cm (12⅜ in)
Manufacturer: Vorwerk, West Germany

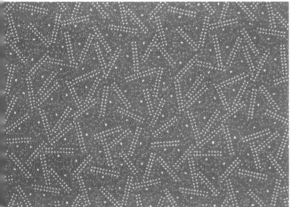

38

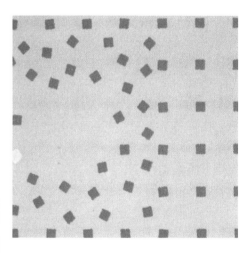

39

Hans-Ullrich Bitsch
Carpet, from the *Dialog* collection
Polyamide
W 400 cm (157½ in). Repeat W 100 cm
(39½ in), L 92.5 cm (36¼ in)
Manufacturer: Vorwerk, West Germany

40

Javier Mariscal
Rug, *León Solitario*
Wool
W 170 cm (67 in). L 240 cm (94½ in)
Manufacturer: Nani Marquina, Spain

The Spanish mascot for the 1992 Olympic Games to be held in Barcelona will become recognized worldwide during the next two years. Hence the battle between graphic artists when the Barcelona Olympic Committee announced a competition to choose the design. Javier Mariscal won with his brilliant caricature of an animated foxy dog belonging to no recognizable breed, though related to the lion illustrated on this rug. So his design for Nani Marquina, *León Solitario*, takes on a new stance, albeit a wistful one. Amid a sea of blue stands this tiny, solitary lion, "only a lion, waiting for you to caress it with your feet."

Since 1977 Javier Mariscal has been a graphic designer whose illustrations have been used in comic books (now collectors' items) and textiles, rugs, lamps, porcelain, sculpture and furniture. He often collaborates with the illustrator Pepe Cortés. It is possible to spot a Mariscal from a distance at the international textile fairs; nobody else can get so much apparently freehand work into the manufacturing process, and with such invigorating charm.

41

Marc Van Hoe
Carpet, *W. Ross*
Wool, linen
A rug woven using the Jacquard
technique. Limited batch production
W 120 cm (47¼ in)
Manufacturer: Deweer, Belgium

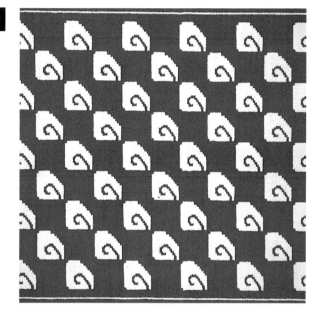

42

Marc Van Hoe
Rug, *Odessa*
Wool, linen
A rug woven using the Jacquard
technique. Limited batch production
W 120 cm (47¼ in)
Manufacturer: Deweer, Belgium

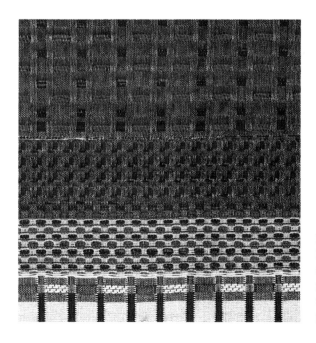

43

Mark Van Hoe
Fabric, *Cogitat A*
Cotton, wool
Prototype
W 140 cm (55⅛ in)
Manufacturer: Ter Molst, Belgium

Fujiwo Ishimoto
Fabric, *Atlas*
52% linen, 48% printed cotton
W 145 cm (57 in). Repeat 96 cm (37¾ in)
Manufacturer: Marimekko, Finland

44

Fujiwo Ishimoto
Fabric, *Aatto*
52% linen, 48% printed cotton
W 145 cm (57 in). Repeat 90 cm (35½ in)
Manufacturer: Marimekko, Finland

46

45

Fujiwo Ishimoto
Fabric, *Lainehtiva*
Printed cotton
W 145 cm (57 in). Repeat 109 cm (43 in)
Manufacturer: Marimekko, Finland

47

Fujiwo Ishimoto
Fabric, *Kalliomaa*
Printed cotton
W 145 cm (57 in). Repeat 96 cm (37¾ in)
Manufacturer: Marimekko, Finland

48

Fujiwo Ishimoto
Fabric, *Itkuraita*
Printed cotton
W 140 cm (55⅛ in). Repeat 240 cm
(94½ in)
Manufacturer: Marimekko, Finland

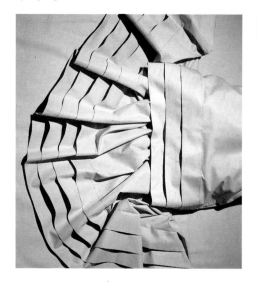

On dress labels Sybilla's distinctive signature is an exaggerated line that plunges up and down like a temperature chart. It is as elegant as the clothes she designs. Born in New York in 1963, she lived in Madrid until her first job took her to Paris and the haute couturier Yves St Laurent. In 1983, she was successful with her first collection of demure, tailored clothes that have unexpected, subtle details such as twirls and flounces that draw attention to the line. Gymslips they may be, but provocative ones. Sybilla's first venture into furnishing design is this project for Bures Industries of embroidered and printed cotton sheets that sport the same motifs as her fashion collections.

This page:
Sybilla
Sheets
Printed cotton
W 50 cm (19⅝ in). L 80 cm (31½ in)
W 160 cm (63 in). L 260 cm (102¼ in),
265 cm (104¼ in)
W 210 cm (82¾ in). L 265 cm (104¼ in),
270 cm (106¼ in)
Manufacturer: Bures Industries, Spain

53

54

This page:
Javier Mariscal
Sheets
Cotton
W 50 cm (19⅝ in). L 85 cm (33½ in)
W 160 cm (63 in). L 260 cm (102¼ in),
265 cm (104¼ in)
W 210 cm (82¾ in). L 265 cm (104¼ in),
270 cm (106¼ in)
W 240 cm (94½ in). L 275 cm (108¼ in),
280 cm (110¼ in)
Manufacturer: Bures Industries, Spain

Top:
Reiko Sudo
Fabric, *Film Stripe*
Cotton, polyurethane
Made using the double-weave Jacquard
technique. The double layers of the wide
coloured stripes create a billowing effect
when the white polyurethane yarn in the
narrow stripes shrinks during finishing.
W 60 cm (23½ in). Repeat 21 cm (8¼ in)

Bottom:
Sayuri Shimoda
Fabrics, *Sashiko*
Cotton, polyester
Made using the double-weave Jacquard
technique. One side of the fabric is
polyester and the other side is cotton.
Binding yarns make embroidery patterns
on each side.
W 108 cm (42⅝ in). Repeat 1.25 cm
(½ in)
Manufacturer: Nuno, Japan

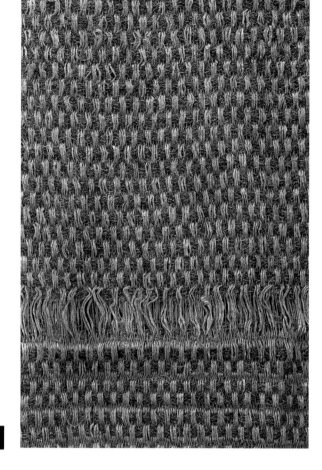

55

Eiji Miyamoto
Fabric, *Ancient Look*
Silk, wool
One-off
W 110 cm (43½ in). Repeat 70 cm
(27½ in)
Manufacturer: Miyashin, Japan

56

57

Eiji Miyamoto
Fabric
Polyester, cupra, wool, acrylic
Three-layered quilting, highlighted with
looped wool thread. One-off
W 110 cm (43½ in). Repeat 1.5 cm (⅔ in)
Manufacturer: Miyashin, Japan

Eiji Miyamoto
Fabric
Linen, cotton
Made using the crimped Jacquard
technique. One-off
W 90 cm (35½ in). Repeat 6 cm (2½ in)
Manufacturer: Miyashin, Japan

Eiji Miyamoto
Fabric
Linen
Made using the tie-dye technique.
One-off
W 150 cm (59 in)
Manufacturer: Miyashin, Japan

58

60

59

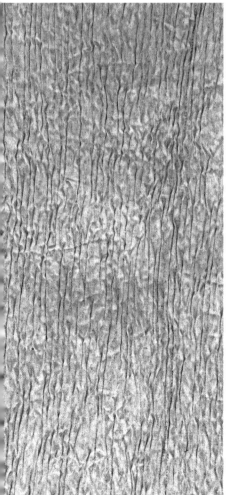

Eiji Miyamoto
Fabric
Linen, cotton
Crimped effect created by pulling the
weft thread tightly on the back of the
fabric. One-off
W 60 cm (23½ in)
Manufacturer: Miyashin, Japan

61

Eiji Miyamoto
Fabrics
Left to right:
Silk
One-off
W 130 cm (51⅛ in). Repeat 2 cm (¾ in)
Cotton
One-off
W 130 cm (51⅛ in)
Wool
W 130 cm (51⅛ in)
Manufacturer: Miyashin, Japan

62

Gavino Falchi
Fabrics/bedcovers
Left to right:
Brummel
Cotton
Cashmere design, made using the
Jacquard technique.
W 256 cm (100¾ in). L 285 cm (112¼ in)
Ofelia
Cotton damask
The central band is patterned with ribs.
W 256 cm (100¾ in). L 285 cm (112¼ in)
Fedra
Flemish linen
W 256 cm (100¾ in). L 285 cm (112¼ in)
Nelia
Cotton piqué
W 256 cm (100¾ in). L 285 cm (112¼ in)
Otto
Damier silk, wool, satin
W 256 cm (100¾ in). L 285 cm (112¼ in)
Coppelia
Cotton piqué
W 256 cm (100¾ in). L 285 cm (112¼ in)
Manufacturer: Driade, Italy

"It is nonsense to ignore the potential of computers and high-tech materials in this age," says Junichi Arai. "To follow ancient craft techniques is pointless." This is why every year his fabrics from Japan startle *The International Design Yearbook's* selection committee with their sheer beauty. While other designers submit yet more reworkings on familiar patterns of birds or flowers, braids or stripes in the same screen-printed fabrics, Junichi Arai tests the stresses, strains and breaking points of various mixes. "Some designers think that pattern is the most important thing about textiles," he says, "but I love texture."

Born into a traditional weaving community, Junichi learned a great many conventional techniques. His admiration for the printing and weaving of Indonesia and Mexico also encouraged him to experiment with ethnic variations, from *ikat* weaves to Mexican embroideries. Now his fabrics are woven from unlikely combinations of polyester, silk, linen and cotton with aluminium metallic strips. He particularly admires the drawn-thread effect which he achieves by subjecting his fabrics to intense heat. The puckered, bobbled or gossamer results can be seen in the selection shown here.

63

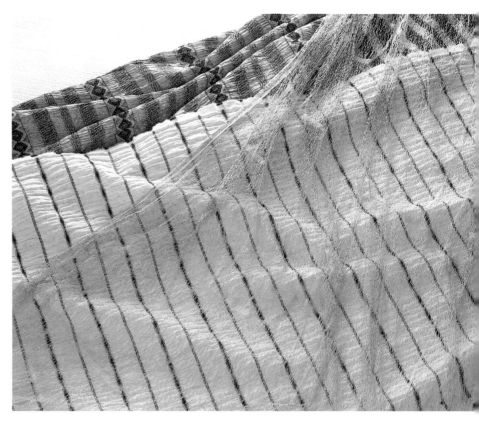

Junichi Arai
Fabrics
Top: *Tube*
Polyester
Made using the Jacquard technique with
several different kinds of polyester
yarns.
W 50 cm (19⅝ in). Repeat 12 cm (4¾ in)
Middle: *Striped Pucker*
Polyester
Made using the Jacquard technique with
several different kinds of polyester
yarns.
W 95 cm (37½ in). Repeat 9 cm (3½ in)
Bottom: *Silk Lace*
Silk
Made using the Raschel technique.
W 100 cm (39½ in). Repeat 135 cm
(53¼ in)
Manufacturer: Nuno, Japan

64

Junichi Arai
Fabrics
Top: *Metal*
Polyester and aluminium
W 50 cm (19⅝ in). Repeat 12 cm (4¾ in)
Middle: *Bubble Pucker*
Polyester and Cotton
W 90 cm (35½ in). Repeat 21 cm (8¼ in)
Bottom: *Spaced Weft Fringe*
Wool and Cotton
W 85 cm (33½ in). Repeat 10 cm (4 in)
Manufacturer: Nuno, Japan

65

Junichi Arai
Fabric, *Spaced Warp*
Cotton, wool
Made using the Jacquard technique with
different textures created by the
omission of warp yarns.
W 120 cm (47¼ in). Repeat 13 cm (5⅛ in)
Manufacturer: Nuno, Japan

The emergence of the designer rug has been one of the spin-offs of the retreat from wall-to-wall carpeting in fashionable interiors. While background flooring fades into anonymity, rugs are being given the most artistic treatments, with manufacturers reviving hand-tied knotting to cope with the changes of pattern that these demand. Marcello Morandini's experimental, rigorous geometry on a series of shapely rugs, made in Switzerland by Melchnau, has brought a new perspective to floor covering. Morandini cut out the geometric shapes, using *trompe l'œil* gradations of tone to distort the parameters. Arranging or inter-weaving these squares, circles, triangles and rectangles becomes the owner's artistic endeavour.

Melchnau have used the classic Axmin-ster technique for Morandini's *Progetto* series. In use since 1880, this method, which is the same as that used for hand-tied Oriental carpets, allows for any number of colours. Morandini's other rugs have been hand-tufted to give even freer rein. Hand-tufting permits differences in yarn sizes, pile or loop surface structure, variations in height from 9 to 30mm, and practically every motif from the 17th-century Gobelin period to Abstract Modern. Morandini's juxta-positions of black and white have a distinctive Op Art effect, akin to Kinetic Art.

Marcello Morandini
Rug, *Progetto 21*
Wool
W 240 cm (94½ in). L 240 cm (94½ in)
Manufacturer: Teppichfabrik Melchnau,
Switzerland

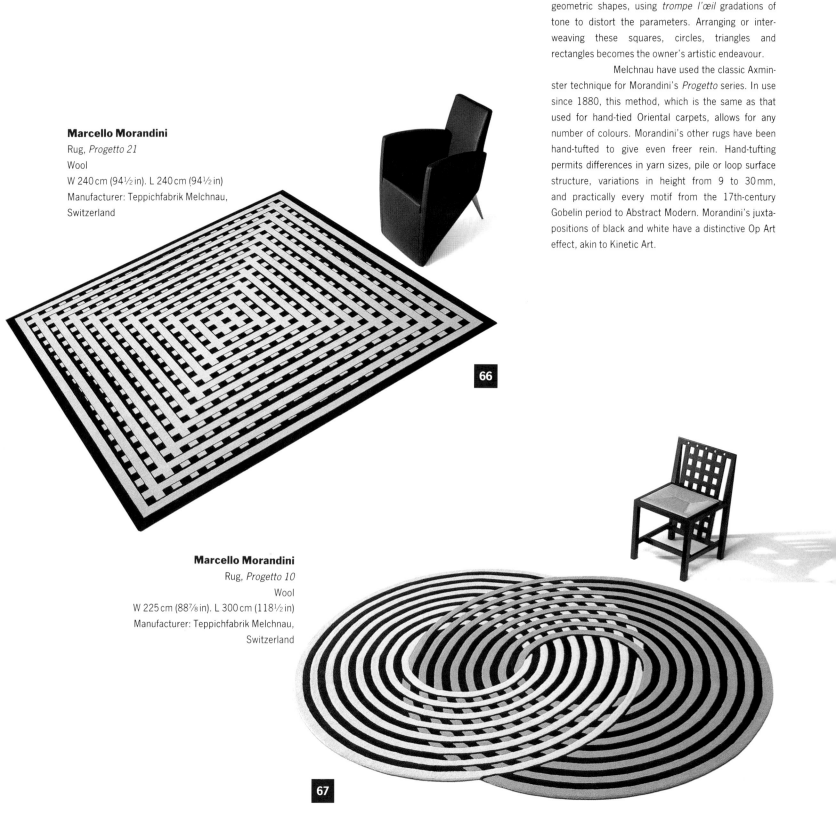

66

Marcello Morandini
Rug, *Progetto 10*
Wool
W 225 cm (88⅞ in). L 300 cm (118½ in)
Manufacturer: Teppichfabrik Melchnau,
Switzerland

67

Marcello Morandini
Rug, *Progetto 6*
Wool
W 300 cm (118½ in). L 300 cm (118½ in)
Manufacturer: Teppichfabrik Melchnau,
Switzerland

68

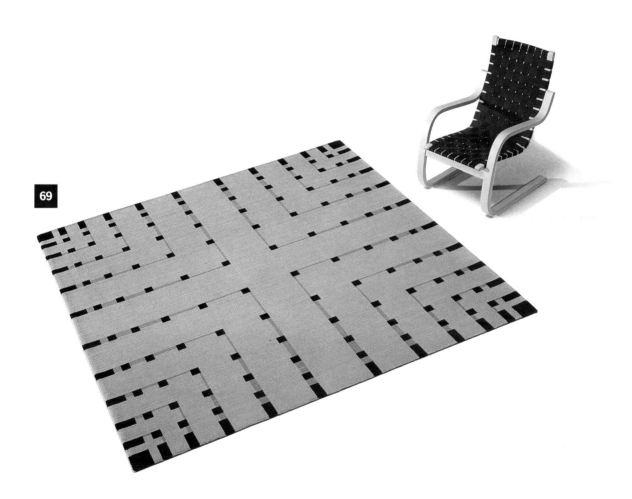

69

Marcello Morandini
Rug, *Progetto 22*
Wool
W 240 cm (94½ in). L 240 cm (94½ in)
Manufacturer: Teppichfabrik Melchnau,
Switzerland

All is not peaceful in Silicon Valley. As industrial designers rely more upon laser and microchip technology, few can meet the challenge of creating new shapes that humanize the products. "I can see the inventor," says Oscar Tusquets Blanca, "but where is the designer?" Many entries for this section were rejected because they were clumsy attempts at packaging products "differently" – for example a toaster on clunky feet in pastel plastic.

As gadgetry and gimmickry are eliminated, the products that remain are very often characterless. Many conform to a black box anonymity: televisions are barely distinguishable from micro-wave ovens, video recorders from tape decks. Much design has a corporate look, with brand names the only differentiating feature between one fax machine and another. Inevitably, designers who design like machines will be replaced by machines. To humanize technology, which becomes increasingly sophisticated, it is neces-sary to have a "high-touch," not a high-tech, approach. Kenneth Grange's perfect pouring spout for a kettle that can be filled without removing the lid could be made only in plastic, while Alan Fletcher's supremely simple letter holder for Oun in Japan illustrates crafsmanship in professional design. The kitchen appliances generically known as "white goods" have turned black. It is not the colour difference which qualified them for inclusion here, however, but the thoughtful design of the illuminated control panels.

Product semantics characterizes all these designs for everyday products whose shapes are not predictable. Richard Sapper, designer of that 20th-century icon, the *Tizio* light for Artemide, applies product semantics to his authoritative watch for Alessi. Watches used to be prized, not thrown away like Sony's *Gotta Watch*. Since quartz crystals are so cheap, watches have become a disposable fashion accessory. But Sapper's "precise instrument of measurement," as he calls it, is to be worn as jewellery; like a business card, it makes a deliberate statement of status, and becomes the "companion which human beings look at more often than any other."

Marketing strategies can bring a certain style to product design. The *My First Sony* sound system for children has intrinsic obsolescence as well as brand loyalty, while the Philips flat-pack television heralds the company's development of viewing screens on the backs of seats in aircraft. Some industrial designers view themselves as problem-solvers: Oscar Tusquets Blanca sees them as the artists of industry. Design has always provided evi-dence of a culture's values, its "life-style." Future archaeologists will find here an eclectic collection of artefacts, including a significant product in the age of conspicuous consumption – the garbage can.

PRODUCTS 5

Ajin Togashi
Stereo amplifier, *LA-1*
Aluminium, glass, rubber
Works with any CD, tape player or
speaker system.
H 9 cm (3½ in). Di 27.6 cm (10¾ in)
Manufacturer: Sasaki Glass Co., Japan

°1

2

Ajin Togashi
Speaker system, *Clearball CB160M*
Glass, iron, rubber
Hi-fi speaker system with rigid spherical
enclosures made of thick glass. The
speakers can be pointed in any direction
for good amplification.
H 16 cm (6¼ in). Di 16 cm (6¼ in)
Manufacturer: Sasaki Glass Co., Japan

Michael Graves
Mantel clock
Ebonized wood, maple-veneered ABS
H 24 cm (9⅜ in). W 9 cm (3½ in). L 16 cm
(6¼ in)
Manufacturer: Alessi, Italy

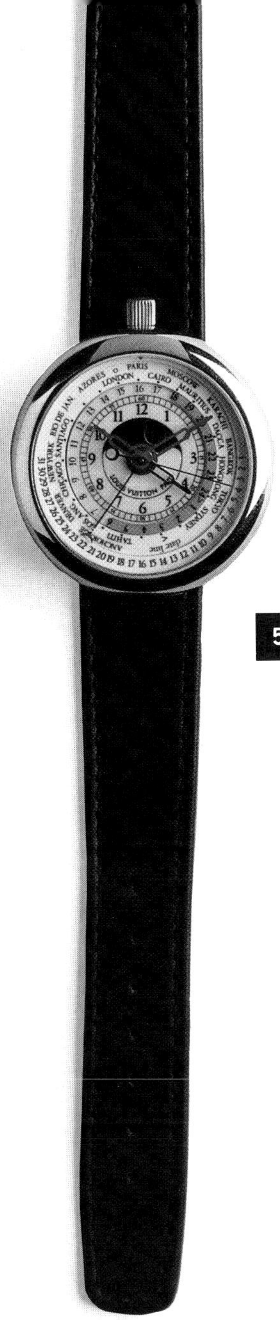

Gae Aulenti

Wrist-watch, *Louis Vuitton II*
Zirconium oxide ceramic, sapphire glass
Watch with an alarm function. The newly discovered ceramic is waterproof, and does not scratch or tarnish.
D 1.27 cm (⅝ in). Di 3.7 cm (1⅕ in)
Manufacturer: Louis Vuitton, France

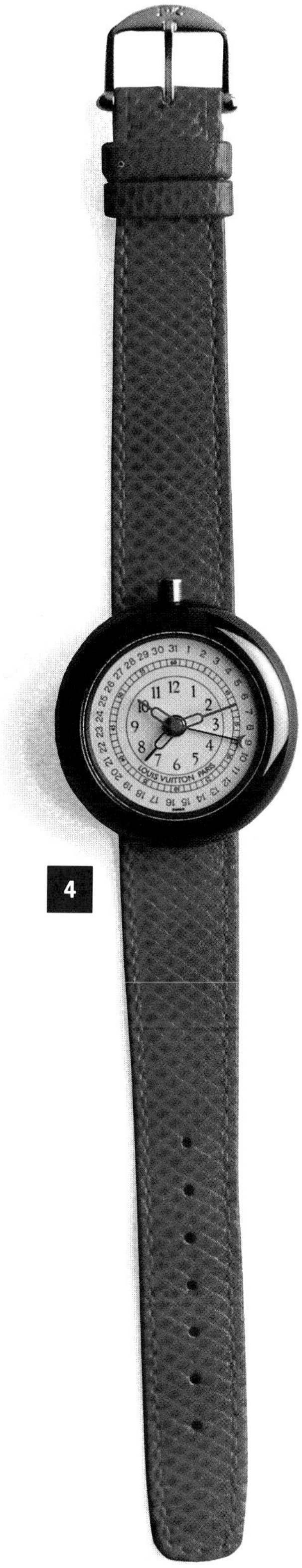

5

Richard Sapper

Wrist-watch, *Uri-Uri*
Stainless steel, black chromium-plated brass, titanium, gold, sapphire glass
Quartz watch, water-resistant to 30 metres.
D 0.5 cm (¼ in). Di 3.5 cm (1⅜ in)
Manufacturer: Alessi, Italy

4

Gae Aulenti

Wrist-watch, *Louis Vuitton I*
18 carat gold case
Anti-magnetic with a quartz mechanism.
As well as local time, this watch displays the date, the current phase of the moon, and the time in each of the cities named.
D 1.45 cm (⅗ in). Di 4 cm (1⅖ in)
Manufacturer: Louis Vuitton, France

6

7

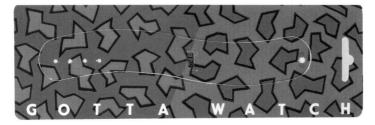

Sony Design Team
Disposable digital wrist-watch,
Gotta Watch
Paper, stainless steel, quartz mechanism
L 22 cm (8⅔ in)
Manufacturer: Sony, Japan

Ever since tiny quartz crystals and liquid crystal displays started to replace the cogs and winders of the traditional timepiece, watches have increasingly been attracting designers' attention. The watch with no moving parts, with endless functions from a calculator to an alarm, can sell for no more than a few dollars. The packaging, therefore, is highly valued. In this design for a throwaway called *Gotta Watch*, Sony have emphasized the packaging aspect. They have dispensed with the conventional watch strap and case, merely printing a variety of graphics on strong paper which can be clipped around the wrist with a plastic catch. The watch itself has a cheap, simple, quartz mechanism and a digital face.

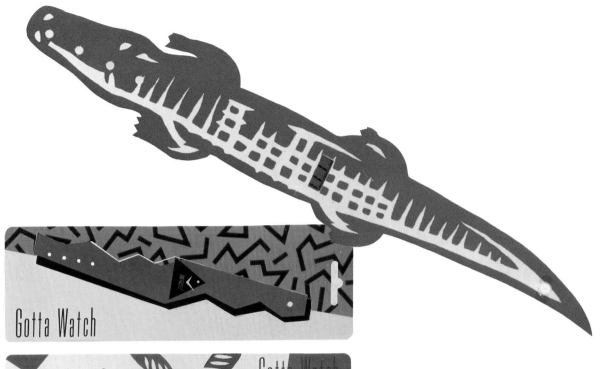

Gotta Watch

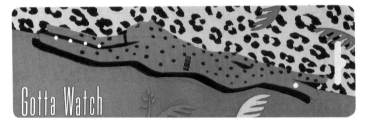

Gotta Watch

Gotta Watch

GOTTA WATCH

Gotta Watch

GOTTA WATCH

Helle Damkjaer
Stacking paper holder, *Linial*
Stainless steel, nickel- or copper-painted
brass
Prototype
H 6 cm (2⅜ in). W 26 cm (10¼ in).
L 31 cm (12¼ in)
Manufacturer: Anthologie Quartett, West
Germany

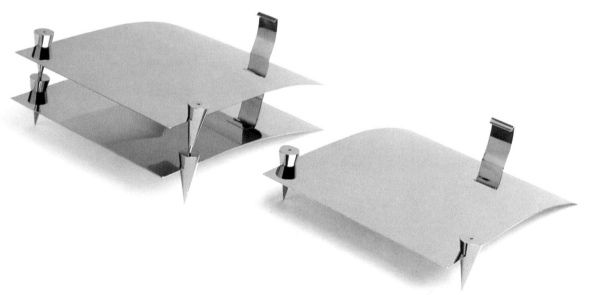

Gae Aulenti
Pen
18 carat gold
Monogrammed with a fine, medium or
broad nib.
L 15.5 cm (6⅛ in). Di 1 cm (⅖ in)
Manufacturer: Louis Vuitton, France

9

10

Erik Magnussen
Paper knife
18/8 stainless steel
W 1.5 cm (⅔ in). L 22 cm (8⅔ in)
Manufacturer: Stelton, Denmark

11

Alan Fletcher
Letter holder, *Massimo*
American walnut, chrome-plated steel
Base H 4 cm (1½ in). W 15 cm (6 in).
L 15 cm (6 in). Di of each ball 4.5 cm
(1¾ in)
Manufacturer: Oun, Japan

Corporate Industrial Design

Pocket colour television, *LCD 3 in*
Anodized pressed aluminium
Active matrix, high-resolution liquid
crystal display in a compact flat design.
H 16 cm (6¼ in). W 8.8 cm (3½ in).
D 2.5 cm (1 in)
Manufacturer: Philips, Netherlands

12

Christopher Alviar, Sohrab Vossoughi and Terry Jones for Ziba Design

PC Viewer
Injection-moulded ABS, infra-red glass
Portable, lightweight plastic viewer
system. When placed on an ordinary
overhead projector, the LCD technology
presents a high-contrast image of the
stored information. It has a remote
control facility and is compatible with
most personal computer systems.
Main housing: H 4 cm (1½ in). W 30 cm
(11⅞ in). L 31.5 cm (12⅓ in)
Memory module: H 8.75 cm (3½ in).
W 27.5 cm (10⅞ in). D 7.5 cm (3 in)
Manufacturer: Infocus Systems, USA

Pioneer in compact disc technology, Philips is clearly
moving into the screen world. Their Corporate Industrial Design unit have had an interesting year. With
Warner Brothers, USA, they experimented on small
liquid crystal display panels, such as this one, for the
backs of aircraft seats. This folding television, with a
7.5 cm (3 in) screen and a liquid crystal display, can be
easily slipped into a jacket pocket.

14

13

Sony Design Team

Portable hand-held photocopier, *HCP-C8*
Plastic, metal
Prints on paper and plastic.
H 10 cm (4 in). W 7.2 cm (2⅞ in).
D 2.7 cm (1¹⁄₁₀ in)
Manufacturer: Sony, Japan

Canon Design Team

Personal workstation, *NAVI*
ABS
Multi-functional piece combining
telephone, facsimile, word processor
and personal computer. The choice of
modes is made by touching the icons
appearing on the screen. Simultaneous
operations in different modes are
possible.
Main unit: H 35.2 cm (13⁷⁄₁₀ in). W 37 cm
(14½ in). D 32.5 cm (12¾ in)
Keyboard: H 5 cm (2 in). W 30.4 cm
(11⁹⁄₁₀ in). D 15.9 cm (6⅕ in)
Manufacturer: Canon, Japan

16

Matsushita Design Team

Personal television
Plastic
8 in colour television with magenta-
coloured screen and single flex for
power and aerial.
H 20.2 cm (7⅞ in). W 22.6 cm (8⅞ in).
D 31.9 cm (12½ in)
Manufacturer: Kyushu Matsushita
Electric Co., Japan

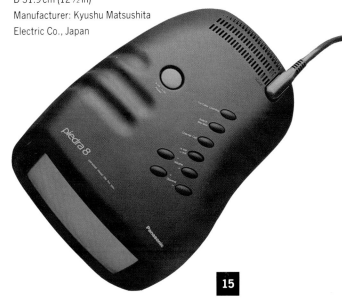

15

17

I·DE·A Institute Design Team

Television
Plastic
700-line horizontal resolution with a
12-hour on/off timer and a remote
control unit. The piece is designed to
house two video recorders and to store
video tapes.
H 107.9 cm (42¹⁄₁₆ in). W 68.8 cm
(27¹⁄₁₆ in). D 51 cm (20 in)
Manufacturer: Toshiba, Japan

18

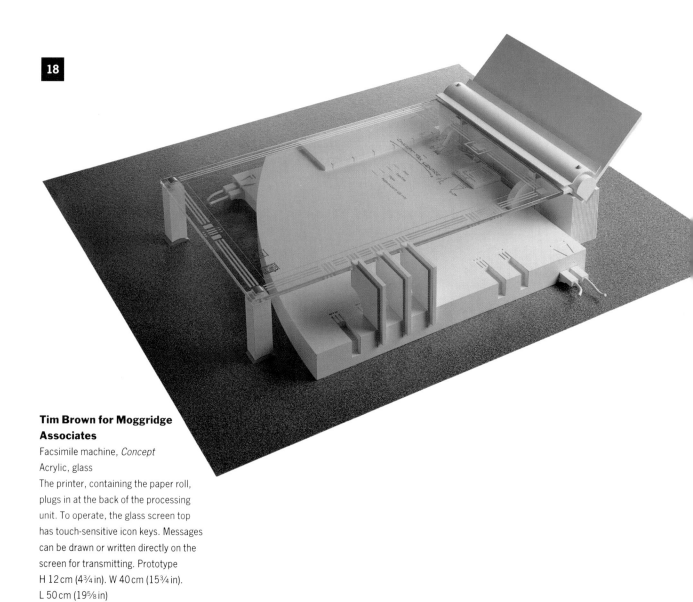

**Tim Brown for Moggridge
Associates**
Facsimile machine, *Concept*
Acrylic, glass
The printer, containing the paper roll,
plugs in at the back of the processing
unit. To operate, the glass screen top
has touch-sensitive icon keys. Messages
can be drawn or written directly on the
screen for transmitting. Prototype
H 12 cm (4¾ in). W 40 cm (15¾ in).
L 50 cm (19⅝ in)
Manufacturer: IDM, UK

**Isao Hosoe in collaboration
with Alessio Pozzoli**
Floppy disk container, *Space 540*
Makrolon, Plexiglass, ABS
Antistatic, impact-resistant, lightweight
portable box to contain 40 floppy disks.
Equipped with a double-locking system,
it can be used both vertically and
horizontally.
W 19 cm (7½ in). D 6 cm (2⅜ in). L 40 cm
(15¾ in)
Manufacturer: Massplast, Italy

19

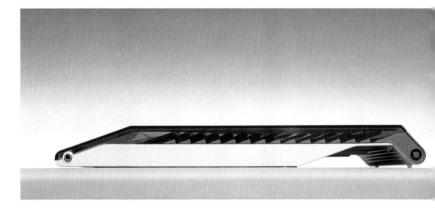

20

**Isao Hosoe in collaboration
with Alessio Pozzoli**
Floppy disk container, *Space 330*
Makrolon, Plexiglass, ABS
Antistatic, impact-resistant, lightweight
portable box to contain 30 floppy disks.
Equipped with a double-locking system,
it can be used both vertically and
horizontally.
W 21 cm (8¼ in). D 4 cm (1½ in). L 37 cm
(14½ in)
Manufacturer: Massplast, Italy

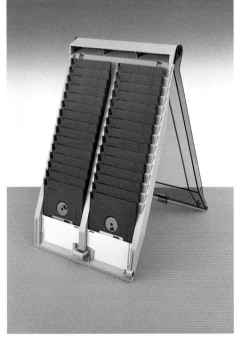

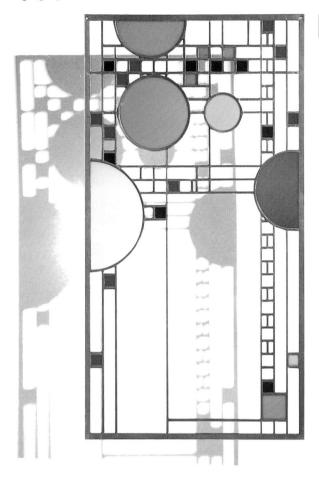

21

22

Frank Lloyd Wright
Window, *Clerestory No. 2*
Glass, zinc
Available for use as a panel with optional
frame for hanging or mounted display, or
as an installation-ready window.
Reproduced from The Coonley
Playhouse, Riverside, Illinois, designed in
1911.
H 86 cm (33¾ in). W 46 cm (17⅞ in)
Manufacturer: Oakbrook Esser Studios,
USA

Frank Lloyd Wright branded his style "Usonian," for United States Own. He did not concede any influence at all from across the Atlantic. "No practice by any European architect to this day has influenced mine in the least," he stated in his *Testament* published in 1957 when he was 88 years old. These stained glass windows graphically illustrate his original approach. At a time when the Arts and Crafts glass makers in the UK were producing Art Nouveau lilies and sinuous vines, Wright's stained glass showed the same angularity and geometric formalism as his buildings. His rectilinear designs in primary colours now reach record prices at auction: in 1988 a small sconce with the initials FLW sold at Sotheby's for $13,000.

His showpiece architectural door panels exactly suit the kind of home he pioneered: suburban houses that spread outwards instead of upwards (unlike their European counterparts, terraced houses); concrete breeze-block latticed screens to form a link between the outside and the indoors; glass walls and open-plan living. His architecture remains representative of America today. "In organic architecture," Wright wrote, "it is quite impossible to consider the building as one thing, its furnishings another and its setting and environment still another." Architectonic furniture and fittings, so closely linked with their setting, seldom travel, so it is enterprising of the Frank Lloyd Wright Foundation, guardian of his designs, to release the original plans which made these reproductions possible, and available through mail order.

Frank Lloyd Wright
Window, *Lake Geneva Tulip*
Glass, zinc
Available for use as a panel with optional
frame for hanging or mounted display, or
as an installation-ready window.
Reproduced from The Lake Geneva Inn,
Wisconsin, designed in 1911.
H 34 cm (13⅜ in). W 53 cm (20⅞ in)
Manufacturer: Oakbrook Esser Studios,
USA

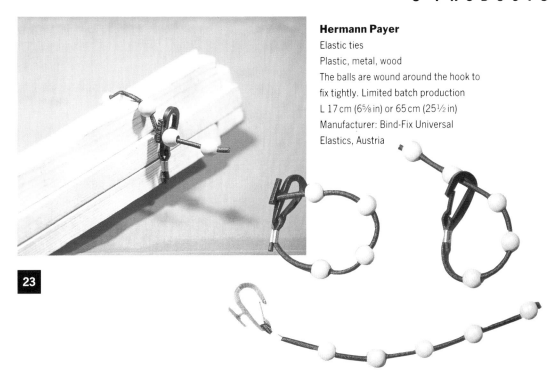

Hermann Payer
Elastic ties
Plastic, metal, wood
The balls are wound around the hook to
fix tightly. Limited batch production
L 17 cm (6⅝ in) or 65 cm (25½ in)
Manufacturer: Bind-Fix Universal
Elastics, Austria

23

24

**Olavi Lindén and Timo
Sunila**
Knife sharpener, *Roll Sharp*
Fibreglass-reinforced polyamide 6,
polycarbonate, ceramic aluminium
oxide, polyacetal
The ceramic wheels grind both sides of
the knife blade.
H 6 cm (2⅜ in). W 6 cm (2⅜ in). L 16 cm
(6¼ in)
Manufacturer: Fiskars Oy Ab, Finland

Paolo Nava
Coat rack and umbrella stand, from the
Twist collection
Sheet steel
Limited batch production
Coat rack: H 180 cm (70⅝ in). Base Di
40 cm (15¾ in)
Umbrella stand/waste-paper basket:
H 50 cm (19⅝ in). D 27 cm (10½ in)
Manufacturer: Airon, Italy

25

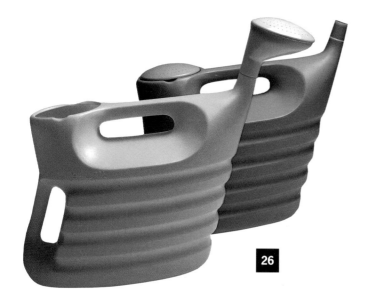

26

Kenneth Grange
Garden watering cans, *Jetcan*
Moulded polypropylene
The body is heavily ribbed to improve
rigidity and aid water-level assessment
and the spout can be stored in the filling
aperture.
H 33 cm (13 in). W 44 cm (17¼ in).
D 18.8 cm (7⅖ in)
Manufacturer: Geeco, UK

Kenneth Grange is the designer behind that 20th-century British landmark, the parking meter, as well as the British Intercity train, the Parker pen and a range of appliances for Kenwood. His career began in the heady days of the Fifties when the Festival of Britain aimed to get design back into industry, and Ernest Race used resmelted aircraft wings for his aluminium stacking chair. Grange, an admirer of what he calls "the innovation and audacity of the Fifties," has expressed disappointment that British consumers have since been prevented from enjoying innovative products by manufacturers trying to hold down prices. This persistent policy has resulted only in a marked reduction of quality. "Whether it is merely the thicker gauge of metal or the thicker plastic of the Germans, or the finer machining of the Japanese, there is a highly visible difference, and in the open market of Europe the British product made to domestic standards will be unacceptable to the European home."

The huge success of his Kenwood *Chef* mixer created its own problems, since attempts to replace it were resisted. Even when it was redesigned in 1975, the change to its appearance was very small. "To designers whose stock-in-trade is innovation," wrote Grange in 1983, "this situation is at the same time flattering and depressing." Fortunately, Kenwood has commissioned him to design new products, which still give the company a distinctive style in an age when electric goods are plentiful and cheap. Two of his latest designs illustrate his appreciation of the tactile quality of materials in daily use in the home.

27

Kenneth Grange
Kettle
Moulded plastics
An automatic jug kettle with a large
spout and a lockable lid guarding against
spillage, with twin-level sight tubes
allowing for left-hand or right-hand
operation.
H 22.4 cm (8⅜ in). W 23 cm (9 in).
D 12.5 cm (5 in)
Manufacturer: Kenwood, UK

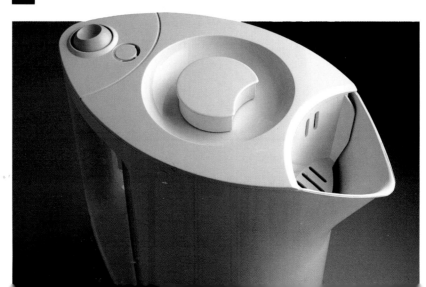

28

Ikuo Kobayashi
Thermos bottles, *HSK-1000*
Stainless steel, polypropylene,
enamelled finish
The light, unbreakable stainless steel
liner and the steel outer shell assist
insulation performance.
H 27.6 cm (10⅘ in). Di 9.5 cm (3¾ in)
Manufacturer: Nippon Sanso, Japan

Enrico Baleri
Garbage cans, *Patti*
Polyethylene, polypropylene, iron plate,
sheet zinc
H 95 cm (37½ in). W 42 cm (16½ in).
Di 42 cm (16½ in)
Manufacturer: Vanini, Italy

29

30

Canon Design Team
Camera, *Canon EOS 750 QD*
ABS, polycarbonate
A compact 35 mm single lens reflex
camera with autofocus, automatic
exposure and automatic built-in flash.
The date and time are imprinted directly
on to each frame.
H 10 cm (4 in). W 15 cm (6 in).
D 7 cm (2¾ in)
Manufacturer: Canon, Japan

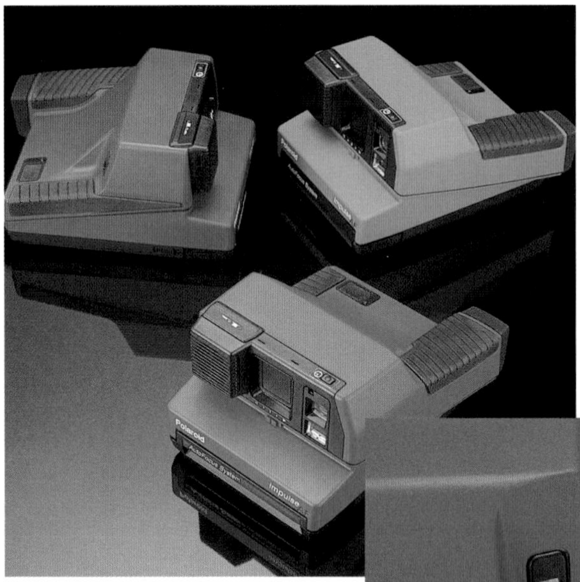

**James Ryan and John Betts for
Henry Dreyfuss Associates**
Camera, *Polaroid Impulse*
Noryl, santoprene, Lim silicone
Instant Polaroid camera, with a one-
touch pop-up strobe that automatically
opens the internal lens cover and
activates the electronic control circuitry.
H 9.5 cm (3.7 in). W 13 cm (5.2 in).
D 17.2 cm (6.8 in)
Manufacturer: Polaroid, USA

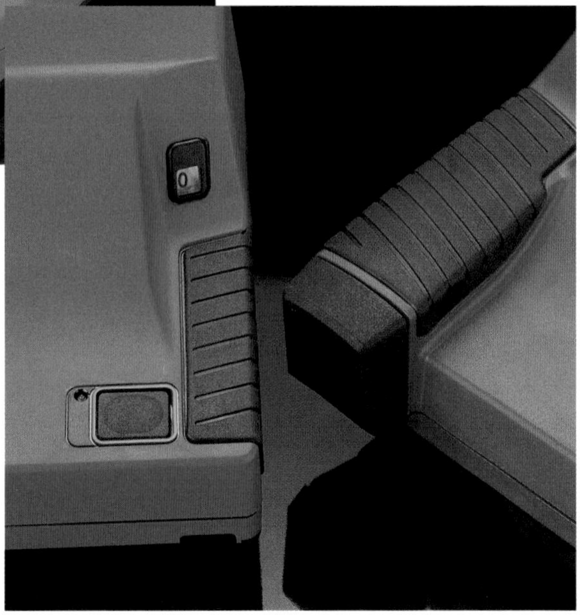

31

32

Giugiaro Design

Camera, *Nikon F4*
Rubber compound, copper siluminum alloy, plastic
High-performance 35 mm single lens reflex camera.
H 13.8 cm (5²⁄₅ in). W 16.8 cm (6⁷⁄₁₀ in).
D 7.6 cm (3 in)
Manufacturer: Nikon, Japan

New technology renders objects obsolete faster in product design than in most other areas. Nikon is a good example of a company dedicated to long-term performance and user loyalty, with new camera cases that are still compatible with existing lenses and accessories. The man behind the design of the *Nikon F4*, Giorgetto Giugiaro, has given the solid die-cast case rugged good looks as well as providing sufficient protection for the controls. No water or dust can penetrate the case, and the ultra-tough shutter has been tested to withstand 150,000 firings. This is the camera to meet the technical requirements of professional photographers.

Kyocera Design Studio

Cine camera, *Samurai*
Polycarbonate, acrylic
Single lens reflex cine camera with autofocus, autozoom, autowind and rewind.
H 12.5 cm (5 in). W 7.3 cm (2⁷⁄₈ in).
D 14.6 cm (5⁷⁄₈ in)
Manufacturer: Kyocera, Japan

33

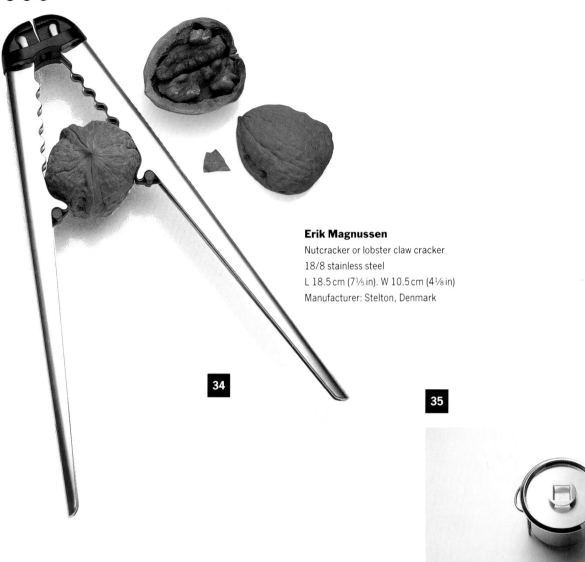

34

35

Erik Magnussen
Nutcracker or lobster claw cracker
18/8 stainless steel
L 18.5 cm (7⅕ in). W 10.5 cm (4⅛ in)
Manufacturer: Stelton, Denmark

Erik Magnussen
Sauce server with lid and tray,
casseroles with stands
18/8 stainless steel
Server: H 8 cm (3⅛ in). Di 10 cm (4 in)
Tray: Di 14 cm (5½ in)
Casseroles: H 11.5 cm (4½ in). Di 18 cm
(7 in). H 10 cm (4 in). Di 25.5 cm (10 in)
Manufacturer: Stelton, Denmark

Alessandro Mendini
Cookware
Stainless steel, plastic
Part of a range of 25 items.
Prototypes
Big stockpot: H 30 cm (11⅞ in).
Di 34 cm (13⅜ in)
Small stockpot: H 19 cm (7½ in).
Di 24 cm (9⅜ in)
Saucepan: H 15 cm (6 in). Di 30 cm
(11⅞ in)
Small casserole: H 13 cm (5⅛ in).
Di 24 cm (9⅜ in)
Manufacturer: Alessi, Italy

36

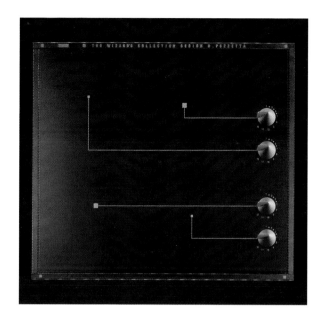

These days practically every domestic appliance is given a facing to match the units in that mythical place, the dream kitchen. But it is quite inappropriate that, behind door fronts with whimsical, nostalgic paint finishes, there is concealed labour-saving technology that is wholly modern. The *Wizard* collection addresses this problem of presentation by boldly upturning the conventional taste for white goods, making the entire object – oven and hob – matt black. Illuminated controls graphically illustrate their function with symbols that at last make obsolete those lengthy and often badly translated instruction manuals.

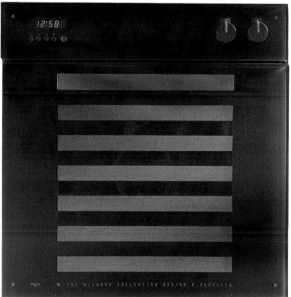

37

Roberto Pezzetta
Electric oven, *Wizard Multiblack*
Glass, melamine resin, enamelled steel, aluminium
A multi-function oven with an electronic timer and programmer, using 2.5kW.
H 59.5 cm (23⅜ in). W 59.5 cm (23⅜ in).
D 56 cm (22 in)
Manufacturer: Zanussi, Italy

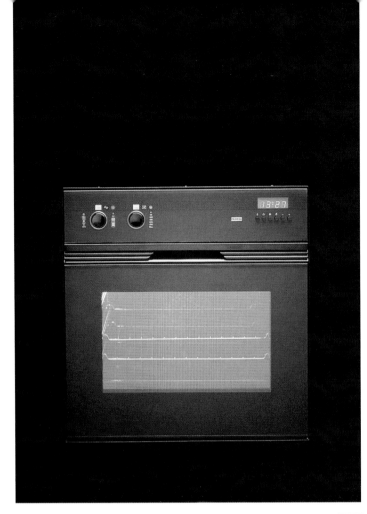

Marcello Cutino

Electric oven, *Ottomatic*
Stainless steel, glass
The concave knobs are flush with the
panel and pop out for use when touched.
H 59.5 cm (23½ in). D 55 cm (21½ in).
L 59.5 cm (23½ in)
Manufacturer: Franke, Italy

38

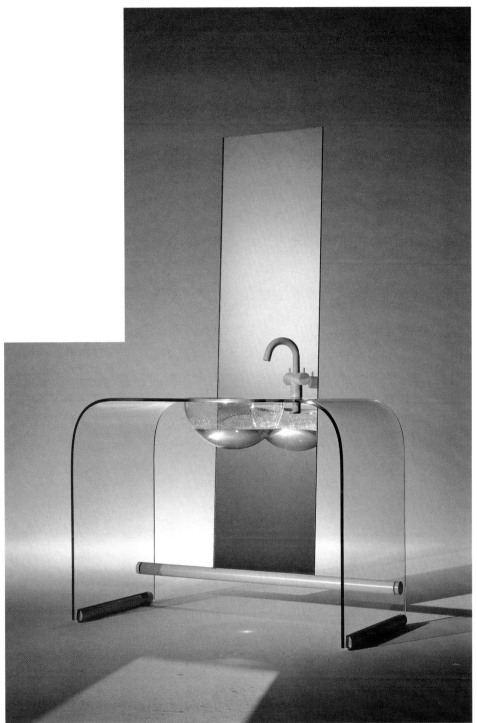

39

Shiro Kuramata
Washbasin, *Coup de Foudre*
Glass, mirror, steel
H 170 cm (67 in). W 500 cm (197½ in).
D 100 cm (39½ in)
Manufacturer: Toyo Sasshi, Japan

40

41

Philippe Starck
Coat-hook, *Chab Welington*
Aluminium
L 12 cm (4¾ in). Di 5.3 cm (2¹⁄₁₆ in)
Manufacturer: Owo, France

Philippe Starck
Door handle, *Mimi Bayou*
Aluminium
L 5 cm (2 in). Di 3 cm (1⅓ in)
Manufacturer: Owo, France

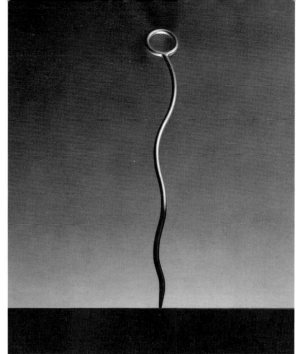

43

Philippe Starck

Poker, *Picfeu*
Iron
W 1 cm (²⁄₅ in). L 59 cm (23¼ in).
Handle L 6.5 cm (2½ in)
Manufacturer: Owo, France

42

Philippe Starck

Firedogs, *Tito Lucifer*
Cast iron
H 28.5 cm (11¼ in) and 13 cm (5⅛ in).
D 8 cm (3⅛ in) L 38.5 cm (15¼ in)
Manufacturer: Owo, France

44

Elisabeth Garouste and Mattia Bonetti

Firedogs
Bronze
H 33 cm (13 in). W at back 15 cm (6 in).
L 50 cm (19⅝ in)
Manufacturer: Barthélemy, France

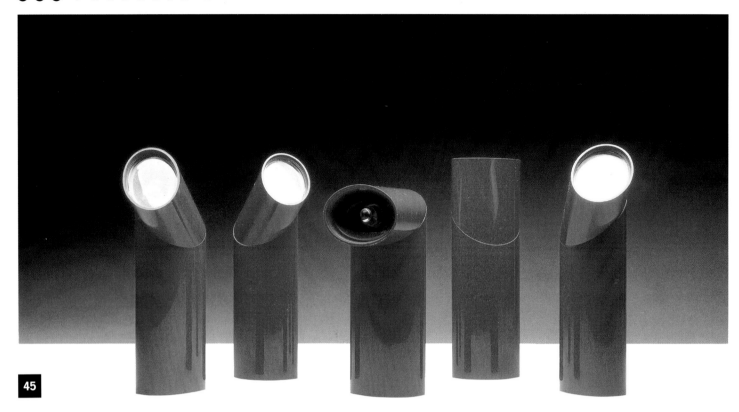

45

Emilio Ambasz
Flashlight, *Polyphemus*
Injection-moulded ABS
The angled swivel head allows for
rotation of 360 degrees. It can be bent in
an L-configuration for easy hand grip.
H 10 cm (4 in). D 2.9 cm (1¼ in)
Manufacturer: G.B. Plast, Italy

Last year it was candlelight, harnessed in the form of
sconces or candelabras, that attracted the most
surprising number of entries to the lighting section of
The International Design Yearbook. This year, there
was a similarly high entry for the products section in
the category of flashlights, with submissions from
round the world for this simple, hand-held tool. Not all
the designs were based on battery-operated
flashlights: one was solar-powered – the world's first.
Designed for expeditions into the wilderness, it was
finally rejected for its cumbersome packaging.

Ambasz's torches address a simpler
need. His collection illustrates his earlier recognition
of the importance of colour, texture, pattern and
ornament. In his foreword to *The International Design
Yearbook 2* he wrote: "Design, once perceived as yet
another means of achieving redemption through sen-
sory deprivation, has now begun to open its tightly
closed fist to embrace fashion and caress ornament.
So a breed of designer has appeared who frankly
takes joy in the exercise of his stylistic gifts."

46

Paul Cockburn
Pocket torch, *Bobby Dazzler*
Polystyrene, polypropylene
High-output 9V halogen pocket torch.
The sprung switch allows flashing or
extended lighting use. Battery and bulb
removal is via side buttons.
W 5 cm (2 in). D 3.5 cm (1⅜ in). L 10.5 cm
(4⅛ in)
Manufacturer: Union Carbide, Australia

47

Paul Cockburn
Work lantern, *Dolphin Mark III*
ABS, polyethylene, rubber
A shock-resistant, waterproof, high-
output 6V lamp.
H 14 cm (5½ in). W 12.5 cm (5 in).
L 19.5 cm (7¾ in)
Manufacturer: Union Carbide, Australia

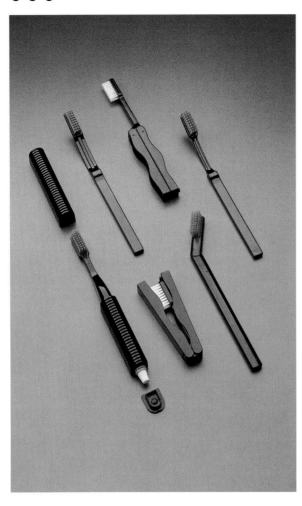

Emilio Ambasz
Toothbrushes
Polypropylene, nylon
W 1.2 cm (½ in). L 16 cm (6¼ in) to
18 cm (7 in)
Manufacturer: Sunstar, Japan

48

49

Corporate Industrial Design
Electric shaver, *Roltronic*
ABS, platinum-refined shaver foil
The rolling cover protects the shaving
head when not in use; opening it turns
the shaver on.
H 12.6 cm (5⅟₁₆ in). W 6 cm (2⅜ in).
D 3 cm (1⅓ in)
Manufacturer: Grundig, West Germany

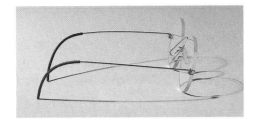

50

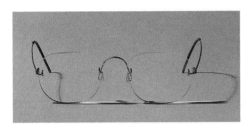

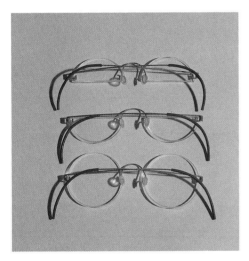

Hans Dissing and Otto Weitling

Spectacles, *Air Titanium*
Titanium, silicone rubber, glass
Lightweight frame made of allergy-proof
titanium wire using no soldering joints,
screws or rivets. The lenses are mounted
using a loop/slot system. The weight of
the frame is less than 3 g (¹⁄₁₀ of an
ounce). The dimensions are variable.
Manufacturer: Lindberg Optik Design,
Denmark

51

Shiro Kuramata

Handbag, *Copacabana*
Leather, metal
Designed for the exhibition "Petites
Architecture Nomades" produced by
Martine Bedin.
Base H 31 cm (12¼ in). W 23 cm (9 in)
Manufacturer: J & F Martell Diffusion,
France

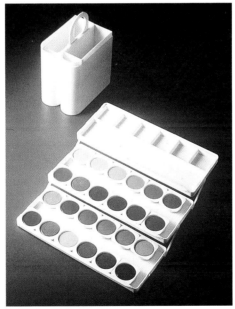

Emilio Ambasz

Water colour paints, *Acqua Color 24*
Polystyrene, polypropylene
The set includes a three-tiered hinged
palette and the storage box doubles as a
water container.
H 4.5 cm (1¾ in). W 9 cm (3½ in).
L 20.5 cm (8 in)
Manufacturer: Herlitz, West Germany

52

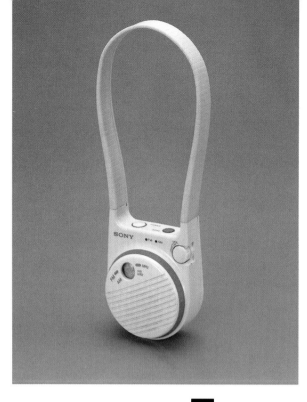

Sony Design Team

53

Shower radio, *ICF-S78*
Plastic
Waterproof radio with digital clock and
alarm facility designed for use in the
shower.
H 31.7 cm (11⁴⁄₅ in). W 9.4 cm (3⁷⁄₁₀ in).
D 5.8 cm (2³⁄₁₀ in)
Manufacturer: Sony, Japan

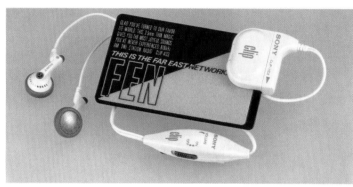

54

Sony Design Team

Personal radio
Plastic
One credit-card sized plastic card is
slotted into the clip for each radio
station.
Card: W 5.4 cm (2¹⁄₁₆ in). L 8.85 cm
(3⁵⁄₁₀ in)
Manufacturer: Sony, Japan

55

Sony Design Team

Drum pad, *DRP-1*
Plastic, metal, wood
Hand-held, battery-operated unit with
internal speakers.
H 3 cm (1¹⁄₃ in). W 11 cm (4³⁄₈ in). D 12 cm
(4³⁄₄ in)
Manufacturer: Sony, Japan

Children will be both seen and heard with Sony's new line dubbed *My First Sony*. It includes a cassette player, with a microphone for recording which switches off automatically after use; an AM/FM radio cassette player, with one operating button and a built-in microphone; a personal FM radio to fit a small hand; and the classic *Walkman* packaged in red with a Perspex window so that children can see how it works, and with a "limiter" button to reduce volume.

What makes these products new, apart from the colourful packaging, is that each product features protective rubber trims, extra large buttons for small fingers, and sturdy outer cases with big, firm handles. They are all designed for hard wear, so that, according to Sony, "even the most careless person need not be afraid." The planned obsolescence is a brilliant marketing strategy: each child will want to trade up in due course to the grown-up version.

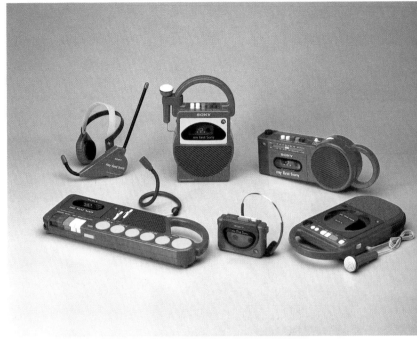

56

Sony Design Team
Personal music system, *My First Sony*
Plastic
A range of matching items designed
especially for children.
Left to right, back row:
Radio transmitter and receiver:
W 25 cm (9⅞ in)
Cassette player with microphone:
H 30.4 cm (11⁹/₁₀ in). W 18.3 cm (7⅙ in).
D 9.5 cm (3¾ in)
Radio cassette player: H 14.5 cm (5¾ in).
W 37.5 cm (14⅝ in). D 8.2 cm (3⅕ in)
Left to right, front row:
Cassette player with microphone and
keyboard: H 5.5 cm (2⅛ in). W 46 cm
(18 in). D 17.7 cm (6⁹/₁₀ in)
Personal stereo cassette player:
H 9.5 cm (3¾ in). W 13.5 cm (5³/₁₀ in).
D 4 cm (1½ in)
Compact disc player with microphone:
H 6.4 cm (2³/₁₀ in). W 18.7 cm (7³/₅ in).
D 36.2 cm (14⅛ in)
Manufacturer: Sony, Japan

57

Products Industrial Design:
Roland Schmidt and Klaus
Lackner
Cassette storage box, *Tape Me*
Polypropylene, nylon
Cassette box with a removable strap
which can be used for 12 cassettes or 6
cassettes and a personal stereo.
H 9 cm (3½ in). W 14.5 cm (5¾ in).
L 36.5 cm (36¼ in)
Manufacturer: Reisenthel, West Germany

BIOGRAPHIES

Every effort has been made to obtain details about each designer whose work is represented in the book, but in some cases information was not available. The figures following each entry refer to the illustrations in which the designer's work is represented (the number before the full point indicates the chapter number).

Ad Us Berlin see *Manuel Pfahl* and *Bettina Wiegandt*.

Leo Aerts is a Belgian designer, working with *Ingrid Wijnen*. 1.130

Christopher Alviar was born in Manila, Philippines, in 1961 and moved to the United States in 1977. A graduate in Industrial Design from the University of Washington in 1986, he was a freelance designer for various firms in the Seattle area including O'Brien International and Walter Dorwin Teague Associates before joining Ziba in 1987. He was a recipient of IDSA's Merit Award (1985, 1986) and recently IDSA's NW Design Invitational and Design Excellence Awards 1988, both for his work on an electronic transparency system. 5.13

Emilio Ambasz earned a Master's degree in Architecture at Princeton University, where he was subsequently a professor. While still in his twenties he helped to found New York's Institute for Architecture and Urban Studies, and served as Curator of Design at the Museum of Modern Art. He has since won international recognition for his work as architect, interior and industrial designer, as well as for his lectures and writings on design. Among his buildings, several of which have won awards, the Museum of American Folk Art and Houston Center Plaza are especially well known. With Giancarlo Piretti he designed the *Vertebra* seating system (winner of the Compasso d'Oro) and the *Logotec* track spotlight range (winner of the American National Industrial Design Award in 1980). 5.45, 48, 52

Ron Arad was born in 1951 in Tel Aviv, Israel. He studied at the Jerusalem Academy of Art and at the Architectural Association, London, graduating in 1979. After working for a firm of London architects, he founded the design company One-Off Ltd in 1981. He has exhibited widely and designs furniture, products and interiors. He has contributed to furniture collections for Vitra and Aram Design Ltd. 1.10–14

Junichi Arai, born in 1932 in Gunma Prefecture, Japan, is a textile designer and manufacturer specializing in sculptural, heavily textured fabrics. He has supplied Issey Miyake and Comme des Garçons, among other leading Japanese designers. In 1987 he was made an Honorary Member of the Faculty of Royal Designers for Industry. 4.63–65

Ramon Arbos is a Spanish industrial designer, born in 1938, whose work has won several awards and been exhibited at exhibitions in Barcelona. 1.116

Robert Arko graduated from the Cleveland Institute of Arts in 1982 with a degree in Industrial Design. With GVO, a consulting firm based in Palo Alto, he was involved in projects ranging from office electronics and consumer products to exhibition design. Since 1984 he has been a member of the design group at Metro. He has designed and managed construction of Metro's showrooms in New York, Chicago, Houston and Los Angeles. He is now concentrating on the design of furniture and managing a new textile and finishes programme for the company. His designs have won many awards and been featured in several exhibitions, including an Exhibition of Bay Area Furniture Designers at the San Francisco Museum of Modern Art. 1.124

Sergio Asti is an Italian architect who has lectured and exhibited extensively, and has sat on a number of award juries since he completed his studies at the Milan Polytechnic in 1953. In the mid-Sixties he studied glass techniques in Murano, Italy. His designs have won many awards and have been displayed in several Venice Biennale exhibitions as well as permanent museum collections. 3.11–13; 4.22–24

Gae Aulenti graduated in architecture from the Milan Polytechnic in 1954. As well as her architectural projects, she has designed stage sets and costumes for opera and drama, lectured extensively on architecture, had exhibitions throughout the world and received many awards. She was responsible for the Musée National d'Art Moderne at the Centre Georges Pompidou and for the interior architecture of the Musée d'Orsay, both in Paris. In September 1987 President Mitterrand conferred on her the title of Chevalier de la Légion d'Honneur. 1.125; 2.40; 5.4, 5, 9

Hiroshi Awatsuji, a textile designer, was born in Kyoto in 1929 and graduated from the Kyoto Municipal College of Fine Arts, establishing his own design studio in 1958. Since 1964 he has collaborated with the Fujie textile company. His principal commissions in Japan include textiles for the government pavilion at Expo 70, and tapestries for the Keio Plaza and Ginza Tokyu hotels. He exhibited at the Victoria and Albert Museum's "Japan Style" exhibition in 1980, and at the "Design Since 1945" exhibition in Philadelphia. 4.1–5

Enrico Baleri, born in Bergamo in 1942, is an Italian designer and entrepreneur. He studied in Milan without graduating; since then he has been involved with a number of companies including Pluri and Alias, where he held the position of art director until 1983. He then set up Baleri Italia, a firm which has commissioned work from, among others, *Philippe Starck*, Hans Hollein and *Alessandro Mendini*. 5.29

Fabrizio Ballardini was born in Asmara, Ethiopia, in 1953. He graduated from the Faculty of Architecture at the University of Florence in 1977. Since 1979 he has worked as an industrial designer while continuing to maintain close professional contacts with the Plants Nursery & Farming Company Ethiopia, designing advertising panels. He has worked with *Fulvio Forbicini* since 1987. 1.132

Francis Ballu was born in Champagne, France, in 1950 and studied cabinet-making. In 1979 he was awarded the Meilleur Ouvrier de France in recognition of his manual work. He now works with *Xylos*. 1.19

Michele Barro is an Italian designer, born in 1959. He attended the Milan Polytechnic, but his real approach to art and design started with *Ettore Sottsass* and later, with *Shiro Kuramata*. For two years he worked at the Kuramata Design Office in Japan as well as other Japanese companies. In 1986 he returned to Italy to work with Sottsass Associati. 1.50

Arlon Bayliss, an English designer, was born in 1957. He studied at Solihull Technical College, Bristol Polytechnic and the Royal College of Art in London, and has worked as a glass designer and glass-maker. A former assistant of Charlie Meaker, he has received many international awards for his work, including the 1980 Swiss Glass Design Award in Lucerne. Bayliss has been working for Rosenthal since 1982. His designs include the *Harlequin* and *Sinus* series of glassware. 3.40

Martine Bedin was born in Bordeaux, France, in 1957. She studied architecture in Paris, and in 1978 was awarded an Italian scholarship and worked at the Superstudio in Florence. She has worked with *Ettore Sottsass*, designing lamps and furniture for Memphis. Since 1982 she has been a freelance industrial designer as well as a teacher of design at the Ecole Camondo, Paris. 2.16; 3.63, 64; 4.9, 10

Bellefast is a design partnership of *Andreas Brandolini* and *Joachim Stanitzek*, founded in 1982. Their work has been shown at the Museum für Kunst und Gewerbe, Hamburg; the Kunstmuseum, Düsseldorf; many interior design exhibitions in Berlin and Hamburg, and at the "Phoenix: New Attitudes in Design" exhibition of 1984 in Toronto. 1.197

Mario Bellini was born in Milan in 1935 and graduated in architecture from the Milan Polytechnic in 1959. He works in architecture and industrial design for firms such as Artemide, B & B Italia, Cassina, Erco, Ideal Standard, Poltrona Frau and Rosenthal. Since 1965 he has been a consultant with Olivetti on electronic machines, and is now editor of *Domus*. He has won several awards, including the Compasso d'Oro in 1986. 1.52, 53; 3.66

Ward Bennett is an American polymath designer whose contributions to pottery, tableware, furniture, interiors and sculpture have long been recognized as classics. In 1947

he began to design interiors, which led to work on furniture and tableware. Some of his best architectural work has been on his own homes, notably his inspired country house, for which he also designed the gardens, in the Springs, East Hampton, Long Island. 3.9

Gemma Bernal was born in Barcelona, Spain, and trained at the School of Industrial Design. She now works as an independent designer, in collaboration with *Ramon Isern*, for such manufacturers as Disform, Gruppo T, Garcia Garai and Fellex. 1.48

Guen Bertheau-Suzuki was born in Paris in 1956 and has a diploma from the Institute of Architecture in Tournai, Belgium, and a Master's degree from Tokyo University. An industrial and graphic designer, Bertheau-Suzuki has worked in architectural offices in Paris, Brussels and Tokyo, and currently lives in Tokyo. 2.33

John Betts is a designer with Henry Dreyfuss Associates in New York where he has worked since 1984. 5.31

Nicholas Bewick was born in Newcastle upon Tyne, UK, in 1957, and studied architecture at Canterbury School, Kent, and the RIBA. He worked with the architect Michael Hopkins in London 1979–80 and 1982–84. After qualifying at the Domus Academy, Milan, in 1985 he collaborated with *Michele De Lucchi*. In 1986 he contributed to the Memphis collection and was a founder and designer for the group Solid. He designed a collection for Cappellini International in 1987 and is now a partner with De Lucchi. 3.73

Hans-Ullrich Bitsch was born in Essen in 1946 and studied architecture and design in Saarbrücken and Chicago. He lives and works in Düsseldorf. His clients in the field of corporate identity include WDR, a radio and television corporation. In the best Bauhaus tradition, he cultivates the unity of architecture, interior design and industrial design. 4.39

Ricardo Blanco was born in Buenos Aires in 1940 and has a degree in architecture from Buenos Aires State University. He is currently Professor of Industrial Design at the universities of La Plata, Cuyo and Buenos Aires. He specializes in furniture, lighting and graphic design, and has won numerous awards. 1.140, 141

Vicente Blasco is a freelance designer, working in Valencia where he was born. He studied architecture, graduating in industrial design, and also has a degree in design and production by computer. In 1988 he began his studies for a Master's in industrial design at the Domus Academy. 1.115

Michael Boehm was born in Germany in 1944. He attended the Hadamar School of Glass-making and studied at the College of Art in Kassel and then rounded off his studies by visiting the main glass-making centres of Europe. Boehm has been working for Rosenthal ever since he joined the company as a young designer in 1966. Typical of his high standards are the series of glassware such as *Papyrus*, *Snowdrop* or *Maitre 13/66*, the series of glass dishes, *Galaxis* and *Glas-Collage*, a large dish in a limited edition. 3.39, 40

Mattia Bonetti is a Swiss designer and photographer, born in Lugano in 1952. He now lives in Paris, and has collaborated with Elisabeth and Gerard Garouste since 1980, exhibiting in Bordeaux, Barcelona, New York, Paris and Copenhagen. 2.39; 5.44

Mario Botta was born in 1943 in Mendrisio, Switzerland. He attended the Academy of Fine Arts in Milan, then graduated in architecture from the University of Venice. He gained practical experience in Le Corbusier's studio, and established his own architectural practice in Lugano in 1969. He has completed a number of private houses and commercial buildings in Switzerland generally categorized as "rationalist." Since 1982 he has also designed furniture for Alias. Two of his chairs are in the study collection of the Museum of Modern Art in New York. 1.72; 2.27

Andreas Brandolini was born in Germany in 1951. He studied architecture in Berlin and has been a lecturer in Industrial Design at the Hochschule der Künste, Berlin, visiting lecturer at the Architectural Association in London and visiting professor at the Hochschule für Gestaltung, Offenbach. He has been part of a design workshop with *Joachim Stanitzek* and exhibited in Brazil, France, Germany and Italy. 1.97–99

Marianne Brandt (1893–1983) was born in Chemnitz, East Prussia. She studied painting and sculpture at Weimar and joined the Bauhaus in 1923, working with Laszlo Moholy-Nagy in the metal workshop, where she produced a number of light fittings. When Hannes Meyer took over the running of the Dessau Bauhaus, she left to work for Walter Gropius in Berlin on furniture and interior design. 3.71

Andrea Branzi, born and educated in Florence, is educational director of the Domus Academy. He has consistently been a representative of the radical tendency in Italian design. His work was awarded the Compasso d'Oro in 1987. Until 1974 he was with Archizoom Associati, the first avant-garde Italian group. He was involved in the establishment of Studio Alchimia, the Milan-based group which has created pieces closer to artworks than to conventional pieces of design, and with Memphis, collaborating with *Ettore Sottsass*. 2.18

Marcel Breuer (1902–1981) was born in Pecs, Hungary, and studied at the Bauhaus, Weimar. After three years as a teacher at the Bauhaus he produced his first furniture out of tubular steel. During the mid-Thirties he worked in London as an architect and between 1937 and 1946 was Professor of Architecture at Harvard University. During that time he set up a studio with Walter Gropius in Massachusetts and in 1946 set up his own studio in New York. 1.100

Tim Brown was born in Britain in 1962. He studied at Newcastle upon Tyne Polytechnic and the Royal College of Art, London, and won a Royal Society of Arts Bursary Award for business office equipment. He joined Moggridge Associates in 1987 where he has worked on business and office equipment and computer systems. His designs for fax machines for Dancall in Sweden were on show at the "Leading Edge" exhibition at the Axis Gallery, Tokyo, in December 1988. He is currently on a year's transfer from Moggridge Associates in London to ID Two, their office in San Francisco. 5.18

John Caldwell attended Chouinard Art Institute and the Art Center College of Design in Los Angeles and established his own design studio in 1962, specializing in furniture, lighting and graphic design. Design awards have been numerous: the most recent include the IBD Gold Award, the Annual Design Review Gold Award for *Industrial Design* magazine, PIA awards, *Interiors* magazine award and the Pacifica Award. 1.34

Canon Design Team is based in Tokyo. 5.16, 30

Giulio Cappellini was born in 1954, and studied architecture at Milan Polytechnic, graduating in 1979. In 1979 he entered into Cappellini International Interiors for whom he produced a range of products, including the *Colombia* system and *Aliante* in collaboration with *Rodolfo Dordoni*. With Dordoni and *Paola Navone*, he founded Mondo in 1987. 1.49

Anna Castelli Ferrieri graduated in architecture at the University of Milan and worked as a lecturer in industrial design there, as well as an assistant editor of the magazine *Casabella*. Since then she has worked as an architect, planner and industrial designer. Since 1976 she has worked as art director for Kartell, specializing in the design of injection-moulded plastic furniture, for which she was awarded the Compasso d'Oro in 1979. Her designs are on show at the Museum of Modern Art, New York. 1.114

Achille Castiglioni was born in Milan in 1918. He began his work as a designer in partnership with his brothers, Livio and *Pier Giacomo Castiglioni*, specializing in interiors, furniture and lights. He is particularly well known for the latter, notably the *Toio* uplighter. Castiglioni is one of the foremost talents in Italian design, and has been honoured no less than seven times by the Compasso d'Oro, as well as having six of his pieces selected for exhibition at the Museum of Modern Art, New York. 1.51; 2.44

Pier Giacomo Castiglioni (1913-1968) trained as an architect and worked closely with his brother *Achille Castiglioni* from 1945 until his death. 1.51

Piero Castiglioni was born in Lierna, Italy, in 1944. He graduated in architecture and since 1980 he has been working as a technical consultant for Fontana Arte. He collaborated with his father, *Achille Castiglioni*, on the *Scintilla* system which Fontana Arte has been producing since 1983. With *Gae Aulenti* he set up the Musée d'Orsay in Paris. He is currently working on structures for the Olympic Games to be held in Barcelona in 1992. 2.40

Pierluigi Cerri, born in 1939, is an Italian architect and founder-member, with *Vittorio Gregotti*, of Gregotti Associati. He is director of the publishing firm Electa, member of the editorial staff of *Rassegna* and *Casabella*, and has contributed to many books and magazines, among them the Italian edition of *Vers une Architecture* by Le Corbusier (Milan, 1972). Cerri has been responsible for the design of many exhibitions in Europe and Tokyo and for the graphic design of the Palazzo Grassi in Venice. 2.7

Antonio Citterio was born in Italy in 1950. He studied at the Milan Polytechnic, and has been involved in industrial and furniture design since 1967. He opened a studio with *Paolo Nava* in 1973. Jointly and individually they have worked for B & B Italia, Flexform and others. In 1979 they were awarded the Compasso d'Oro. 3.14

Lluís Clotet was born in Barcelona in 1941 where he graduated in architecture. In 1964 he founded Studio PER together with the architects Pep Bonet, Cristian Cirici and *Oscar Tusquets Blanca*. With the last rlamed, he collaborated on numerous projects until 1983. He is a founder-member of BD Ediciones de diseño, for which he has designed furniture and products. As an architect he received the FAD award for the best interior in Barcelona in 1965 and 1972, and for the best building in 1978 and 1979. He was awarded the Delta de Oro for the best industrial design in 1974, 1979 and 1980, and in 1985 for his last 25 years' work. 1.85

Nigel Coates was born in 1949 and graduated from the Architectural Association with the year prize in 1974. He formed an architectural practice with Doug Branson in 1985, which has undertaken commercial and domestic commissions in the UK and Japan, including shops for Jasper Conran, Katharine Hamnett and Jigsaw, and restaurants in Japan and London. He has taught at the AA since 1976 and was a founder-member of the expressionistic and influential NATO (Narrative Architecture Today) group. Despite his increasing international reputation, his furniture has until recently been sold commercially only in Japan. 1.106, 107

Paul Cockburn is a designer/film-writer who founded an industrial design consultancy in 1969. The company now works with clients internationally, and is unique in the breadth of its projects, ranging from film, art, graphics and design through to engineering and product development. 5.46, 47

Joe Colombo (1930–1971) was born in Milan. He studied architecture at the Milan Polytechnic but gave up his studies to manage his father's company. He returned to architecture during the Fifties when he also began to paint. In 1964 he won the In-Arch Prize for his design of the interior of a Sardinian hotel and was also awarded gold medals for objects exhibited at the Thirteenth Triennale. He was twice awarded the Compasso d'Oro and in 1968 received the Design International Award in Chicago. His work has been exhibited in museums and galleries throughout the world. 2.14

Denis Conrady is an American designer currently working for *Studio Naço* in Paris. 1.30

Jean-Michel Cornu is a French designer, born in 1958 in Saigon. He studied at the Ecole des Beaux Arts, Paris, and later travelled to Japan and Egypt. His work is greatly influenced by his wide travels and his interest in anthropology. In 1984 he won the Bourse Médicis Hors les Murs for an engineering project in Ethiopia. His motto is "Japan revisited via Africa!"

Corporate Industrial Design (CID) is the design team for the multi-national electronics organization Philips. Headed by R. Blaich, the managing director, CID consists of 115 designers based in Philips' Eindhoven headquarters in The Netherlands as well as an additional 110 designers located worldwide. 5.12, 49

Pepe Cortès was born in Barcelona in 1945. He has collaborated on numerous projects, including lights, furniture and interiors, with *Javier Mariscal*. 1.41

Marcello Cutino was born in Castelfranco Veneto, Italy, in 1956. After his studies in applied art at Verona and design in Milan he set up a studio with Susanna Brugnoli that creates products for clients worldwide. 5.38

Remi Colmet Daage is a French architect, born in Paris in 1949, who studied first in Belgium and then in Paris. In 1978 he became a founder-member of *Xylos*. 1.19

Walter Dahn is a German textile designer living and working in Cologne, whose work has been exhibited in Paris, Amsterdam, New York, Switzerland and Stockholm. 4.18

Riccardo Dalisi was born in Potenza, Italy, in 1931. Since 1962 he has been conducting experiments on architectural forms using light and geometry, and taking part in various competitions connected with building construction at an academic level. He has written a number of books and teaches at the University of Naples. In recent years he has been developing the theme of the Neapolitan coffee pot for which he won the Compasso d'Oro in 1981. He is credited with revitalizing research into design in southern Italy and has been described by Alessandro Mendini as "the brains behind design in the South." 1.138

Helle Damkjaer was born in Denmark in 1965. In 1983 she began work as a graphic designer with McCann Erickson in Copenhagen, continuing with them in Milan where she moved in 1987. She has also worked for Esprit de Corp, Noto and Zeus as a graphic designer, but more recently has turned to product design. 5.8

Paolo Deganello was born in Este, Italy, in 1949. He studied in Florence and from 1963 to 1974 worked as a town planner for the Florence municipality. In 1966 he founded, with *Andrea Branzi*, Gilberio Corretti and *Massimo Morozzi*, the then avant-garde group Studio Archizoom. In 1975, with Corretti, Franco Gatti and Roberto Querci he founded the Collettivo Tecnici Progettisti. He has taught widely, including at Florence University and the Architectural Association, London, and has published several books and articles. He has designed products for Marcatrè, Vitra, Driade and Cassina and has taken part in many international exhibitions and competitions. 1.55; 3.28

Philippe Delaflotte is a French designer, born in Paris in 1951, who has worked on prototype design for Citroën. His interest in furniture design led him to join *Xylos* in 1982. 1.19

Michele De Lucchi was born in Ferrara, Italy, in 1951. He studied first in Padua and then at Florence University, where he founded the Gruppo Cavat, which produced avant-garde and radical architecture projects, films, texts and happenings. He graduated from Florence University in 1975 and subsequently taught there. In 1978 he left teaching and began a close collaboration with *Ettore Sottsass*. He worked and designed for Alchimia until the establishment of Memphis in 1981, for whom he designed and carried out some of their best-known products. In 1979 he became a consultant for Olivetti Synthesis in Massa and in 1984 for Olivetti SpA in Ivrea; under the supervision of Sottsass he designed their *Icarus* office furniture. With Sottsass Associati he designed more than fifty Fiorucci shops in Italy and abroad. Currently he is designing for a wide range of important furniture manufacturers: among others, Acerbis, Artemide, Vistosi, RB Rossana and Fontana Arte. 1.148; 2.48

Margit Denz is a student at the Academy of Applied Arts in Vienna. 3.54, 55

Bernhard Dessecker was born in Munich in 1961. He studied interior design and then worked in New York at Studio Morsa from 1983 to 1984. Since 1984 he has been a freelance designer and a collaborator in the design team of *Ingo Maurer*. 2.24

Sergi Devesa is a Spanish designer born in 1961. Following his studies in applied art he has worked with Metalarte on lighting and has now turned his attention to furniture design. 1.86

Jane Dillon was born in the UK in 1943. She trained in interior design at Manchester, and then in furniture design at the Royal College of Art, London. After graduating in 1968, she worked for Knoll International and for Olivetti under *Ettore Sottsass*. From 1973 she has worked as a design consultant on furniture for the Barcelona firm Casas, and on lighting for Disform. She has been a design consultant for many major companies and currently works with *Floris Van Den Broecke* and *Peter Wheeler* in London. 1.145

Dissing & Weitling is a consulting firm of architects, planners and designers, established in 1971 as a continuation of the firm of Arne Jacobsen, architect and designer. They operate in a number of European and Middle Eastern countries and their clients include private companies, public authorities and governments. 5.50

Donghia Design Studio see *John Hutton* and *Glenn Peckman.*

Rodolfo Dordoni is an Italian designer. He graduated in 1979 from Milan Polytechnic and has worked for Cappellini, Vistosi, B Ticino and Fontana Arte. 1.49

Gillo Dorfles was born in Trieste in 1910. He studied medicine at Milan University, transferring to Rome where he graduated in 1935. In the years 1929–30 he travelled through Germany and Northern Europe, where he encountered the works of the Expressionists, Klee and Kandinsky. A specialist in psychiatry, he found time to paint, study philosophy and write on art and architecture. From 1955 he taught aesthetics at Milan, Florence, Cagliari and Trieste, and was a visiting professor at many foreign universities. As a painter, he was one of the founders of the Concreta Art Movement with Gianni Monnet, Bruno Munari and Atanasio Soldati. His painting has recently had its first public acknowledgement with an exhibition organized by the Valle d'Aosta Regional Government. 4.21

Marie-Christine Dorner was born in Strasbourg, France, in 1960. She graduated in 1984 in Paris, and has worked for Patrick and Daniel Rubin and for Jean-Michel Wilmotte. In 1985 her table won a prize from Galeries Lafayette; in 1986 a collection of her work was produced by Idée and shown at the Axis Gallery, Tokyo. 1.121, 122; 4.20

Henry Dreyfuss Associates, founded in 1929 and based in Manhattan, provides industrial design services for many national and international clients. 5.31

Christian Duc is a French designer. After studying English literature and fine arts, he lived in Amsterdam and then Berlin. He returned to Paris in 1979 and set up DCA Co. which produces his own furniture and tableware designs, and he also works as an interior designer. In 1985 he won the interior design prize at the Decorative Artists' Exhibition, Paris. 4.19

Peter Dudley is an American designer who studied materials engineering. He has an associate degree from Wendell Castle School, New York, and is a faculty assistant there. He has exhibited several times and won the Ruby Gordon Award at the Finger Lakes Exhibition. He is the author of a book on fine woodworking. 1.29

Andrzej Duljas was born in Poland in 1958. He studied laser microanalysis and researched powders metallurgy before moving to the areas of fine arts and design. In the USA he spent two years with the lighting firm of Louis Baldinger and Sons and in 1987 joined the Koch & Lowy Design Team. 2.31, 32

John Dunnigan designs and builds one-off art furniture in his studio in West Kingston, Rhode Island. Since 1972 his company has completed many commissions covering the full range of furniture design. His work is in several galleries in the USA and is part of the permanent public collection at the Museum of Fine Arts, Boston. Since 1980, he has been on the faculty of the Rhode Island School of Design in the departments of interior architecture and industrial design. 1.28

Gavino Falchi is an Italian designer, born in 1959. He graduated in applied art from the Sassari school and studied architecture at Turin Polytechnic. He worked first in interior design, and in 1985 turned to fashion, producing a collection for the Biennial Art Exhibition in Barcelona. Recently he has worked in furniture and textile design. 4.62

Alan Fletcher was born in 1931 and trained at the Royal College of Art, London, and Yale University. He began his career in New York, then moved to London where he co-founded Fletcher, Forbes, Gill in 1959, serving such clients as Pirelli, Cunard, Olivetti and Reuters. He is a founder-member of Pentagram, formed in 1972. He has received gold awards from the D & AD and the New York "One Show." In 1977 he shared with Colin Forbes the Designers and Art Directors Association President's Award for outstanding contributions to design. The Society of Industrial Artists and Designers awarded him the 1982 medal for outstanding achievement in industrial design and in the same year he was elected International President of AGI. Among the books he has co-authored are *Identity Kits*, *Graphic Design*, *A Sign System Manual* and *Living by Design*. 5.11

Fulvio Forbicini was born in Ravenna in 1952 and graduated in industrial design in Florence in 1974/75. Following an association with Roche Bobois, he opened a studio with *Fabrizio Ballardini* where they continue to explore the needs of industry in an aesthetically satisfying way. 1.132

Sam Francis, Abstract Expressionist painter, was born in San Mateo, California, in 1923. He studied medicine 1941–1943 and painting and the history of art, under Mark Rothko, 1948–1950. His work is considered subtler and more European than his American colleagues: he is known in America as a "homo transatlanticus." Important exhibitions include those at Los Angeles County Museum of Art; Whitney Museum of American Art, New York; Louisiana Museum, Copenhagen/Humblebaek; Musée National d'Art Moderne, Centre Georges Pompidou, Paris. 4.30

Gianfranco Frattini, architect and designer of exhibitions, interiors and furniture, was born in Padua, Italy, in 1926. He studied architecture at the Milan Polytechnic, graduating in 1953. He worked as an assistant to Giò Ponti until 1957, when he left to establish his own studio. Since then he has worked for most of the major Italian furniture and lighting manufacturers, including Cassina, Artemide and Arteluce. He has won the Compasso d'Oro six times as well as many

other medals and awards, and his work is exhibited in museums throughout Europe and America. 2.25, 26

Elisabeth Garouste lives in Paris and works with *Mattia Bonetti*. 2.39; 5.54

Luciano Gaspari was born in Venice, where he lives and works, and studied at the Universities of Fine Arts in Venice and Bologna. He was one of the subscriber–artists of the Bologna Cultural League of 1948. He writes articles and takes part in many collective shows, and has won numerous prizes. Among the most important are: the Micchotti Prize at Francavilla al Marco, 1951; the Strosa Prize, 1956; the Bergamo Prize, 1959; the Triennale di Milano Prize, 1960; the Giorgione–Poussin Prize and the Autostrada del Sole, 1961. He has exhibited at the Venice Biennale for many years and his work has been shown at major exhibitions and galleries throughout Europe. 3.41, 42

Gaston & Daniela is a Spanish textile company, established in Bilbao in 1876. 4.16

Ernesto Gismondi is an Italian designer, engineer and industrialist. He was born in San Remo in 1931 and studied aeronautical engineering at the Milan Polytechnic and the School of Engineering, Rome. He established the lighting company Artemide in 1959, initially producing lamps in small quantities using hand-craft techniques and later working on the lighting of large areas for institutional customers. As well as employing some of the world's foremost designers to work for Artemide, Gismondi has himself produced a number of successful lights for the company. He is also managing director of Reglar, a company involved in the production and moulding of SMC (sheet moulding compound), a thermoplastic he developed in 1966, suitable for use in the production of furniture and industrial articles. 2.28

Giorgetto Giugiaro was born in Italy in 1938. After studying briefly at the Academy of Fine Arts in Turin he was apprenticed to Fiat, leaving to work as a stylist for Bertone. In 1968 he established his own car design studio, ItalDesign, working on such important models as the Fiat Panda and the Golf for Volkswagen. Recently he established Giugiaro Design to design products, furniture, cameras, watches and even pasta. 5.32

Gaspar Glusberg is an Argentinian architect, born in 1959 in Buenos Aires. He is head of the industrial design department of Modular Design in Buenos Aires, specializing in light fittings. 2.37, 38

Elisabeth and Mikael Goldstein are Swedish designers born in 1947 and 1948. Elisabeth, an arts graduate, is a self-taught painter; Mikael, a psychology graduate, is a self-taught designer. 1.21

Kenneth Grange is a British designer, born in 1929. He trained as a technical illustrator, and worked as an assistant in various architectural offices. In 1971 he founded the Pentagram design consultancy with *Alan Fletcher*, Forbes, Gill and the architect Theo Crosby. Grange has worked primarily as an industrial designer, producing cameras for Kodak, parking meters for Venner, food mixers for Kenwood and pens for Parker. In 1983 his work was the subject of a special exhibition at the Boilerhouse Project at the Victoria and Albert Museum, London. 5.26, 27

Michael Graves, the Princeton architect famed for his Post-Modern classicism, was born in 1934. His work, which has received numerous awards, includes the Newark Museum, the Whitney Museum, a library in San Juan Capistrano, the Humana Headquarters in Louisville and a winery in California's Napa Valley. His painting and murals are in several major museums and he has designed furniture for Memphis and Sawaya & Moroni, and products for Alessi and Swid Powell. 3.67–70; 4.34, 35; 5.3

Alfredo Pizzo Greco, a painter, sculptor and designer, was born in 1942. Since 1959 he has exhibited on an international level with more than 140 one-man shows and group exhibitions. He has been a member of many selection committees, associations and study centres, working with architects, historians and anthropologists in the field of environmental and landscape design. From 1964, he has worked in his own studio, creating numbered and signed engravings, linocuts, silkscreen prints and lithographs on stone. Currently he is involved with the restoration and conservation of historical buildings, including a 16th-century building in the Piazza Mercato delle Scarpe in Bergamo. 2.50

Vittorio Gregotti runs Gregotti Associati with *Pierluigi Cerri*. For many years he was chief editor of *Casabella* and is now director of both *Casabella* and *Rassegna*, and is attached to *Edilizia Moderna*. He has been a visiting lecturer at various institutes in Tokyo, Buenos Aires, São Paulo and Lausanne, and Professor of Architectural Composition at Venice University of Architecture. He was one of the prize winners in the Compasso d'Oro in 1968 and has sat on many committees, including the Thirteenth Triennale in 1964. He has been director of the visual arts and architecture section of the Venice Biennale, and in 1982 he was commissioned to work on Expo 1989 in Paris. 1.35; 2.7

Silvia Gubern studied art and graphic design at the Elisava School, Spain, but decided to concentrate on painting. She now lives and teaches in Barcelona and works in graphic, interior, industrial and textile design. 4.13, 14

Zaha Hadid was born in Baghdad, Iraq, in 1950. She graduated from the Architectural Association, London, in 1977 and in the same year joined the Office of Metropolitan Architecture. In 1982 she was awarded a gold medal in the *Architectural Digest* British Architecture Awards for an apartment conversion in London and in 1983 she won first prize in the Peak International Competition, Hong Kong. Her work is published worldwide and is frequently exhibited. She lives in London. 1.67, 68

Masaya Hashimoto was born in Tokyo in 1964. He moved to Milan in 1986 and collaborates with *Isao Hosoe*. 1.147

Renate Hattinger is a student at the Academy of Applied Arts in Vienna. 3.56

Robert and Trix Haussmann studied architecture in Zurich and began a practice together in 1967. Their work covers a wide variety of projects, including interior design, restoration work, textiles, furniture and ceramics. 1.71

Matthew Hilton, born in the UK in 1957, studied furniture design at Kingston Polytechnic and then worked with the product design consultancy CAPA for five years on a variety of high-technology products. He became an independent furniture and interior designer in 1984, producing lights as well as furniture. In 1986 he designed a range of furniture for Sheridan Coakley which was shown in Milan, and in 1987 held an exhibition in Tokyo with *Jasper Morrison*. 1.82, 83

Darryle Hinz, born in 1949, is an American living in Denmark. He was educated in ceramics and art history at the California State University and studied the techniques of working with glass in Sweden in 1973–1978. Since 1983 he has worked with Anja Kjaer in their own studio. He is represented in various museum collections throughout Europe and the USA. 3.37

David Hockney, painter, was born in Bradford, England, in 1937 and now lives in California. He studied at Bradford College 1953–1957, at the Royal College of Art in London 1959–1962, and has held various teaching posts in the USA. He is an exponent of the English variation of Pop Art, his work being divided into three parts: painting, stage design and photography. In 1988, a large retrospective exhibition of his work was held in the Los Angeles County Museum of Art, the Metropolitan Museum of Art, New York, and the Tate Gallery, London. 4.31, 32, 33

Josef Hoffmann (1870–1956), an Austrian architect, was born in Pirnitz, Moravia. He studied under the architect Karl Hasenauer, the so-called "Ringstrassenbaron," and Otto Wagner at the Academy of Fine Arts, Vienna. His involvement with the works of Charles Rennie Mackintosh promoted his individual development towards a severe style, based upon straight lines. A creative genius of the last era of grand Austrian architecture between 1899 and 1914, he designed the Purkersdorf Sanatorium and the Palais Stoclet in Brussels. The latter was the creation of the group of architects, designers and craftsmen brought together by Kolo Moser in 1903, whose aim was to create a "comprehensive work of art." 1.104

Torben Holmbäck is a Danish industrial designer, born in Copenhagen in 1933. He was educated in advertising and marketing in Denmark and England, and held several leading positions in newspaper and magazine publishing prior to taking up design in 1980. He is represented in the permanent design collection of the Museum of Modern Art, New

York; in Die Neue Sammlung, Museum für angewandte Kunst, Munich, and in the Museum of Applied Arts, Copenhagen. He was awarded the Japanese G-Prize for Good Design in 1986 and the Danish ID Prize in 1988. 2.22

Alfred Homann was born in Denmark in 1948 and is a graduate of the Royal Danish Academy and a member of Industrial Designers of Denmark. Versed in varied aspects of building and product design, he has completed restaurant, showroom, retail, museum, transportation and historical renovation projects as well as residential and public housing jobs. He has designed furniture, and lighting for Louis Poulsen and has won many awards. He has offices in Copenhagen and Washington, DC. 2.10, 11

Bibs Hosak-Robb, an industrial designer, was born in Neu-Ulm, West Germany, in 1955. He worked for Siemens, Munich, 1980–1981 and in that year moved to London to study at the Royal College of Art. In 1984 he was awarded third prize at the International Spring Fair in Frankfurt, and obtained a similar Design Plus prize for his cutlery in 1985. He has exhibited in Dallas, London and Munich and produced a variety of work for both commercial and public clients. 3.2, 3

Isao Hosoe was born in Tokyo in 1942. His initial interests lay in science, and he took a Master's degree in aerospace engineering at the Nihon University of Tokyo. From 1967 to 1974 he collaborated with the architect Alberto Rosselli. He became a member of the Italian Association of Industrial Designers, the Japan Design Committee and the Italian Society of Ergonomics. In 1985 he founded his own design company. Since 1970 he has won many awards for his designs which cover such diverse projects as transport, furniture, robots, business machines and aircraft. His work has been shown at numerous exhibitions in Japan, Europe and America. He has lectured in America and Italy and been a jury member for the Italia Cup in Milan in 1986/87 and for the Alex Award in Tokyo in 1987. Following a period as visiting professor to the Domus Academy in Milan 1984–1987, he now teaches there full time. 1.147; 5.19, 20

Jörg Hundertpfund was born in Zurich in 1960. He studied industrial design at the Hochschule der Künste in Berlin 1985–1988, and his work has been shown at several exhibitions in Berlin. 1.91

John Hutton is an American designer who joined Donghia Furniture in 1978. His interest lies in producing furniture "stripped to its very essence to avoid being typecast by trends and periods." 1.73, 74

Christian Hvidt was born in Copenhagen in 1946. He was a toolmaker and a product development engineer before setting up his own design practice in 1980. Since then he has been a member of the executive of the Industrial Designers of Denmark Association and its President since 1985, and is also a member of the Danish Art Foundation Council. He won the industrial design prize, Die Gute

Industriform, IF, three times (1981, 1982 and 1984), and the Klint Scholarship in 1984. 2.29, 30

I·DE·A (Institute of Development in Automotive Engineering), formed in 1978 by Franco Mantegazza, is a team of experts specializing in product engineering, manufacturing engineering and, since 1983, product design. The first assignment of the Design Department, headed by Ercole Spada and Justin Norek, was a new family of earth-moving machines for the Japanese firm, Komatsu. Cooperation with Toshiba on TV sets started in 1987. 5.17

Massimo Iosa Ghini is an Italian designer working in furniture, textiles, fashion and advertising. Born in 1959 in Borgo Tossignano, he studied in Florence and graduated in architecture in Milan. In 1981 he joined the group Zak-Ark, and from 1984 has collaborated with the firm AGO. Since 1982 he has worked on a number of discotheques, video projects and magazines. In 1986 he took part in the Memphis group's 12 New Collection. 1.79

Ramon Isern was born in Barcelona, Spain, in 1944 and trained as an industrial designer. He has worked with *Gemma Bernal* for, among others, the furniture manufacturers Disform, Gruppo T, Garcia Garai and Fellex. 1.48

Fujiwo Ishimoto was born in Ehime, Japan, in 1941 and studied design and graphics in Tokyo. From 1964 to 1970 he was a commercial artist, from 1970 to 1974 a designer at Decembre and from 1974 a printed textile designer for Marimekko, Finland. In 1983 he was awarded both the Roscoe Prize and an honourable mention at the Finland Designs Exhibition. 4.44–48

Arata Isozaki was born in Kyushu in 1931 and obtained his diploma at the University of Tokyo. He founded his own studio in 1963 and continued to collaborate with other architects and studios as well. Among his most famous projects are the Gunma Prefectural Museum of Modern Art at Takasaki (1971–2), the Kitakyshu City Museum of Art (1972–4), the Shukosha Building at Fukoba (1975), the Fujimi Country Clubhouse at Oita (1972–4), the new City Hall in Tokyo and the Museum of Contemporary Art in Los Angeles (both 1986). 2.23; 4.37, 38

Dakota Jackson was, in his early twenties, a professional magician. His sense of mystery and illusion was invested in early pieces of one-off furniture, expressed in moving parts and hidden compartments. His work is included in several private and corporate collections, and has been featured in the Whitney Museum's "High Styles: Twentieth Century American Design," and in other museum and gallery exhibitions in the USA, Canada and Europe. Dakota Jackson is the recipient of a National Endowment for the Arts Design Fellowship, and has lectured at universities and industry events. 1.154–156

Ehlen Johansson was born in Sweden in 1958 and studied design at Göteborg University between 1979 and 1984. Since

1985 she has been working for Ikea, designing furniture and interior products. 3.46

Terry Jones was born in Montgomery, Alabama, in 1957, and graduated in mechanical engineering from the University of Washington in 1980. He joined Ziba Design in 1985, having worked for such companies as Tektronix, Intel, Metheus and Pro-Form. He has been involved in projects ranging from computer hardware and electro-mechanical packaging to mechanisms for exercise equipment. He has also designed and produced a human-powered boat for a company in which he is a partner. 5.13

Carsten Jørgensen was born in 1948 in Denmark. He graduated from the School of Arts and Crafts, Copenhagen, in 1973 and has been art director of the Bodum design workshop since 1978, working as an industrial designer on a range of household goods. 3.17

Angel Jové is a Spanish painter and art teacher. He has been an actor, art director and scenic designer for the theatre, as well as a designer of textiles and lights. 4.11

Sachiko Kawabe was born in Tokyo in 1958. Following her graduation from the Women's Art University, Tokyo, she worked as a fashion stylist for several years and then set up her own design office. Although interested in modern production methods, she is concerned to maintain traditional Japanese craft techniques. She retains an interest in fashion styling and in her work as a make-up artist. 3.26, 27

Perry A. King was born in London in 1938 and studied at the School of Industrial Design, Birmingham. He moved to Italy to work as a consultant to Olivetti, designing among other things the *Valentine* typewriter in collaboration with *Ettore Sottsass*. For the last 13 years he has worked with *Santiago Miranda* from their office, King–Miranda Associati, in Milan, where they are active in industrial design, furniture, interiors, lighting and graphics. Their work has received several awards and has been exhibited and published in Italy and abroad. 1.15, 16, 84; 2.3; 3.24, 25

Toshiyuki Kita was born in 1942 in Osaka, Japan, and graduated in industrial design in 1964. Since 1969 he has divided his time between Osaka and Milan where he has worked on furniture and accessories for many of the major manufacturers. He has received the Japan Interior Design Award, the Kitaro Kunii Industrial Design Award and the Mainichi Design Award. The *Wink* armchair and *Kick* table which he designed for Cassina are in the permanent collection of the Museum of Modern Art, New York. In 1987 he took part in the celebrations for the tenth anniversary of the Centre Georges Pompidou in Paris. 1.149–151; 2.19

Bernd Axel Kluge was born in Bremen, Germany, in 1954. Following industrial design studies at the Hochschule der Künste in Berlin from 1978–1984, and a variety of design activities, he joined the design team of *Ingo Maurer* in 1986. 2.24

Ikuo Kobayashi was born in Kyoto, Japan, in 1947. After postgraduate work in art and design at the Musashino Art University, he joined the Wada Design Group in 1969, where he remained until 1972. He then joined Kyoto Design Center and was involved in industrial and domestic product design. Since 1987 he has been Director of Product Design with GK Kyoto. 5.28

Makoto Komatsu was born in 1943 in Tokyo. He graduated from art school there, then went to work for the Swedish glass-maker Gustavsberg. After returning to Japan he began work as an independent designer. His work is in the permanent collections of the Museum of Ceramics, Faenza, the New York Museum of Modern Art and the Victoria and Albert Museum, London. 3.29, 31

Rainer Krause was born in 1952 in Lübeck, West Germany. In 1984 he established the company Anthologie Quartett to bring together international avant-garde designers. He has organized many international exhibitions and writes on architecture, design and aesthetics. 3.14

Lisa Krohn graduated in studio art and art history from Brown University, USA, in 1985. She also studied industrial design at the Rhode Island School of Design. She has worked as a freelance designer in New York for Walker Group/ CNI, the Richard Penney Group and Smart Design. In 1986 she entered the MFA programme at the Cranbrook Academy of Art. She is editor of the newsletter of the New York chapter of the Industrial Designers' Society of America and has written for various design magazines. In her spare time she produces and markets her jewellery designs. 2.17

Shiro Kuramata was born in Tokyo in 1934. He started an independent practice as a furniture designer in 1965, having served an apprenticeship in cabinetmaking. Apart from his celebrated glass armchair of 1976, and a number of other equally elegant but quirky pieces of furniture, Kuramata has designed interiors for the fashion designer Issey Miyake and for the Siebu stores. In 1981 he received the Japan Cultural Design Prize. 1.87, 88, 112; 3.75, 76; 5.39, 51

Masayuki Kurokawa was born in Nagoya, Japan, in 1937. He graduated from the Department of Architecture at the Nagoya Institute of Technology in 1961 and completed his training in the Graduate School of Architecture at Waseda University in 1967. That same year he established Masayuki Kurokawa Architect and Associates. He has been accorded numerous prizes for his work. In 1970 he won first prize in the International Design Competition for a mass-production house; in 1973 he won first prize in the Competition for Interior Vertical Element of House, and in 1976 he won the annual prize of the Japan Interior Designers' Association for a series of interior elements. He has won six IF prizes for his designs of tables and lighting fixtures. 1.117; 2.41, 42

Kyocera Design Team are based in Tokyo, Japan. 5.33

Klaus Lackner see *Products Industrial Design.*

Marcelo Lagares was born in Argentina in 1962 and studied in Paris, graduating in urban design in 1980. His projects include work on the urban development of Mexico; photographic exhibitions for the Ministère de la Coopération, and a collection of vases for Daniel Hechter. He has worked with *Philippe Starck*, and is now part of *Studio Naço*. 1.30

Danny Lane was born in 1955 in the USA. He moved to Britain in 1975 to work with the stained-glass artist Patrick Reyntiens, and then studied painting at the Central School of Art, London, until 1980. The following year he set up his first studio in London's East End. In 1983 he established Glassworks, using glass in unfamiliar and challenging ways in one-off pieces, furniture and interiors. In 1986 his studio was equipped to handle large-scale architectural installations. 1.80, 81

Michaela Lange is a student at the Academy of Applied Arts in Vienna. 3.59

Roberto Lazzeroni is an Italian designer, born in Pisa, where he lives and works. He studied art and architecture in Florence and is now committed to industrial and interior design. 1.20

Max Leser, a Canadian designer, was born in London. He studied ceramics at the Banff School of Fine Arts, Alberta, and glass-working at Georgian College, Barrie, Ontario, the Sheridan School of Design, Mississauga, Ontario, the Alberta College of Art and the Pilchuck Glass Center, Stanwood, Washington. In 1984 he was commissioned by the city of Toronto to create a limited edition sculpture for the Gardiner Award, and in 1986 he created a transparent time capsule for the lobby of the new North American Life tower in Toronto. His work has been exhibited worldwide and is in permanent collections in Canada and the USA. He currently lives in Toronto where he is president of Leser Design Inc. which specializes in the design and manufacture of modern glass products. 3.18

Roy Lichtenstein, Pop Art painter, was born in New York in 1923. He will go down in the history of art as the man who brought Mickey Mouse and Donald Duck into galleries throughout the world. Between 1957 and 1963 he was lecturer at New York State University and Rutgers University. His work has been exhibited at the most important galleries in Europe, Japan and America. 4.29

Olavi Lindén is a Finnish designer, born in 1946. He is both an engineer and designer and since 1984 has been Product Development Manager for Fiskars. 5.25

Stefan Lindfors was born in Mariehamn, Finland, in 1962 and studied interior and furniture design at the University of Industrial Arts, Helsinki, 1982–88. His work has received many awards in Finland and Europe, including the silver medal at the 1986 Milan Triennale; he had his own exhibition of sculpture at the Gallery Titanik in Turku in 1988. His design interests also extend to the stage. He

designed the studio and furniture for the Finnish Broadcasting Company's television evening news programme in 1988 and the interior and furniture for the café of the Museum of Industrial Arts in Helsinki in 1989. 2.15

El Lissitzsky (1890–1941), the Russian designer, studied engineering and architecture at Darmstadt in Germany. He was a fervent supporter of the Russian Revolution and in 1918 designed a Soviet flag that was carried in procession across Red Square. During his career he taught architecture and graphic art; designed books, the Lenin podium and typography for a book of poems by Mayakovsky; collaborated with artists, such as Hans Arp and Kurt Schwitters, and wrote *The Isms of Art* in collaboration with Arp. He designed little furniture, even though he was for a time professor of interior decoration and furniture in Moscow, his output consisting mainly of some bent-plywood chairs for the Leipzig 1930 International Fur Trade Exhibitions and the items featured here. 1.69, 70

Antoni Llena is a Spanish designer, born in Barcelona in 1942. He studied philosophy and painting and was the first conceptual artist in Spain. His work has been exhibited in Spain and Europe and he is currently organizing an exhibition at the Miró Foundation. 4.12

Josep Lluscà was born in Barcelona in 1948. He studied design at the Escola Eina, Barcelona, and the Ecole des Arts et Métiers, Montreal. He was vice-president of the Adi-Fad (Industrial Designers' Association) 1985–7. He was also a member of the Design Council of the Catalonian government. He is now a professor at the Escola Eina. He has won several awards and has taken part in international conferences and exhibitions. 1.129; 2.6

Alex Locadia was born in Brooklyn, New York, in 1958. In 1982 he began to study under James Hong, who recruited him for his shop where he trained and developed his own work. In 1986 he was invited to participate in a group exhibition for Art et Industrie. He has had exhibitions in New York, Brussels and Paris, and in 1987 one of his sculptures was acquired by the Louvre. 1.131

Steven Lombardi has designed numerous residential and commercial buildings, but since 1979 the design of furniture and lighting, and fine art, have also played an important part in his working life. His pieces include stainless-steel clocks, modular seating and a series of whimsical robots. His work has been exhibited in galleries and museums in Italy and abroad. 1.146; 2.21

Lumiance Design Team is based in Haarlem, The Netherlands, under the direction of Chris Hiemstra, head of the research and design department. Born in 1942, Hiemstra studied graphic, interior and industrial design and was co-owner of Hiemstra/Swaak, an industrial design office, before joining Lumiance in 1970. 2.8, 9

Vico Magistretti was born in Milan in 1920. He took a degree in architecture in 1945 and subsequently joined his father's studio. Until 1960 he was mainly concerned with architecture, town planning and the interior layout of buildings. He began designing furniture and household articles for his buildings in the Sixties and collaborates closely with the companies that produce his designs, including Alias, Artemide, Cassina, Conran Habitat, De Padova, Knoll International and OLuce. He has participated in nearly all the Triennales since 1948 and has won numerous awards. Fifteen of his pieces are in the permanent collection of the Museum of Modern Art in New York. 1.123

Erik Magnussen, born in Copenhagen in 1940, was trained as a potter and graduated in 1960 with a silver medal from the Danish School of Arts and Crafts and Industrial Design. Formerly a teacher at the Royal Academy of Fine Arts, in 1983 he was chosen Designer of the Year by the Danish Design Council. For a number of years he has designed porcelain tableware for Bing & Grondahl, Copenhagen Porcelain and furniture for Kevi A/S Copenhagen. He has been awarded several grants for his work and won the Lunning Prize in 1967, the Furniture Prize in 1977 and the ID prize from the Danish Society of Industrial Designers three times. 5.10, 34, 35

Joey Mancini is an architect, designer and graphic artist born in 1953 in New York City. He has a degree in the applied arts of interior design from the Fashion Institute of Technology, and studied architecture and product design at the Royal College of Arts, London. Between 1971 and 1975 he worked in Milan for *Joe Colombo*, Studio Dallago, *Giotto Stoppino* and *Gae Aulenti*. He has received many awards for product design, has written for magazines, and carried out research for films on the development of American design. His book, *The Extreme Flow of Consciousness*, is a manual on light projection and light machines. 1.40

Angelo Mangiarotti was born in 1921 in Milan and educated there, graduating from the Polytechnic in 1948. He has worked as a designer in America and in Italy, as well as teaching at the Illinois Institute of Technology's design school. He has specialized in small sculptural objects, often intended for the table top, including a stainless-steel clock for Portescap and other pieces for Knoll and Munari. 2.4, 5; 3.77

Ann Marinelli was born in Southbridge, Massachusetts, in 1950 and received her B.F.A. degree in Interior Architecture from the Rhode Island School of Design in 1972. She has been living and working in Milan since 1972, originally working with Alberto Rosselli and now as part of the *Isao Hosoe* Design team. Ann Marinelli is a contributing editor to the American magazine *ID*. 1.147

Javier Mariscal, a Spanish designer, was born in 1950. He trained as an artist and graphic designer and collaborated on the Memphis collection of 1981. He has designed

lights in collaboration with Pepe Cortès for the Barcelona firm BD Ediciones de diseño, textiles for Marieta and carpets for Nani Marquina. 1.113; 2.6–8; 4.15, 28, 40, 53, 54

Ingo Maurer was born in West Germany in 1932. After training as a typographer and graphic artist in Germany and Switzerland, he emigrated to America in 1960. He moved back to Europe in 1963 and started his own lighting design firm, Design M, in 1966. His work has been collected by museums in Israel and Japan, by the Museum of Modern Art, New York, and by the Neue Sammlung, Munich. 2.20, 24

Nanny Still McKinney is a ceramicist, born in Helsinki, who now lives in Brussels. She has received many international awards for her work including the Diplome d'Honneur of the Milan Triennale, the International Design Award, USA, and the Pro Finlandia Medal. Since 1977 she has been working with Rosenthal and her creations include *Taiga*, *Rhapsody in White* and *Raining Blossom* in glass, as well as her *Wave* series of vases in ceramic. 3.40

Antoon Meerman is an Australian designer who has taught design and cabinet-making. In 1986 he was awarded a diploma with distinction by the Canberra School of Art's wood workshop. 1.108

David Mellor was born in Sheffield, UK, in 1930. He trained as a silversmith, but subsequently specialized in metalwork, veering more and more towards mass production. Early in the Seventies he set up a factory to manufacture cutlery. Mellor has won eight design awards from the Design Council of Great Britain, five of which have been for cutlery. His work is in the collections of the Victoria and Albert Museum, London, and the Museum of Modern Art, New York. 3.10

Marco Mencacci is an Italian architect and designer who grew up in Genoa and studied at the Sorbonne and the Université d'Architecture in Paris. 1.139

Alessandro Mendini was born in Milan in 1931. He was a partner of Nizzoli Associates until 1970, and a founder-member of Global Tools. He then edited *Casabella* and *Modo* and, until 1985, *Domus*. He has collaborated with a number of companies, has written widely and received the Compasso d'Oro in 1979. 1.64–66; 3.35, 36; 5.36

Pedro Miralles is a Spanish architect, born in Valencia in 1955. He has participated in many exhibitions in Madrid and Valencia and in 1987 won the IMPIVA scholarship from the Domus Academy in Milan. In 1988, the Ministry of Industry awarded him a scholarship to work in Paris for the company *Xo*. Following collaboration with Andreu Est he won the 1987 Valencia Innovation award and in the same year was awarded the Colegio de Arquitectos de Madrid for the best design of that year. He has worked for many major companies, including Punt Mobles, Arflex, BD Ediciones de diseño, Santa & Cole, Akaba, Artespana and DeSedie. 1.142, 143; 4.6–8

Santiago Miranda is a Spanish designer, born in Seville in 1947. He trained at the Escuela de Artes Aplicadas in Seville before moving to Italy where he has worked ever since with *Perry A. King*. 1.15, 16, 84; 2.3; 3.24, 25

Eiji Miyamoto was born in 1948 near Tokyo and graduated from Hosei University in 1970. Miyamoto began developing and designing fabrics in 1975 and now supplies leading Japanese fashion designers, including Issey Miyake. 4.55, 57–61

Marcello Morandini was born in Mantua in 1940 and has lived in Varese since 1947. He was educated at the Brera Academy in Milan. In 1963 he opened his own studio and exhibited his first three-dimensional structures in Genoa in 1965. He has subsequently had many exhibitions in Italy and throughout the rest of the world. In 1979 he was invited to Sydney, Australia, and lived and worked for a short time in Singapore. He has been designing ceramics for Rosenthal for several years and was commissioned by them to design the façade of their new offices in Selb, West Germany. 3.65; 4.66–69

Masahiro Mori was born in 1927 in Saga-Ken, Japan. He is a ceramics and industrial designer whose awards include the gold medal of the International Competition of Contemporary Art Ceramics, Faenza, in 1975 and the Grand Prix of the 13th Annual Industrial Design Competition, Valencia. 3.21–23

Massimo Morozzi was born in Florence, Italy, in 1941. Trained as an architect, until 1972 he was a member of Archizoom Associati, the leading avant-garde architectural group of the day in Italy. During this period Morozzi collaborated on the design of the *Aeo* chair for Cassina. For five years he ran Montedison's textile design research centre. After 1977 he worked with the CDM group on a corporate identity programme for Rome airport. In 1982 he opened his own studio specializing in consumer goods. 1.22, 23

Jasper Morrison is a British furniture designer, educated in New York, Frankfurt and England. He graduated from the Royal College of Art, London, in 1985. Since then he has designed and made small-batch production pieces. In 1986 he started in private practice and took part in Zeus's exhibition in Milan. He has also produced a number of projects for SCL Ltd, London, and Idée, Japan. 1.118–120

Thomas Müller studied architecture at the Staatliche Akademie der Bildenden Künste in Stuttgart. From 1985 to 1987 he studied at the Department of Furniture Design at the Royal College of Art, London. He currently lives in Berlin. 3.34

Bruno Munari was born in Milan in 1907 and was active as a second-wave Futurist painter around 1930. After 1945 he was an Abstract painter and in 1948 a founder of the Movimento Arte Concreta, with which *Gillo Dorfles* and *Joe Colombo* were also associated. He published much avant-garde theorizing on communication and design as well as being active as a designer himself. His cube ashtray for Danese was much admired, as were many lights and

toys. He won the Compasso d'Oro and has been honoured by the Academy of Science in New York and the Japan Design Foundation. 1.46, 47

Eckart Muthesius was born in Berlin, the son of Hermann Muthesius, architect and founder of the Deutsche Werkbund, and could claim the Scottish painter Frank Newberry and the architect and designer Charles Rennie Mackintosh for godfathers. The latter presented Eckart with a spoon and fork especially designed for his christening. He attended a school of applied arts in Berlin-Charlottenburg and, later, a polytechnic school in London. It was in London that he gained his first practical experience as an architect after which he returned to Germany as apprentice in his father's office. When he set up his own offices in Berlin, the firm's first commission was a private house for Carl August Von Gablenz, founder of Lufthansa. In the Thirties Muthesius was commissioned to build and decorate the new palace for his friend the Maharaja of Indore; among the items was this trolley. 1.101, 102

Studio Naço see *Denis Conrady* and *Marcelo Lagares*. 1.30

Paolo Nava was born in Italy in 1943 and studied at Milan Polytechnic and in Florence. He worked for various design studios in England. His designs encompass furniture, kitchen systems and lights. 5.23

Paola Navone was born in 1950 and graduated in architecture from Turin Polytechnic. She has written for several magazines, including *Casabella*, *Domus* and *Modo*, and worked as design consultant for many Italian and international companies. In 1987 she founded Mondo with *Giulio Cappellini* and *Rodolfo Dordoni*. 1.49

Nemo is a design team comprising Alain Domingo and François Scali. Domingo was born in Paris in 1952 and Scali in Boulogne-Billancourt in 1951; both studied architecture at the Ecole des Beaux Arts, Paris. They have designed lights, jewellery, furniture, carpets and rugs, products, stationery, luggage, packaging and postmen's uniforms. Their designs can be seen in many museums in Europe and the USA, Canada and Japan, and have been featured in many books and articles. They received awards from Mobilier National 1983, the French Ministry of Culture, the Musée des Sciences et Techniques de la Villette and the Janus de l'Industrie. 3.72

Susanne Neubohn is a Swedish designer born in 1960 who studied industrial design in Berlin and works with John Hirschberg and Inge Sommer as Berlinetta Industrial Design. Their work has been shown at many exhibitions, including "1988 Avant Garde Furniture, Berlin" at the Centre Georges Pompidou, Paris. They also work in urban development and the protection of the environment. 1.95

Annabel Newham is a British designer who graduated from the West Surrey College of Art and Design in ceramics. Her work has been exhibited in West Germany, Holland, Switzerland, Japan and Malaysia as well as in

London where she is an associate member of The Glasshouse. 3.32

Marc Newson was born in Sydney, Australia, in 1963. He graduated from Sydney College of the Arts in 1984. He held his first exhibition in 1986 and in 1987 designed and made prototypes of furniture for Idée in Tokyo. 1.109–111

Klara Obereder is a student at the Academy of Applied Arts in Vienna. 3.60

Svend Onø was born in Copenhagen in 1960, and educated in arts, craft and design. In 1988 he designed a deck-chair for Kircodan and collaborated on the decoration of a conference room for Nykredit with Frank Olieu. He is a member of the Danish furniture and interior designers' professional organization. Since 1983 he has been part of a group of furniture designers primarily involved with exhibiting prototypes. 3.1

Paolo Pallucco is an Italian furniture designer, architect and manufacturer born in 1950 in Rome. He established Pallucco in 1980, producing new designs and re-editions of modern classics and putting his own creations into production. In 1984 he started Pallucco Design to work on designs independently of his other company. He works in conjunction with *Mireille Rivier*. 1.75–78

David Palterer is an architect born in Haifa, Israel, in 1949. He graduated from the University of Florence in 1979 where he then taught and lectured. He has also taught at Syracuse University, Werk Bund at Stuttgart and the Bezalel Academy for Art and Crafts in Jerusalem. His recent projects include the restoration and enlargement of the Theatre of San Casciano with Professor L. Zangeri, the Florence Air Terminal, a park in Pesaro and a bird park in Tel-Aviv. He has produced designs for many international companies, including Artemide, Swid Powell, Factotum Vistosi and Zanotta. Many of his designs have been exhibited worldwide and his work is in the permanent design collections of the Vienna Kunstgeverbe Museum, the Prague Museum and the Israel Museum in Jerusalem. 3.43–45

Perico Pastor is a Spanish designer born in 1953, who divides his time between Spain and New York, where he works as an illustrator. 4.25, 26

Hermann Payer is an Austrian designer, born in Vienna in 1961. After finishing his education in communication engineering, he studied at the Vienna University of Agriculture, where he developed a new kind of plant-tie. This development of the idea has received an Austrian industrial award. 5.24

Glenn Peckman lives and works in New York and Italy. Originally a painter, he was apprenticed in Italy with Rati Silks in the late Seventies, and now works extensively in home furnishings. His work has been acquired by the Cooper-Hewitt Museum of Decorative Arts, and his designs have been produced in the USA, Europe and India. 1.73, 4.17

Jorge Pensi is a Spanish architect and industrial designer, born in 1946 in Buenos Aires, Argentina. In 1977 he formed Grupo Berenguer, Design, Form and Communication with Alberto Lievore, Norberto Chaves and Oriol Pibernat. Since 1979 he has been associated with Perobell, the SIDI group and the magazine On Diseño. His chair *Toledo* won first prize at SIDI in 1988 as well as a silver prize at the Amat Muebles para Colectividades. His products have been selected for design exhibitions in Barcelona, Valencia and Cataluna, and his work has been featured in many Spanish and international publications. 1.54; 2.1, 2

Maurizio Peregalli, an Italian designer, was born in 1951 in Varese. He studied in Milan and, after graduating, started work on designing shops for Giorgio Armani. In 1984, along with five other designers, he established Zeus in Milan, a gallery showing avant-garde furniture, textiles, ceramics and glass. He is also a member of Noto, an interior design and manufacturing company. 1.152, 153

Roberto Pezzetta was born in Treviso, Italy, in 1946. He has spent most of his career working for household appliance companies. From 1969 to 1974 he worked in the industrial design department of Zoppas, and since then for Zanussi, apart from a brief spell at Nordica. Since 1982 he has been in charge of Zanussi's industrial design department. He was awarded the Compasso d'Oro in 1981 and specially mentioned at the Compasso d'Oro in 1987. He has won gold medals for design in Holland and Ljubljana. 5.37

Manuel Pfahl, an avant-garde German designer, was born in 1958 and studied industrial design at the Hochschule der Künste, Berlin. His work has been exhibited frequently, including shows at the Kunstmuseum in Düsseldorf and the Kunststichting in Rotterdam. 1.90

Christophe Pillet, a French designer, was born in 1959 and now lives and works in Milan. He has worked as a designer and consultant for various French companies and this year has collaborated with *Martine Bedin* on projects involving industrial products, furniture and architecture. 3.30

Christian Ploderer is an Austrian designer, born in 1956, who studied industrial design at the Hochschule für angewandte Kunst, Vienna. He was a guest student of *Ettore Sottsass, Mario Bellini, Alessandro Mendini* and Hermann Czech, before his graduation in 1985. From 1979 to 1985 he had his own design studio, Ploderer & Rollig, and since 1986 has been an independent designer and design consultant for lighting, furniture and interior decoration. In 1987 he received a national award for design. 1.33

Paolo Portoghesi was born in Rome in 1931. He is professor at the Faculty of Architecture, Rome University, and has been a member of the San Luca Academy since 1961. In 1983 he was appointed chairman of the Venice Biennale. His works include Khartoum International Airport, 1973; Amman Royal Court, 1974, and the Mosque and Islamic Cultural Centre, Rome, 1976. He is the author of several publications on criticism of architecture and city planning as well as editor-in-chief of *Controspazio* and *Eualpino*. 3.47

Alessio Pozzoli was born in Milan in 1960 and received a degree from the School of Applied Arts and Design, Turin, in 1983. He has been collaborating with *Isao Hosoe* Design since 1984. 1.147; 5.19, 20

Products Industrial Design was established in 1986 by Roland Schmidt (born 1957) and Klaus Lackner (born 1960) in Heidelberg, West Germany. They work in all fields of consumer products and equipment for international companies, and have received several design prizes and awards such as the Gold Prize, Tokyo International Lighting Design Competition, 1983; Erkundungen, Stuttgart, 1986; International Design Competition, Osaka, 1985, and the Design Centre prize, Stuttgart. 5.57

Jean Prouvé (1901–1984) was born in Paris. He was a pupil of Emile Robert and the blacksmith Szabo. In 1923 he set up his own studio in Nancy undertaking various architectural and furniture commissions. During the mid Twenties he made contact with Le Corbusier, Jeanneret, Mallet-Stevens and Herbe and from the early Thirties worked from his studio in Paris. In 1932 he designed furniture for the University in Nancy, where he had grown up and where he lived. 1.103

Daniela Puppa, architect and designer, was born in 1947 and graduated from Milan Polytechnic in 1970. A former co-editor of *Casabella* and *Modo*, she took part in the Venice Biennale of 1980, and the Milan Triennales of 1981 and 1983. She has worked in theatre design and fashion, and since 1983 has been assistant on the fashion design course at the Domus Academy. 2.12

Andrée Putman was born in Paris. She studied the piano at the Paris Conservatoire under François Poulenc. After several years as a journalist she moved into industrial design and in the Seventies was co-founder of Créateurs et Industriels, bringing together designers such as Issey Miyake and Castelbajac to produce objects as well as fashion. Her interest in the work of Eileen Gray led to the reproduction of previously forgotten 20th-century furniture designs. In 1978 she founded Ecart International, specializing in re-editions, and began her own career as an interior designer. 1.126, 127

Giorgio Ragazzini, an Italian designer, was born at Imola in 1962. He graduated from the Isia di Faenza and was a post-graduate of the Domus Academy in 1987. Between 1983 and 1987 he collaborated with Paolo Zani on industrial ceramics; he also produced headphones for Ross Electronics in London. 1.18

Franco Raggi was born in Milan in 1945, and graduated in architecture from Milan Polytechnic in 1969. He has designed architecture, exhibitions, books and magazines, and is currently a professor at the Faculty of Architecture, Pescara. 2.12, 49

Gerrit Rietveld (1888–1964) was born in Utrecht, The Netherlands, the son of a cabinet-maker. He began work in his father's workshop at the age of 11. In 1911 he started his own cabinet-making business and began to study architectural drawing at evening classes. In 1918 he produced his famous red and blue chair, in cheap wood, simple colours and owing much to the example of *Frank Lloyd Wright*. He became a member of De Stijl movement in 1919. In the Twenties he designed furniture, lamps and a radio as well as working on architectural interiors. He was in contact with many of the international avant-garde including Kurt Schwitters and *El Lissitzky*. The design shown here was originally manufactured and sold by Metz & Co. of Amsterdam in 1935. 1.105

Franz Ringelhan, a member of the *Ingo Maurer* Design Team, was born in Oberhausen, West Germany, in 1957. After studying interior design in Rosenheim 1976–1981, he became a freelance designer for Ingo Maurer. He co-designed *Ilios* and *Oh Jack!* and has collaborated on several lighting and exhibition designs. 2.24

Mireille Rivier was born in 1959 in Lyon, France. She graduated in architecture at the Polytechnic of Lausanne before moving to Rome where she works with *Paolo Pallucco*. 1.75–78

Nancy Robbins is an American designer who has lived and worked in Barcelona since 1972. She graduated from the Rhode Island School of Design in 1964. Between 1964 and 1972 she was involved in many interior design projects in New York and in a chain of shops with restaurants in Belgium. In 1984 she opened her first furniture store, and in 1986 opened a shop in Barcelona. She has exhibited at the European Masters series "Annual of Interior Design" and "Annual of Furniture Designers" as well as at the furniture shows in Valencia in 1987 and 1988. She is at present designing wallpaper, fabrics, display systems for shops and department stores, commercial interiors, domestic interiors and furniture. 1.31, 32

Sylvia Robeck was born in Berlin in 1959. She studied graphics and industrial design at the Hochschule der Künste, Berlin. Exhibition involvements include "The Art of Reading" for the Museum für Kunstgewerbe, Frankfurt, in 1985; "Design Poker" in Austria, 1986, and "To Book a Furniture," Berlin, 1987. 1.91

James Ryan is partner in charge at the New York design consultancy, Henry Dreyfuss Associates. 5.31

Martin Ryan was born in Dublin, Eire, in 1953. After a career as a musician spanning several years, he studied design at the London College of Furniture. He then developed a range of furniture, and launched Portfolio Furniture in February 1986. Under his guidance the company has grown to its present status as one of the leading modern furniture design companies in Britain. In association with Viaduct Furniture, Portfolio has also developed a successful export market. 1.57

Lino Sabattini is an Italian silversmith, born in 1925. His metalwork first attracted international attention in 1956 when it was exhibited in Paris at a show organized by the architect Giò Ponti. Since then he has continued to be closely associated with a simple, sculptural, essentially modern approach to the design of metal and glassware, working for companies such as Rosenthal and Zani. He exhibits at the Milan Triennale and other major exhibitions. In 1979 he was awarded the Compasso d'Oro. His work is in the collections of the Museum of Modern Art, New York, the Cooper-Hewitt Museum of Decorative Arts and Design, and the British Museum, London. 3.4, 5

Pete Sans is a Spanish designer, born in Barcelona in 1947. During 1962 and 1963 he worked in the studios of the architect José Pratmarso while he was studying for his baccalaureate. In 1971 he opened a studio in graphic design, directed the Galeria and the Escuela Nikon, noted in Barcelona for taking up the most combative artistic statements of the moment, and published the magazine *Papel Especial*. In 1979 he carried out a series of prototypes, one of which was to become the germ of the *Lamparaprima*. With the success of this piece and design awards in Spain and abroad, he turned to full-time industrial design. His most outstanding pieces are the *Lampara Lapa*, the *Serie Empuries*, the *Mesa Mesita*, the unit series and the *Mesa Phidea*. 1.37–39

Richard Sapper was born in Munich in 1932. After studying at the University of Munich, he joined Daimler-Benz's styling department in 1956. Two years later he moved to Italy, working initially with Giò Ponti and then in the design department of La Rinascente before joining Marco Zanuso. With Zanuso he worked on several of the best-known pieces of Italian industrial design from the Sixties, in particular portable radio and television sets for Brionvega. After establishing his own studio, Sapper designed the classic modern adjustable light, the *Tizio*, and the *Tantalo* clock, both produced by Artemide. In addition to furniture for Castelli, Molteni and Knoll, Sapper has designed tableware for Alessi. He participated in "Italy: The New Domestic Landscape" at the Museum of Modern Art, New York, in 1972, and has worked in the past with *Gae Aulenti* on transport-planning studies. His numerous awards and distinctions include the Compasso d'Oro and the German Die Gute Industrieform prize. 5.6

Soichiro Sasakura is a Japanese designer born in 1949. Since his graduation from the Kanazawa College of Art, he has been employed by the Sasaki Glass Company. 3.19

William Sawaya was born in Beirut in 1948 and graduated from the National Academy of Fine Arts, Beirut, in 1973. An architect, he is particularly interested in the definition of internal spaces and began his career in the Lebanon, subsequently working in the USA, France and Italy. He moved to Italy in 1978 and in 1984 he established Sawaya & Moroni together with Paolo Moroni. His work has been

published in various magazines and newspapers throughout Europe and the USA. 1.128

Tobia and Afra Scarpa are an Italian husband-and-wife team who have worked together for more than 25 years. Tobia, born in 1935 in Venice, spent a brief time working in the glass industry before their collaboration. Afra, born in Montebelluna in 1937, graduated from the Architectural Institute, Venice. In 1958 they began working in glass with Venini at Murano. They created the *Bastiano* divan and *Vanessa* metal bed for Gavina, and for Cassina the *Sonana* armchair which won the Compasso d'Oro award in 1970 and the *925* armchair which is on permanent display at the Museum of Modern Art, New York. The *Torcello* system, designed for Stildomus, and the *Morna* bed are among their other famous creations. They are responsible for the image of the Benetton shops in Europe and America. They occasionally work as architects as well as designers. Their pieces can be seen in major museums all over the world and many have been chosen for international exhibitions. 2.43

Ali Scherhaufer is a student at the Academy of Applied Arts in Vienna. 3.58

Schlagheck & Schultes Design is based in Munich and is responsible for, among other things, lights for Vereinigte Werkstätten. Its president is Herbert Schultes, a German industrial designer who was born in Freiburg in 1938. He studied in Munich and went on to lecture at the Cologne Technical College and the Fachochschule, Munich. He has been the chief designer at Siemens since 1985. 2.45

Johanna Schmeiser is a student at the Academy of Applied Arts in Vienna. 3.62

Roland Schmidt see *Products International Design*.

Frank Schreiner was born in 1959 in Russelsheim. He studied engineering and visual communication in Berlin and worked on "Outbreak of the Breakthrough – a Show on New German Design," by Christian Borngraber and Bob Rooyens. He has been involved with many exhibitions, including several on the German avant garde. One of his chairs is in the collection of Rolf Fehlbaum of Vitra International, in Basel, Switzerland. 1.93

Phillip Schroeder was born in Pine Bluff, Arkansas, USA, in 1945. He graduated from the College of Journalism, University of Florida, in 1967. He worked in advertising and marketing for 20 years before pursuing his AutoArt career. His *Car's the Star* has been on the television series *Miami Vice*, used as the throne on the Miss Teenage America Pageant, and can now be seen daily on the MTV set. The AutoArt collection was exhibited at the recent Salon de Mobile in Milan. 1.157

Sashiko Shimoda is a Japanese designer, born in Tokyo in 1963. Since graduating from the Musashino Art University, he has worked with Nuno. 4.56

Studio Simonetti was founded by Massimo Simonetti. For 15 years the company has

worked in planning, architecture, marketing, interior and industrial design, and its work can be seen throughout Italy in hotels, restaurant and fast food chains, and tourist complexes. The company has recently completed the Atlas Asni and Amadil Atlas hotels in Morocco. 1.56

Bořek Šípek was born in Prague in 1949. He studied furniture design in Prague, architecture in Hamburg and philosophy at Stuttgart University. His works are included in the collections of the Museum of Modern Art, New York; the Museum of Decorative Arts, Prague; the Kunstmuseum, Düsseldorf, and PTT in Den Haag. He now lives in Amsterdam and designs for Sawaya & Moroni, Driade, Vitra and Cleto Munari. 1.1–9

Torben Skov is a Danish designer born in 1947. He graduated from the Graphic College of Denmark and since 1971 has been working in graphic design, lettering and illustration from his own studio. In 1978 he made his début as a painter but since 1984 he has concentrated on producing geometric furniture. 1.136, 137.

Ingrid Smolle is a student at the Academy of Applied Arts in Vienna. 3.61

Robert Sonneman is an American product designer. He graduated in industrial management from Long Island University, and attended Harvard Graduate School of Design. He is the principal of the Sonneman Design Group, a New York-based product and architectural design firm. 2.46, 47

Sony Design Team is based in Tokyo. 5.7, 14, 53–56

Johnny Sørensen was born in Denmark in 1944. He graduated in crafts and design in 1966, and opened an office with *Rud Thygesen* the same year. Together they have been awarded many prizes and have been the subject of exhibitions. Examples of their work have been purchased by the Danish State of Art Foundation. 1.133, 134

Ettore Sottsass was born in Innsbruck, Austria, in 1917. He graduated as an architect from Turin Polytechnic in 1939, and opened an office in Milan in 1946. Since 1958 he has been a design consultant for Olivetti but is also active in fields as various as ceramics, jewellery, decorations, lithographs and drawings. He has taught and exhibited widely. In 1980 he established Sottsass Associati with other architects, and has designed many pieces of furniture that are part of the Memphis collection. 1.24–27; 2.35, 36; 3.38

Martin Spreng was born in West Germany in 1957. Although initially interested in painting, he turned to cabinet-making and worked in Paris for Rinck and Mercier, creating his own style of veneering and inlaying. He has exhibited in France and West Germany and in 1982 joined *Xylos*. 1.19

Joachim Stanitzek was born in Poland in 1951 and completed an engineering apprenticeship in Hagen. He then studied sociology, history of art, videography and architecture in Aachen and Berlin. From 1982

he has been involved with the *Bellefast* experimental design workshop with *Andreas Brandolini*. In 1985 he worked on "Outbreak of the Breakthrough – a Show on New German Design," by Christian Borngraber and Bob Rooyens. His work has been exhibited at one-man shows and international venues. His cloakroom facilities are in the Design Collection of the Kunstmuseum in Düsseldorf. 1.89, 97

Philippe Starck was born in Paris in 1949 and works as a product, furniture and interior designer. In Paris he was commissioned by President Mitterrand to give a new look to part of the Elysée Palace and designed the Café Costes, together with a number of fashion shops. In New York he remodelled the interior of the Royalton Hotel, and in Tokyo he has designed two restaurants and is currently working on a number of other buildings. His furniture design includes projects for Disform, Driade, Baleri and Idée. Among his industrial design projects are cutlery for Sasaki, clocks for Spirale and mineral-water bottles for Vittel. 1.59–63; 2.51; 3.78–86; 5.40–43

Stiletto Studios was founded in 1981 to provide a wide range of audio-visual services and design projects. See *Frank Schreiner*.

Giotto Stoppino was born in Vigerano, Italy, in 1926, and studied architecture in Milan. From 1953 until 1968, when he opened his own office, he worked with *Vittorio Gregotti* in the partnership of Architetti Associati. Stoppino has designed furniture for Bernini, Kartell and Acerbis, and lights for Arteluce; he took part in the New York Museum of Modern Art exhibition, "Italy: The New Domestic Landscape," in 1972. 1.35

Reiko Sudo was born in Ibaraki Prefecture, Japan, in 1953 and studied at Musashino Art University where she later worked in the textile department. She became a freelance textile designer in 1978, and in 1984 helped to found the Nuno Corporation. 4.56

Minoru Sugahara was born in Tokyo in 1940 and graduated from Wasada University. He joined the Sugahara Glass company in 1963 and since 1973 has headed the design team. One of his most successful designs, *BK & WH*, received a Japanese design award in 1986. 3.20

Timo Sunila is a Finnish product designer born in 1953. In 1987 he was awarded a diploma at the "Form 6" exhibition in Finland. 5.25

Sybilla was born in New York in 1963, daughter of an Argentinian father and a Polish mother; while she was still a child her family moved to Madrid. In 1980 she moved to Paris to undertake an apprenticeship in what was later to become her true vocation, clothing design. She spent a year working at Yves St Laurent's haute couture workshop and then returned to Spain to create her first collection, shown in October 1983. By 1985 she was showing her second winter collection at the Salon Gaudi in Barcelona and in the summer her first footwear collection went on sale. Her international début came with the showing of her winter 1986–7 collection which received much acclaim. Today her clothing and footwear is sold throughout Europe, the USA, the Middle East and Australia. This is her first collection of linen. 4.49–52

Matteo Thun was born in Austria in 1952 and graduated from Florence University. He was a founding member of the Memphis design group and established his own design company in Milan in 1984. His work has been shown in Berlin, Hanover, Düsseldorf, Vienna, Los Angeles and at the 1983 Milan Triennale. He is a professor of product design and ceramics at the Academy of Applied Arts, Vienna. 3.48–53; 4.36

Rud Thygesen was born in Denmark in 1932, and opened an office with *Johnny Sørensen* in 1966. 1.133, 134

Ajin Togashi was born in Tokyo in 1960 and graduated from the Crafts Division of Tokyo National University of Fine Arts and Music. Before taking a master's course in wrought metal, he designed a series of lights for exhibition and public spaces. In 1986 he joined the Sasaki Glass Company and has designed tableware, percussion and wind instruments made of glass and, more recently, the *Clearball* speaker systems which received the Design of the Year award, Japan 1987. This speaker system is an update of that series. 5.1, 2

Jaime Tresserra Clapés was born in Barcelona in 1943. He began studying law but switched to the arts, where he pursued an interest in jewellery making. For 15 years he worked in interior design and architecture and then moved into furniture design. He won the 1986 Casa Viva award for best design at the Mogar Fair in Madrid and then established his own company. At the International Furniture Fair in Valencia in 1987 he received Best Design Award. He has recently designed packaging for the Olympic Games to be held in Barcelona in 1992 and is currently working on designs for furniture, lamps and carpets. 1.17

Oscar Tusquets Blanca was born in Barcelona in 1941. He attended the Escuela Técnica Superior de Arquitectura, Barcelona, and in 1964 established Studio PER with *Lluis Clotet*, with whom he collaborated on nearly all his projects until 1984. He has been a guest professor and lecturer at universities in Germany, France and the USA, and his work has been exhibited in many parts of Europe and the USA. He has received many awards for his work, both as an architect and as a designer. Introduction; 1.42–45, 85; 3.33

Floris Van Den Broecke was born in 1945 in Harlingen, The Netherlands. He was educated at the Arnhem Academy and the Royal College of Art, London. He has been Professor of Furniture Design at the RCA since 1985, and is a furniture-maker and designer. 1.145

Marc Van Hoe was born in Zulte, Belgium, in 1945. He studied industrial design, fine arts and textile history. In 1975 he opened his own workshop. He now teaches and is a freelance designer and technical researcher in industrial textiles and fibre art. His work is part of several

permanent collections and has been exhibited in Belgium, The Netherlands, France, Switzerland, Poland, Hungary and the UK. 4.41–43

Tucker Viemeister founded Smart Design in New York City with David Stowell in 1985. After graduating from the Pratt Institute in 1974 he taught industrial design in Portugal. He worked for three years as a design consultant on environmental graphics, symbols, typography and street furniture for Washington DC's zoo and the National Mall. He has lectured at various colleges and his work was selected for the Presidential Design Achievement Award in 1984 and for *ID* magazine's Design Review in 1983, 1985, 1986 and 1987. His products are in the permanent collection of the Cooper-Hewitt Museum of Decorative Arts and Design. 2.17

Sohrab Vossoughi was born in Tehran, Iran, in 1956 and moved to the USA in 1971 where he was educated at San José State University, graduating in 1979. He worked for Hewlett-Packard and began doing design consultancy work. In 1982 he established Ziba Design in Oregon. He is currently president of Ziba Design and his clients include Nike, Intel Corp. and Dow Chemical Co. He has received many patents and design awards. His work ranges from furniture to computers, from fitness equipment to household appliances, and from consumer electronics to office systems. 5.13

Maarten Vrolijk was born in Oss, in The Netherlands, in 1966. He trained as a designer at the Akademie Industriele Vormgeving at Eindhoven, and has exhibited at various galleries in The Netherlands. Apart from textiles, he designs furniture and also works in fashion. 4.27

Hermann Waldenburg was born in Silesia in 1940. He was apprenticed as a typesetter, then studied painting at the Staatliche Akademie der Bildenden Künste, Stuttgart, and painting and graphics at the Hochschule der Künste, Berlin. From 1978 he has been a member of the Federation of German Artists. In 1985 he worked on "Outbreak of the Breakthrough – a Show on New German Design," by Christian Borngraber and Bob Rooyens, and his work has been shown at many exhibitions in Germany and at the Bienal Internacional de São Paulo in Brazil. One of his armchairs is in the design collection of the Kunstmuseum, Düsseldorf, and at the Kunstgewerbemuseum, Berlin, are an armchair and other objects. 1.92

Christof Walther is a West German designer, born in 1953. Between 1979 and 1983 he studied industrial design in Berlin and in 1985 founded Berlinetta Industrial Design with Inge Sommer, *Susanne Neubohn* and John Hirschberg. He has also worked with *Andreas Brandolini*, and has exhibited in Berlin and at the International Hanover Fair in 1988. 1.96

Hans Wegner was born in Tonder, Denmark, in 1914. Apprenticed as a cabinet-maker from 1928 until 1932, he then worked in Tonder until 1935. From 1936 to 1938 he studied furniture design in Copenhagen, opening his own studio in 1943. In addition to designing

furniture, Wegner has also worked as an industrial designer, producing cutlery, wallpaper and silverware. He was nominated a Royal Designer for Industry in 1959 and was winner of the Danish Furniture prize in 1980. 1.36

Herbert Weinand was born in Wittlich, Eifel, West Germany, in 1953. After an apprenticeship as a cabinet-maker he studied interior, furniture and product design in Germany and Italy. In 1982 he worked on the design for the film *The Flambéed Woman* by Robert Van Ackeren. In 1983 he was involved with the interior design for the Villa Malaparte, Fondazione Ronchi, Capri for which he also created objets d'art. Since 1984 he has designed many interiors for restaurants and shops in Berlin, Mainz and Luxembourg and has opened his own gallery. His work has been exhibited in Germany, Austria and Italy and has featured at the German avant-garde shows. 1.94

Stefan Wewerka was born in 1928 in Magdeburg, Germany, and lives in Cologne and Berlin. Wewerka is a polymath who worked initially as an architect, then moved into sculpture and painting during the course of the Sixties. In 1974 he designed his first chair for Tecta, and since then has produced a number of increasingly elaborate pieces of environment furniture for them, in addition to designing clothes and jewellery. 1.135

Peter Wheeler was born in Bruck a.d. Mur, Austria, in 1947. He studied industrial design at the Central School of Art and Design in London, and Furniture Design at the Royal College of Art. On graduating from the RCA in 1977, he established a design consultancy in London, working on a wide range of commercial and domestic projects. He has received a number of awards in Britain and America; notably two gold medals from IBD in 1983. Since 1986, Wheeler has been collaborating with *Jane Dillon* and *Floris Van Den Broecke* on numerous furniture projects for Spanish and Italian companies. 1.145

Maria Wiala is a student at the Academy of Applied Arts in Vienna. 3.57

Bettina Wiegandt was born in Nienburg, West Germany, in 1957 and took up a joinery apprenticeship in Berlin between 1976 and 1980. Following the completion of this course, she studied industrial design. One of her chairs is in the design collection of the Kunstmuseum, Düsseldorf, and her work has often been exhibited. 1.90

Ingrid Wijnen is a Belgian designer who works with *Leo Aerts*. 1.130

Christopher Williams is an English designer born in 1949 who trained in interior and industrial design. Between 1971 and 1976 he designed domestic products for Conran Associates. He studied glass-making at the Royal College of Art in 1978 and went on to lecture at the High Wycombe College of Art. For seven years he was lecturer in industrial art at the RCA but now works as a freelance designer and teaches part time. He is a director of The Glasshouse. His work has been exhibited throughout England, Europe, Japan and the USA. His pieces are to be seen in the

Victoria and Albert Museum; the Contemporary Fine Art Society, London; the Crafts Council Collection, London; the Museum of Decorative Arts, Paris, and the Corning Glass Museum; New York State. 3.15, 16

Jean-Michel Wilmotte opened his own design studio in Paris in 1975 specializing in interior architecture, furniture, lighting, fabric, carpet and product design. Two years later he founded Academy to produce and sell his own designs and in 1987 opened an office in Japan. He has designed interiors at the Elysée Palace and for the French ambassador in Washington and has designed and renovated many public buildings in Nîmes. He has designed boutiques and large stores throughout France as well as in Japan and the USA, and furniture and fabrics for companies such as Mobilier International and Toulemonde Bochart. 1.58

Dieter Witte was born in Hanover, West Germany, in 1937. He studied industrial design there, graduating in 1961. He worked as a staff designer, specializing in lighting, for Lemgo. Until 1977 he worked as a freelance designer, mainly for Erco and Rosenthal, before joining Osram. 2.13

Frank Lloyd Wright (1867–1956), the American architect, is generally credited, along with Le Corbusier, Mies and Gropius, as one of the founding fathers of the modern movement in architecture. Trained in the offices of Louis Sullivan, Wright established his own firm in 1889, beginning his independent career with a series of highly individualistic houses characterized by spatially dynamic plans. For Wright, architecture was an art that embraced all aspects of a building, and he produced a wealth of original detail for interiors, and a great deal of furniture. For the Larkin Building in Buffalo (1904), he designed the first metal office furniture. Other major buildings include the Imperial Hotel, Tokyo (1916), the Johnson Wax Building, Racine (1936) and the Guggenheim Museum, New York, completed in 1960. 5.21, 22

Joerg Wurmitzer is an Austrian designer born in Klagenfurt in 1966. He is currently a student of the Academy of Applied Arts in Vienna studying industrial design as a pupil of Boris Bodrecca. The lamp shown was created for a competition sponsored by Woka Lamps, Vienna. 2.34

Xylos see *Francis Ballu, Remi Colmet Daage, Philippe Delaflotte* and *Martin Spreng*. Xylos have exhibited in France, West Germany, Italy and the USA. 1.19

Marco Zanuso Jr was born in Milan in 1954, the son of the distinguished Italian designer Marco Zanuso. He graduated in architecture from the University of Florence in 1978 and established his own office in 1980, working on exhibition design, architecture and industrial design. In 1981 he established Oceano Oltreluce, a lighting company. He has participated in many exhibitions and his work has appeared in publications throughout Europe. 3.74

Ziba Design see *Christopher Alviar, Terry Jones, Sohrab Vossoughi.*

SUPPLIERS

Fullest possible details are given of suppliers of the designs featured here; the activities of some outlets and manufacturers, however, are limited solely to the place of origin of their work.

Accademia Via Indipendenza 4, 33044 Manzano, Udine, Italy.

Acerbis International Via Brusaporto 31, 24068 Seriate, BG, Italy. *Outlets* Australia: Arredorama International Pty Ltd, 1 Ross Street, Glebe, NSW 2037. Belgium: Artiscope SA, 35 Boulevard St Michel, 1040 Brussels. France: Agences Générales Reuter, D915 Route de Paris, Domaine de la Pissotte, 95640 Marines. Greece: J. Deloudis AE, 217 Kifisias/2 Parnassou, Amaroussion, Athens. Japan: Atic Trading Inc, 2-9-8 Higashi, Shibuya-Ku, Tokyo. The Netherlands: Modular System, 73 Assumburg, 1081 GB Amsterdam, Buitenveldert. Scandinavia: Interstudio APS, 6-8 Esplanade, 1263 Copenhagen, Denmark. Spain: Axa International SA, 13, 5 Km, Llissa de Vall, Barcelona. Switzerland: Wohndesign AG, 123 Rychenbergstrasse, 8400 Winterthur. UK: Environment Communication, 15-17 Rosemont Road, London NW3 6NG. USA: Atelier International Ltd, 235 Express Street, Plainview, NY 11803.

Airon Via Don Sturzo 10, 20050 Triuggio, Milan, Italy.

Akaba Calle Major, s/n, 20160 Lasarte, Gipuzkoa, Spain. *Outlets* Belgium: Arline SPRL Collections, 1031 Ch. d'Alsemberg, 1420 Braine l'Alleud. France: Nestor Perkal, 8 Rue des Quatre Fils, 75003 Paris. Italy: Halifax: Via Prealpi 13, 20034 Giussano, MI. The Netherlands: Louis Goulmy Agenturen, Postbus 15, 2170 AA Sassenheim. Scandinavia: Teamprodukter, PO Box 30545, 20062 Malmö, Sweden. Switzerland: IMD AG, 460 Eebrunnestrasse, 5212 Hausen. USA: Stendig International, 305 East 63rd Street, New York, NY 10021. West Germany: IMD AG BRD, 11 Flöthbruchstrasse 11, 4156 Willich 2, Anrath.

Aleph see *Driade*

Alessi SPA Via Privata Alessi 6, 28023 Crusinallo, Novara, Italy. *Outlets* Denmark: Gense A/S, 17 Maglebjergvej, 2800 Lyngby. Finland: Casabella OY, 24 Yliopistonkatu, 20100 Turku. France: Société Métallurgique Lagostina, 62 Rue Blaise Pascal, 93600 Aulnay-sous-Bois. Japan: Italia Shoji Co Ltd, 5-4 Kojimachi, 1-Chome, Chiyoda-Ku, Tokyo 102. The Netherlands: Interhal BV, 8 Zoutverkoperstraat, 3330 CA Zwijndrecht. Sweden: Espresso Import, 10E Furasen, 42177 V, Frolunda. Switzerland: Guido Mayer SA, 9 Rue du Port Franc, 1003 Lausanne. UK: Penhallow Marketing Ltd, 3 Vicarage Road, Sheffield S9 3RH. USA: The Markuse Corporation, 10 Wheeling Avenue, Woburn, MA 01801. West Germany: Van Der Borg GMBH, 6 Sandbahn, 4240 Emmerich.

Alias SRL Via Respighi 2, 20122 Milan, Italy. *Outlets* France: Roger von Bary, 18 Rue Lafitte, 75009 Paris. Japan: Casatec Ltd, 2-9-6 Higashi, Shibuya-Ku, Tokyo 150. The Netherlands: Kreymborg, 63 Minervalaan, 1077 Amsterdam. Scandinavia: Design Distribution, 38/A/1 Dobelnstan, 113 52 Stockholm, Sweden. Switzerland: Renato Stauffacher, 2 Capelli, 6900 Lugano. UK: Artemide GB Ltd, 17-19 Neal Street, London WC2H 9PU. USA: International Contract Furniture, 305 East 63rd Street, New York, NY 10021. West Germany: Peter Pfeifer Focus, 87 Leopoldstrasse, 40 Munich 8.

Amat Camino can Bros 8, 08760 Martorell, Barcelona, Spain. *Outlets* Finland: Inno, Merikatu 1, 00140 Helsinki. France: Contrast, 11 Rue de Cambrai, 75019 Paris. Italy: C.I.C. Distribuzione, Loc. Grand Chemin, 1, 11020 Saint Christophe, Aosta. Scandinavia: Miranda of Sweden, Glashuset, Gustavsberg 13400. West Germany: Objekt Koordination, 55 Walter Kolbstrasse, 4018 Langenfeld.

Anthologie Quartett Schloss Huennefeld, Haus Sorgenfrei, 4515 Bad Essen, West Germany. *Outlets* Belgium: Surplus, 9 Zwarte Zusterstraat, B-9000 Ghent. France: Altras, 24 Rue Lafitte, 75009 Paris. Hong Kong: Le Cadre Gallery, 8 Sunning Road g/f, Causeway Bay. Italy: Via R. Drengot 36, 81031 Aversa. Lebanon: Intermeuble Sarl, Boite Postale 316, Beirut. The Netherlands: Binnen, 82 Kaisergracht, 1015 Amsterdam. Switzerland: Andome, 75 Schaffhauserstrasse, 8302 Kloten.

Arflex SPA Via Monte Rosa 27, 20051 Limbiate, Milan, Italy. *Outlets* Argentina: Collección SACIF, Florida 890, 1er Piso, 1005 Buenos Aires. Brazil: Arflex do Brasil, Rua Libero Badaró 377, 20 Andar CJ., 2004 São Paulo. Japan: Arflex Japan Ltd, 2-9-8 Higashi Shibuya-Ku, Tokyo 150.

Artemide SPA Via Brughiera, 20010 Pregnana Milanese, Milan, Italy. *Outlets* Australia: Artemide Pty Ltd, 69-71 Edward Street, Pyrmont, NSW 2009. Canada: Artemide Ltd, 354 Davenport Road, Designers Walk, 3rd Floor, Toronto, M15 RK5. France: Artemide SARL, 4 Rue Paul Cézanne, 75008 Paris. Japan: Artemide Inc, 1-5-10 Sotokanda Chiyodaku, Tokyo 101. The Netherlands: Horas SA, 25 Beemstraat, 1610 Ruisbroek, Belgium. Scandinavia: Renzo d'Este, 1A Brodrevej, 2860 Søborg, Copenhagen, Denmark. UK: Artemide GB Ltd, 17-19 Neal Street, London WC2H 9PU. USA: Artemide Inc, 528 Center One, 30-30 Thomson Ave, New York, NY 11101. West Germany: Artemide GmbH, 60 Königsallee, 4000 Düsseldorf.

Hiroshi Awatsuji Design Studio 1-21-1 Jingumae Shibuya-Ku, Tokyo, Japan.

B & B Italia SPA Strade Provinciale, 22060 Novedrate, Como, Italy. *Outlets* France: Helven Francis, 52 Rue De Lille, 59130 Lambersart. Japan: B & B Japan Ltd, 8F Book Center Building, 2-5-23 Kaigan, Minato-Ku, Tokyo 105. The Netherlands: Wanno Carolo, 14 Houtkoperstraat, 3330 Swijndrecht. Scandinavia: Renzo d'Este, 1A Brodrevej, 2860 Soborg, Copenhagen, Denmark. UK: Keith De La Plain, 5 Sayers Lane, Tenterden, Kent TN30 6BW. West Germany: Klaus Wasche, 266 Bachemer Strasse, 5000 Cologne 41; Bernd Schmidt, 25 Tannenweg, 8000 Munich 50.

BD Ediciones de diseño 291 Mallorca, 08037 Barcelona, Spain. *Outlets* Canada: Triedei, 460 McGill, Montreal, Quebec H2Y 2H2. France: Nestor Perkal, 8 Rue des Quatre Fils, 75003 Paris. Hong Kong: Le Cadre Gallery, 8 Sunning Road G/F. Italy: BD Italia, Piazza San Marco 1, 20100 Milan. Japan: Gendai Kikakushitsu, Koshin Bldg., 302 2-2-5 Sarugaku-cho, Chiyoda-Ku, Tokyo. The Netherlands: Quattro, Centre "Le Bosquet," Jodoigne-Geldenaken B-5900, Belgium. Switzerland: IMD Inter-Marketing Distribution AG, Eerburnestrasse 26, Hausen (AG), CH 5212. UK: The Ikon Corporation, B5L Metropolitan Wharf, Wapping Wall, London E1 9SS. USA: Manifesto, 200 West Superior Street, Chicago, Illinois; Lymnn, 457 Pacific Avenue, San Francisco 94133. West Germany: IMD Inter-Marketing Distribution AG, Flöthbruchstrasse 11, 4156 Willich 2, Anrath.

G.B. Bernini SPA Via Fiume 17, 20048 Carate Brianza, Milan, Italy.

Bieffeplast SPA Via Pelosa 78, 35030 Caselle di Selvazzano, Padova, Italy. *Outlets* Austria: Pro Domo, 35-37 Flachgrasse, 1151 Vienna. Belgium: furniture – Horas, 25 Beemdstraat, 1610 Ruisbroex, Brussels; lighting – Ardeco International Belgium, 47 Avenue Général de Gaulle, 1050 Brussels. Denmark: Interstudio, 6 Esplanaden, 1263 Copenhagen K. France: Protis, 67-101 Avenue Vieux Chemin St Denis, 92230 Gennevilliers. The Netherlands: furniture – as Belgium; lighting – Interlinea, 49 Weeresteinstraat, 2182 Gr Hillegom. Spain: Idea Mueble, 185 Via Augusta, Barcelona. Sweden: Inside AB, PO Box 7689, 10396 Stockholm. Switzerland: Design Agentur, 47 Hafnerstrasse, CH-8005 Zurich. UK: OMK Designs, 12 Stephen Buildings, Stephen Street, London W1. USA: Gullans International Inc, 227 West 17th Street, New York, NY 10011. West Germany: Andreas Weber, 79 Nymphenburger Strasse, 8000 Munich 19.

B.J. Metal AS 20 Nyhavn, 1051 K, Copenhagen, Denmark. *Outlets* Italy: Holmbäck & C Design SRL, Via Della Vigna Nuova 82/R, 50123 Firenze. The Netherlands: Bergers Interieurs, Postbus 107, 2650 Berkel en Rodenrijs. Spain: Pilma, Valencia 1, E-08915 Barcelona. Switzerland: Iff Design Import, Finsterwaldweg 92, 8205 Schaffhausen. West Germany: Teunen & Teunen, Postfach 36, Geisenheim 2, 6222.

Bodum (Schweiz) AG Kantonsstrasse, 6234 Triengen, Lucerne, Switzerland. *Outlets* France: Martin SA, 82-84 Rue de Dessous-des-Berges, 75013 Paris. Italy: Italtrade SA, 10-17 Piazza della Vittoria, 16121 Genoa. Japan: Zojirushi Vacuum Bottle Co, 20-5 Tenma, 1-Chome, Kita-Ku, Osaka 350. The Netherlands: Mepal BV, 1 Kwinkweerd, 7241 CW Lochem. Scandinavia: Peter Bodum AS, 18 Nglegaardsvej, 3540 Lynge, Denmark. UK: Bodum (UK) Ltd, 7 Neal Street, London W2H 9PU. USA: Rosti (USA) Inc, 18 Sidney Circle, New Jersey 07033. West Germany: Peter Bodum, 6 Bochstrasse, 2358 Kaltenkirchen.

Mattia Bonetti 14 Rue Vavin, Paris, France.

Botium Bellacenter STM, 2300 Copenhagen, Denmark. *Outlets* Belgium: Mobica Puba, 50 Gossetlaan, 1720 Groot-Bijgaarden. France: MOM/SEID International, 10 Boulevard des Batignolles, 75017 Paris. Japan: Royal Furniture Collection, Co-op Broadway Center, Room 1003, 5-52-15 Ivakano, Ivakano-Ku, 164 Tokyo. The Netherlands: EK Design Kollekties, 27 Lingedijk Postbus 14, 4196 ZG Tricht (GLD). UK: Zon International Ltd, Norwester House, 12 Fairway Drive, Greenford, Middlesex UB6 8PW.

Brandolini Buro für Gestaltung 4 Oranienplatz, 1000 Berlin 36, West Germany.

Bros's 1 Via Sotto Rive, S. Giovanni al Matisone 33048, Udine, Italy. *Outlets* Austria: Otto Silhavicek, Nussdorferstrasse 36, 1090 Wien. Belgium: Horas International, 22 Rue Copernic, Brussels 1180. France: Jean-Jacques del Valle, Horas International, 136-50 Rue Championet, 75918 Paris. The Netherlands: Hans Vos, Horas International, Cromvoirts Pad 2, 5263 NN Vught. Sweden: J. Giraud, Swedia, Box 138, 376030 Lammhult. Switzerland: O. Daehnel, Zollierstrasse 28, Zollikon, Zürich. UK: Paul Beauchamp, Interior Marketing, 36 Stansted Road, Hockerill, Bishop's Stortford, Hertfordshire CM23 2DY. USA: Emanuel Lacher, Cy Mann Dessigns Ltd, 150 Fulton Avenue, Garden City Park, New York, NY 11140. West Germany: Heinz Mode KG, Oderweg 3, 3501 Zierenberg; Heinz Fassenbender Sedia, Zoppenbroich 1, 4050 Monchengladbach 2; Claus Mansfeld, Taunsstrasse 45, 6200 Wiesbaden; Huberto Essenku, Maxim Wegzger Str. 6, 8000 Munich.

Bures Industries SA 18 Gerona, 08010 Barcelona, Spain. *Outlets* Japan: White House, 151-1-15-12 Tomigaya, Shibuya Ku, Tokyo. UAE: Mohamed Sharief & Bros, PO Box 4446, Deira, Dubai.

Canon Inc PO Box 5050, Shinjuku Dai-Ichi Seimei Building, Tokyo 160, Japan. *Outlets* Austria Canon, Modecenterstrasse 22 A-2, 1030 Wien. Belgium: Canon Copiers Belgium NVISA, Luidlaam 33-Bus 6,100 Brussels. Canada: Canon Canada Inc., 3245 American Drive, Mississauga, Ontario L4V 1N4. Denmark: Christian Bruhn AS, Vasekaer 12, 2739 Herlev. France: Canon, France SA, PO Box 40, 93151 Le Blanc Mesnil. Italy: Canon

Italia SPA, Centro Direzionale, Palazzo Verocchio, 20090 Milan 2-Segrate, MI. The Netherlands: Canon Verkooporganisatie Nederland BV, Cruquiusweg 29, 2102 LS Heemstede, Amsterdam. Norway: Noiseless AS, Tventenveien 30B, Oslo 6. Spain: Canon Copiadoras de España SA, Avd. Menendez Pelayo, 57 Torre Del Retiro, Madrid. Sweden: Canon Svenska AB, Box 2084, Stensatrava gen 13, 12702 Skarholmen. Switzerland: Canon SA, Genève, 1 Rue de Hesse, 1204 Geneva. UK: Canon (UK) Ltd, Canon House, Manor Road, Wallington, Surrey SM6 0AJ. USA: Canon USA Inc., One Canon Plaza, Lake Success, New York 11042-9979. West Germany: Canon Copylux GmbH, Leurriper Strasse 1-13, 4050 Mönchengladbach.

Casas SL Poligono Santa Rita, 08755 Castellbisbal, Barcelona, Spain. *Outlets* Belgium: Quattro, 25 Rue de la Régence, Brussels. France: Casas SL 27 Rue des Tournelles, 75004 Paris. Spain: Casas SL 15 Rodríguez de San Pedro, Madrid. Switzerland: Gatto Difussion, 30 Rue des Chavannes, 2016 Cortaillod. UK: Architectural Trading Company, 219-29 Shaftesbury Avenue, London WC2H 8AR. USA: International Contract Furnishings, 305 East, 63rd Street, New York NY 10021.

Cassina SPA PO Box 102, 20036 Meda, Milan, Italy. *Outlets* Argentina: Interieur Forma SA, 545-55 Paraguay, 1057 Buenos Aires. Australia: Artes Studios – Arredorama, 1 Ross Street, Glebe, NSW 2037. Belgium: Mobica, 50 Gossetlaan, 1720 Groot Bijgaarden. Brazil: Probjeto SA, 8400 Rua Vergueiro, 04272 San Paolo. Japan: Cassina Japan Inc, 2-9-6 Higashi, Shibuya-Ku, Tokyo 105. The Netherlands: Mobica, 31 Middenweg, 3401 MB Ijsselstein. Spain: Mobilplast SL, 40 Calle Milagro, 08028 Barcelona. USA: Atelier International Ltd, The International Design Center, 30-20 Thomson Avenue, Long Island City, NY 11101. Venezuela: Capuy, 69 Chacaito-Apdo. 106.

Central Market Japan Inc. 9-5-12 Akasaka Minato-ku, Tokyo, Japan.

Cidue 32 Via San Lorenzo, 36010 Carre, Vicenza, Italy. *Outlets* France: Cidue France SARL, 32 Rue de Paradis, 75010 Paris. Hong Kong: Executive Design, 53 Wong Nei Chong. The Netherlands: Espaces et Lignes, PO Box 406, 2040 Zandvoort. Scandinavia: Inside AB, PO Box 7689, 10395 Stockholm, Sweden. UK: Atrium, 113 St Peter, St Albans, Herts AL1 3ET. USA: Niels Olehansen Inc, 1129 Magnolia Avenue, Larkspur, 94939.

Colle SRL Località San Marziale, Colle Val D'Elsa 53034, Siena, Italy. *Outlets* Austria: H. Zoller, Graver Stein Weg 38, 6020 Innsbruck. Belgium: Gertraco, Waregen. Dominica: Ital. Des. Edificio Concordia, J.A. Soler, Avenida Abraham Lincoln, Santo Domingo. France: D. Medard, 8 Rue Martel, 75010 Paris; Annette Cros, 94370 Sucy en Brie; Gabriell Ciavarella, 12 Rue Rossignol, 68170 Rixheim. The Netherlands: T. Hoyng, PO Box 145, 5400 AC Uden. Spain: Miguel Graell Mir, Claudio Coello 77 11, 28001 Madrid. Switzerland: T.J. Meier, Lid Wil, 88 52 Altendorf. USA: Colle Inc., 8040 Remmet Avenue 9, Canoga Park, CA 91304.

West Germany: W. Goetz, AM Hec Kacker 30, 8501 Kalchreuth B NBG.; P Mumm Ert, Brackhausenstrasse 22, 2120 Lueneburg; E. Dietzel, St. Josefstrasse 10, 8640 Kronach 2.

Cycsa Sant Andreu de la Barca, Barcelona, Spain. *Outlets* France: Jean Dupeu, 9 Avenue President Wilson, Paris. The Netherlands: Molenaar, Postbus 56, 2100 AB Heelstede. Switzerland: Elvira Handwerker, Muhlonstrasse 8-10, 7766 Gaienhofer. West Germany: H & H Galeria, M. Möhnestrasse No. 14, 5760. UK: Mary Fox Linton Ltd, 249 Fulham Road, London SW3 6HY.

Daum Siège Social 41 Rue de Paradis, 75010 Paris, France. *Outlets* Italy: Corrado Corradi SPA, Via Medici del Vascello 8, 20138 Milan. Japan: Royal Copenhagen Japan Ltd, Mita Kokusai Building, 1-4-28 Mita Minato Ku, Tokyo. Spain: Mr. Pallarol, Florida Blanca 45, 08015 Barcelona. UK: Desmond O'Brien, 28 Chelsea Court, 95 Elm Park Gardens, Chelsea, London SW10 9QE. USA: Daum Inc., 41 Madison Avenue, New York, NY 10010. West Germany: Berndt Wingert, Paul Kleen Str. 79, 5090 Lever Kusen 1.

DeSede AG Oberes Zegli, 5313 Klingnau, Switzerland. *Outlets* Brazil: Cerno Industria, 1320-60 Estrada do Quitungo, 21 211 Rio de Janeiro. France: Robert Nissim, Résidence St Pierre A, 06700 St Laurent-du-Var. Italy: G.M. Mandrini, Via Cesare Battisti 3, 28040 Dormelletto. Japan: Mobilia Co, 2-3-5 Azabudai, Minato-Ku, Tokyo 106. The Netherlands: D.V. Luirink, 15 Korte Bergstraat, 3761 DR Soest. UK: Graham C. Walter, 42 High Street, Daventry NN11 4HU. USA: Stendig International Inc, 305 East 63rd Street, New York, NY 10021.

Design Galerie Weinand 37 Wieland Strasse 37, 1000 Berlin 12, West Germany.

Design Gallery Via Manzoni 46, 20121 Milan, Italy.

Design M Ingo Maurer GmbH 47 Kaiserstrasse, 8000 Munich 40, West Germany. *Outlets* France: Altras, 18 Rue Lafitte, 75009 Paris. Italy: Daverio SRL, Via Canova 37, 20145 Milan. The Netherlands: P.A. Hesselmans, 24 Korfgraaf, 4714 GM, Hellouw. Scandinavia (except Sweden): Finn Sloth, 1 Heilsmindevej, 2920 Charlottenlund, Denmark. Sweden: Sandklef, PO Box 4112, 421 04 V. Frolunda.

Designwerkstatt Berlin c/o Christian Borngräber, Yorckstrasse 88d, 1000 Berlin 61, West Germany.

Deweer NV 6 Tiegemstraat, Otegem 8562, Belgium.

Disform 63 Rda. Gral. Mitre, 08017 Barcelona, Spain. *Outlets* France: Edifice, 27 bis Boulevard Raspail, 75007 Paris. Italy: Design and Design, 5 Via F. Witgens, 20123 Milan. Japan: Eishin Trading Co Ltd, 6-5 Morishita Chome-3, Koto Ku, 135 Tokyo. The Netherlands: AMDA Frans Stroosnijder, 37 Oosterhoutlaan, 1181 Al Amstelveen. Scandinavia: Design (J.J. Lassagne), Dobelnsgatan 38A 1TR, 11352 Stockholm. UK: Maison Designs (Retail) Ltd, 917-19 Fulham

Road, London SW6 5HU. USA: EDEAS, 1 West 64 Street, New York, NY 10023. West Germany: ALTECO, Postfach 56, 8021 Schaftlarn.

Driade SPA Via Padana Inferiore 12, 29012 Fossadello di Caorso, Piacenza, Italy. *Outlets* Belgium: Espaces et Lignes, 55 Rue Ulens, Brussels. France: Arturo Del Punta, 7 Rue Simon Lefranc, 75004 Paris. Japan: Arflex Trading Inc, 2-9-8 Higashi, Shibuya-Ku, Tokyo 105. Scandinavia: Design Distribution, 38 A 1TR Doebelnsg., 11352 Stockholm, Sweden. USA: Modern Living, 4063 Redwood Avenue, Los Angeles, CA 90066. West Germany: Klaus Stefan Leuschel, 2 Beethovenstrasse, 6000 Frankfurt/Main 1.

Dunnigan Co. PO Box 428, West Kingston, Rhode Island 02892, USA.

Edizioni de Padova 14 Corso Venezia, Milan 20121, Italy. *Outlets* Japan: Casatec Ltd, 9-6 Hipashi 2-Chome, Shibuya-Ku, Tokyo. The Netherlands: Koos Rijkse, Pr. Christinelaan, 7437 X2 Bathmen. Spain: Idea Meuble S.A., Via Auguste 185, Barcelona. USA: International Contract Furnishings Incorporated, 305 East 63rd Street, New York, NY 10021. West Germany: Habit, 44, Sürderstrasse, 509 Leverkusen 22.

Edra SPA Via Toscana 11, Perigano 56030, Pisa, Italy.

Elam Via Molino 27, 20036 Meda, MI, Italy.

Elisée Editions 19 Rue de Bassano, 75008 Paris, France. *Outlet* France: Mangau, 153 Avenue Jean Jaures, 93300 Aubervilliers.

ENEA Poligono Industrial S/N, Legorreta, Gipuzkoa, Spain. *Outlets* France: BBL Diffusion, 6 Place Maréchal Leclerc, 35400 St. Malo. Scandinavia: Claes Bauer, Box 30545, S-20062 Malmö, Sweden. West Germany: Flototto Handels, Ringstrasse 38-40, 4835 Rietberg 2.

Equator Productions 21 Aachenerstrasse 21, 5000 Cologne 1, West Germany. *Outlet* Belgium: Ranbir Singh, 114 Avenue Holiere, 1060 Brussels.

Eveready Australia Pty Ltd 30 Harcourt Parade (PO Box 11), Rosebery, NSW 2018, Australia. *Outlets* Canada: Eveready Battery Co., Canada, 6300 Northam Drive, Mississauga, Ontario L4V 1H7. Malaysia: Eveready Battery Co., Malaysia, Regent Hotel, 3rd Floor, Jalam Imbi, Ismail, Kuala Lumpur. USA: Eveready Battery Co. Inc., Checkerboard Square 106A, St. Louis, 63164 Missouri.

Fiam Italia SPA Via Ancona 1/13, 61010 Tavullia, PS, Italy. *Outlet* UK: Casa Bianchi, Roslyn House, Sun Street, Hitchin, Herts. SG5 1AE.

La Ferronerie d'art 12 Rue Gaudray, 92170 Vanvef, France.

50's AutoArt 8060 Monrovia, Lenexa, Kansas, USA. *Outlets* France: Atomic Jukebox, 7 Rue Laromiguiere, 75005 Paris. USA: Car's The Star, Crown Center Shops 202, 2450 Grand Avenue, Kansas City, MO 64108.

Fiskars Oy Ab Billnäs 10330, Finland. *Outlets* Belgium: 17 Panoramalaan, 3110 Rotselaar. France: Fiskars SARL, 374 Rue de Vaugirard, 75015 Paris. The Netherlands: Fiskars Nederland BV, 2a Kellenseweg, 4004 JD Tiel. Spain: Bra SA, 9, 3 Carretera Calatell KM, Sant Boi de Llobregat, Barcelona. UK: Fiskars Ltd, Brocastle Avenue, Waterton Industrial Estate, Bridgend, Mid Glamorgan CF31 34N, Wales. USA: Fiskars Manufacturing Corp., 7811 W. Stewart Avenue, WAUSAU, 54402-8027 Wisconsin. West Germany: Wilhelm Boos Jr. GmbH & Co., 311-15 Mangenberger Strasse, 5650 Solingen 1.

Flos SPA Via Moretti 58, 25121 Brescia, BS, Italy. *Outlets* Belgium: Flos SA, Gossetlaan 50, B-1720 Groot-Bijgaarden. France: Flos SARL, 23 Rue de Bourgogne, 75007 Paris. Japan: Flos Co. Ltd, Dowa Building 4F, 18-18 Roppongi 5-Chome, Minato-Ku, Tokyo. Spain: Flos SA, c/ Bovedillas 16, San Just Desvern, 08960 Barcelona. Switzerland: Flos SA, 1204 Genève, 36 Place du Bourg de Four. UK: Flos Ltd, The Studio, 120 High Street, South Milford, Leeds LS25 5AQ. USA: Flos Inc., 200 McKay Road, Huntington Station, New York, NY 11746. West Germany: Flos GmbH, Am Probsthof 94, 5300 Bonn 1.

Fontana Arte SPA Alzaia Trieste 49, 20094 Corsico, Italy. *Outlets* Austria: Einrichtungs-Verkaufs GmbH Co KG, 27 Hagenstrasse, 4020 Linz. Belgium: M. Frank PVBA, 25 Wijngaardstraat, 2000 Antwerp. Canada: Angle International, 296 St Paul West, Montreal. France: Giuseppe Cerutti, 1 Loc Grand Chemin, 11020 Aosta, Italy. The Netherlands: Silvera BV, Postbus 163, 1250 AD Laren. Switzerland: Formatera AG, 54 Stockerstrasse, 8022 Zürich. USA: Interna Designs Ltd, The Merchandising Mart, Space 6-168, Chicago, IL 60654. West Germany: Fr. Von Der Beck, 52 Bahnhofstrasse, 3472 Beverungen 1.

Franke SPA 2 Via Pignolini, Peschiera del Garda 37019, Verona, Italy.

Gallery 91 91 Grand Street, New York, NY 10013, USA.

Geeco Gore Road Industrial Estate, New Milton, Hampshire BH25 6SE, UK.

David Gill 60 Fulham Road, London SW3 6HH, UK.

Richard Ginori SPA Via Pio La Torre 4-C, 20090 Vimodrone, Milan, Italy. *Outlet* UK: ICTC, Unit 2, Worton Industrial Estate, Fleming Way, Isleworth, Middlesex.

Giorgetti SPA 20 Via Manzoni, Meda 20036 MI, Italy. *Outlets* Japan: Sansei Kosan Co. Ltd, 5-1 Nishi-Azabu 3 Chomi, Minato-Ku, Tokyo. The Netherlands: Giorgetti Benelux BV, 11 Smidswater, 2514 B.W. Den Haag. Scandinavia: Inside, Box 7689, Stockholm, Sweden. Spain: De La Prida, 5 Colmenares, 28004 Madrid. UK: Intermobel Ltd, Ward Street, Guildford, Surrey GU1 4NA. USA: Designer Imports Int. Inc., 4202 W. Jefferson Boulevard, Los Angeles, California 90016. West Germany: Buero Klaus Hoehne, 16 Murrer Strasse, 7141 Steinheim, Murr.

The Glasshouse 65 Long Acre, London WC2, UK.

Grundig Elektrogeräte GmbH Kurgartenstr. 37, 8510 Fürth, Bayern, West Germany. *Outlets* France: Grundig France SA, 33-35 Boulevard de la Paix, 78104 Saint Germain-en-Laye. Italy: Melchioni SPA, Via P. Colletta 37, 20135 Milan. The Netherlands: Grundig Nederland BV, Ind. gebiet Amstel, Joan Muyskenweg 22, 1007 AB Amsterdam. Scandinavia: Scan Electgro AS, Knud Bryns Vei 10, 0581 Oslo 5, Norway. Spain: Inter Grundig Comercial SA, Traversa de las Corts 312-314, Barcelona 14. UK: Grundig International Ltd, Millroad, Rugby, Warwickshire CV2 1FR.

Grupo T SA 37 Casanova, Barcelona 08011, Barcelona, Spain. *Outlets* Belgium: Tradix SA, 104 Av. Louis Lepoutre, 1006 Brussels. France: Sommet SA, Le Bourg, Serbannes, 03110 Escurolles. The Netherlands: AMDA BV, 37 Oosterhoutlaan, 1181 AL Amstelveen. Scandinavia: Pasta Lab. 54 Duevej, Copenhagen, Denmark 2000. UK: Maison Designs, 917-19 Fulham Road, London SW6 5HU. West Germany: Traudel Comte, 1 Alfred Drexel Str., 8000 Munich 50.

Hakusan Porcelain Co. Ltd Uchinomi, Hasami-Machi, Nagasaki-Ken, Japan.

Fritz Hansen 3450 Allerød, Denmark.

Herlitz AG 10-17 Reuchlinstrasse, 1000 Berlin 21, West Germany.

Matthew Hilton 87 Shrubland Road, London E8, UK. *Outlet* Japan: Kiya Gallery, 9-2 Sarugaku-Cho, Shibuya-Ku, Tokyo.

IDEA SPA Ville Cantamerla, 82 Via Ferrero di Cambiano, 10024 Moncalieri, Turin, Italy. *Outlets* Japan: Mitsui & Co., 2-1 Othemachi 1-Chome, Chiyoda-Ku, Tokyo. Spain: c/o Sircom SA, Núñez de Balboa 118, 28006 Madrid. USA: 34442 Jefferson, Unit 27B, Mt. Clemens, Michigan 48045. West Germany: I.V.S. Industrieberatungen C. Schmid, Schlosstrasse 77, 7000 Stuttgart 1.

Idée 5-4-44 Minamiaoyama, Minato-Ku, Tokyo 107, Japan.

Idiom Argus Building, Elizabeth & Latrobe Street, Melbourne, 3000 Australia.

IDM 7-8 Jeffreys Place, Jeffreys Street, London NW1 9PP, UK.

Ikea of Sweden AB 34300 Almhult, Sweden.

Infocus Systems 7649 S.W. Mohawk Street, Tualatin, 97062 Oregon, USA.

Intent 27 Llull, Barcelona 08005, Spain. *Outlets* France: B.B.L. Diffusion, 6 Place Maréchal Leclerc, Saint Malo 35400. Japan: Tanifuji Co. Ltd, 1-6-7 Shinyokohama-Cho Kohoku-Ku, Kanagawa-Ken 222. Scandinavia: Palk, 72A Drottninggatam, Helsingborg 25003 Sweden. USA: Domus Massini Inc., 123 Townsend Street, Suite 470, San Francisco, California 94107. West Germany: Kare, 10 Augustenstrasse, 8000 Munich.

InterProfil GmbH Karl Theodor Strasse 91, 8000 Munich 40, West Germany.

Ishimaru Co. Ltd 202 Maison Akashi, 7-3-24 Roppongi, Minato-Ku, Tokyo, Japan.

Itoki Co. Ltd 15-1 Shibuya 2-Chome, Shibuya-ku, Tokyo 150, Japan. *Outlets* USA: 89 Fifth Avenue, New York, NY 10017. West Germany: Königinstrasse 43, 8000 Munich.

Dakota Jackson Inc. 306 East 61st Street, New York, NY 10021, USA.

Kartell SPA Viale delle Industrie 1, 20082 Noviglio, Milan, Italy. *Outlets* Australia: Plastex, 85 Fairbank Road, 3168 Clayton, Victoria. Austria: Eugen Leopold, 19 Grunauerstrasse, 4020 Linz. Belgium: Tradix SA, 104 Avenue Louis Lepoutre, 1060 Brussels. France: Marais International Group, 5 Rue du Faubourg St. Antoine, 75011 Paris. Japan: Kartell Japan Co. Ltd, Dowa Building 4F, 18-18 Roppongi, 5-Chome, Minato-Ku, Tokyo 106. The Netherlands: Modular Systems, Assumburg 73-1, 1081 GB Amsterdam. Scandinavia: John Anker, 6 Esplanaden 1263 Copenhagen, Denmark. Spain: Grupo T SA, 37 Casanova, Barcelona 08011. Switzerland: Piermilio Gatto, 3 Ch. des Graviers, 2016 Cortaillod. UK: Ideas for Living, Lin Pac Mouldings, 5 Kensington High Street, London W8 5NP. USA: Canada: Kartell USA, PO Box 1000, Easley SC 29640.

Kenwood Manufacturing Ltd New Lane, Havant, Hampshire PO9 2NH, UK. *Outlets* Austria: Kenwood Manufacturing GmbH, Erzherzog Karl Strasse 57, 1-1221 Wien. France: Société Kenwood France, 14-16 Avenue de Stalingrad, Zone Industrielle 94262, Fresnes Cedex. New Zealand: Kenwood Appliances Ltd, 560 Rosebank Road, Auckland 7. Scandinavia: Thorn Kenwood A/S, Brogrenen 8, 2635 Ishoj, Copenhagen. South Africa: Kenwood Home Appliances Pty Ltd, PO Box 43425, Industria 2042.

Kjaer & Hinz Glasvaerkstedet 34B Kronprinsessegade, Copenhagen 1306 K, Denmark.

Koch + Lowy 21-24 39th Avenue, Long Island City, NY 11101, USA.

George Kovacs Lighting Inc. 24 West 40th Street, New York, NY 10018, USA.

Leitner Interior Design Leitnersiedlung 1, St. Lambrecht 8813, Austria. *Outlets* Belgium: L. Kreymborg Belgie N.V., Av. Molière Laan 66, 1180 Brussels. Canada: Macvista Importing Inc., 1657 Bayview Avenue, Toronto, Ontario M4G 3C1. France: Protis, 153 Rue du Faubourg Saint-Honoré, 75008 Paris. Hong Kong: Le Cadre Gallery, 8 Sunning Road G/F, Causeway Bay. Japan: European-Asian Trade Service Company Ltd, Daimon Sano Bldg. 5 F, 1-1-35 Shiba Daimon, Minato-ku, Tokyo 105. The Netherlands: Binnen, Egelantiersgracht 31, 1015 RC Amsterdam. Scandinavia: Möbelgalleri Anna, Övre Husargatan, 32, 14 Göteborg, Sweden. Singapore: Abraxas Designs Pte. Ltd, 300 Orchard Road, 02-01 The Promenade, Singapore 0923. USA: City, 213 West Institute Place, Chicago, IL 60610; Current, 1201 Western Avenue, Seattle, WA 98104; Inside, 838 G Street, San Diego, CA 92101; Limn, 457 Pacific Avenue, San Francisco, CA 94133; Modern Living, 4063 Redwood Avenue, Los Angeles, CA 98104. West Germany: Rudolf Brombeiss, Rotmoosstrasse 15, 8990 Lindau; Heribert Ertl, Wittelsbacher Strasse 9, 8068 Pfaffenhofen/Ilm; R.V. Kunze & Partner, Gartenstrasse 14, 3061 Luhden.

Leser Design Inc. 499 Adelaide Street West, Toronto, Ontario M5V 1TA, Canada.

Lindberg Optik Design Frederiksgade 2, 8000 Aarhus C, Denmark. *Outlets* France: Pierre Marly Opticien, 25 Rue Royale et 50 Rue François 1er, 75000 Paris. The Netherlands: Visser & Noorman, Energiweg 7, 9743 An Groningen. Switzerland: Bartschi & Co., Zeitglockenlaube 4, 3000 Berne 7. USA: Kentucky Optical Company, Post Box 1063, Louisville, KY 40201.

Lombardi Inc. 2264-146 Caminito Pajarito, San Diego, California 92107, USA.

Lombardi Project SPA 80 Via Papa Giovanni XXIII, Rezzato, Brescia 25086, Italy.

Lumiance BV 155 Oudweg, PO Box 6310, 2001 HH Haarlem, The Netherlands. *Outlets* Australia: Lumiance Pty Ltd, 53 Coppin Street, Richmond, Victoria 3121. Austria: Zumtobel AG, 8 Hochsterstrasse, PO Box 72, 6850 Dornbirn. Belgium: Lumiance NV, 249 Staatsbaan, 9780 Zulte. Denmark: Uniline National AS, 10 Sankt Knudsvej, 1903 Copenhagen. Finland: Lumiance OY, 50 Kulosaaren Puistotie, PO Box 20, 00570 Helsinki. France: Lumiance, 4 Rue Sadi Carnot, 93170 Bagnolet. Iceland: Interco SF, 17 Sidumula, PO Box 8635, 128 Reykjavik. Italy: Lumiance Italia, Via delle More 1, 24030 Presezzo, Bergamo. Norway: Lumiance Norge AS, 33 Vagsgt., 4300 Sandnes. Portugal: Tecnicon SARL, 40-A-40-C Avenue do Brasil, 1700 Lisbon. Spain: Ildo SA, 21 C de la Sofora, 28020 Madrid. Sweden: Marelco AB, 16 Askims Verksradsvag, PO Box 30070, 40043 Göteborg. Switzerland: Regent Beleuchtungskorper AG, 390 Dornacherstrasse, 4018 Basel. UK: Lumiance, Tetbury Hill, Malmesbury, Wiltshire SN16 9JX. USA: Basic Concept, 141 Lanza Avenue, Garfield, New Jersey 07026. West Germany: Lumiance GmbH, 48 Feldheider Strasse, 4006 Erkrath 2.

Marieta Textil SA 15 Ballester, 08023 Barcelona, Spain. *Outlet* UK: Inhouse, 28 Howe Street, Edinburgh, Scotland.

Marimekko 4 Puusepänkatu, 00810 Helsinki, Finland.

Nani Marquina 3 C. Bonavista, 08012 Barcelona, Spain. *Outlets* France: Marie Bacou, 200 Rue La Fayette, 75010 Paris. Italy: Tisca, Via Donizetti 6, 24050 Lurano, Bergamo. Switzerland and West Germany: IMD, Franz Baars, 26 Eebrunnestrasse, 5212 Hausen AG, Switzerland.

J. & F. Martell Diffusion 18 Rue Royale, 75008 Paris, France.

Massplast Via Merulo 1, Reggio Emilia 42100, Italy.

Matsushita Electric Co. Ltd 4-1-62 Minoshima, Hakata-Ku, Fukuoaka, Japan.

Mazzei SPA 80 Livornese Est, Perignano, Pisa 56030, Italy. *Outlets* Sweden: Unicum Hans Sinee, Thorburnsgatan 5, Box 141 52, S-400 20 Göteborg. Switzerland: Intercollection Haseli AG, Churerstrasse 18, 8808 Pfäffikon.

Antoon Meerman 19 Mueller Street, Yarralumca, ACT 2600, Australia.

Teppichfabrik Melchnau AG 4917 Melchnau, Switzerland. *Outlets* Austria: Einrichtungshandel, Ing. Manfred Prunnbauer, Seizergasse 10, 1150 Wien. Belgium: Bureau Roger C. van Oppens, Bieve des plns 54, B-1420 Braine-L'Alleud. Italy: Sergio Maria Parisi, Proposto d'Arte, C. so Matteotti 106, 20038 Seregno. Japan: Massomi Unagami, Unac-Tokyo, 1-1-20-112 Azabudai, Minato-Ku, Tokyo. Switzerland: Theo Jakob AG, Gerechtigkeitsgasse 23, 3011 Berne; Wohnbedarf AG Basel, Aeschenvorstadt 48, 4010 Basel; Wohnshop SA, Rue Neuve 8, 1000 Lausanne; Zona Inneneinrichtungen, Sladelhoferstrasse 28 C, 8001 Zürich. West Germany: Licht und Raum Design, Albertusstrasse 26, 5000 Köln 1; Cubus, Kantsstrasse 141, 1000 Berlin; Frick, Goethestrasse 19, 6000 Frankfurt A/M 1; Beckmann Internationale Möbel, Klosterstern 4, 2000 Hamburg 40; Focus, Leopoldstrasse 87, 8000 München 40; 3 F. Design, Calverstrasse 26, 7000 Stuttgart.

David Mellor Design Ltd Broom Hall, Broomhall Road, Sheffield, South Yorkshire S10 2DR, UK.

Memphis SRL Via Olivetti 9, 20010 Pregnana Milanese, Italy. *Outlets* Australia: Artemide Pty Ltd, 69 Edward Street, Pyrmont, NSW 2009. Austria: Prodomo, 35-7 Flachgasse, 1150 Wien. Belgium: Horas SA, 25 Beemdstraat, 1610 Ruisbroek. Canada: Artemide Ltd, 354 Davenport Road, Designers Walk, 3rd Floor, Toronto, M15 RK5. France: Roger von Bary, 18 Rue Lafitte, 75009 Paris. Hong Kong: Le Cadre Gallery, 8 Sunning Road G/F, Causeway Bay. The Netherlands: Copi, 90A Prinsestraat, 2513 CG, Den Haag. Scandinavia: Renzo d'Este, 1A Brodrevej, 2860 Söborg, Copenhagen, Denmark. Switzerland: Bell'Arte C. Arquint, 13 Loostrasse, 6430 Schwyz. UK: Artemide GB Ltd, 17-19 Neal Street, London WC2H 9PU. USA: Memphis Milano, International Design Center, Center One, Space 525, 30-30 Thomson Avenue, Long Island City, NY 11101. West Germany: Agentur Brunnbauer, 51 Ehmckstrasse, 2800 Bremen 33.

Carl Mertens Krahenhöher Weg 8, 5650 Solingen, West Germany.

Metalarte SA Avda. de Barcelona 4, 08970 Saint Joan Despi, Barcelona, Spain. *Outlets* France: Electroama, 11 Boulevard St. Germain, 75006 Paris. The Netherlands: Hooge Products, 12 Bebers Pijken, 5221 ED Hertogenbosch. UK: Direct Light Ltd, 275 Fulham Road, London SW10 9PZ. USA: California Artup Corporation, 3000 Shanon, Santa Ana, CA 92704; Hansen Lamps Inc., 121 East 24th Street, New York, NY 10010. West

Germany: Altalinea, 6 Sandhof, 4040 Neuss 21 Norff.

Metropolitan Furniture Corp. 245 East Harris Avenue, South San Francisco, California 94080-6807, USA. *Outlets* Australia/New Zealand: Michael Statham Interiors Ltd, Nat West House, 132 The Terrace, PO Box 3177, Wellington, New Zealand. UK and Europe: Seid International, Fabriksvej 15c, 5467 Rojle, Denmark.

Migoli Studios Karlsviksgatan 10, 11241 Stockholm, Sweden.

Miyashin Co. Ltd 582-11 Kitano-Machi, Hachioji-Shi, Tokyo 192, Japan.

Mobles 114 Enric Granados 114, 08008 Barcelona, Spain.

Modular SA 4070 Elpidio González, 1407 Buenos Aires, Argentina.

Ter Molst 40 Molstenstraat, Oostrozebeke 8780, Belgium.

Mondo SRL Via Vittorio 25, 22060 Carugo, Italy. *Outlets* Austria: Wolfgang Bischoff, Judenplatz 6, 1010 Wien. Belgium: Rika Andries, 144B Turnhoutsebaan, Borgerhout 2200. France: Giuseppe Cerutti, Loc. Grand Chemin 1, 11020 Saint Christophe AO, Italy. The Netherlands: Koos Rijkse Agency, P.R. Christinalaan 1, 7437 XZ Bathmen. Spain: Jose Martinez Medina SA, Camino del Bony S/N, Catarroja Valencia. Sweden: Mobile Box AB, Hargs Saeteri, 19490 Upplands Vasby. Switzerland: Yves Humbrecht Diffusion, Salève 10, 1004 Lausanne. UK: Essential Business Contacts, Lawnfield House, Westmorland Road, Maidenhead, Berkshire SL6 4HB. West Germany: Novus, 26 Gartenstrasse 26, 7959 Achstetten 3.

Jasper Morrison 16a Hilgrove Road, London NW6, UK.

Thomas Muller 150 Kantstrasse, 1000 Berlin 12, West Germany.

Néotù 25 Rue du Renard, 75004 Paris, France. *Outlets* Italy: Dilmos, Via Solferino, 20121 Milan. Japan: Shibuya, Seibu Department Store, Tokyo. Switzerland: Gallery Margine, Stampfenbachstrasse 59, 8006 Zürich. UK: Ikon, B5L Metropolitan Wharf, Wapping Wall, London E1 9SS. USA: Furniture of the 20th Century, 227 West 17th Street, New York.

Nikon Corporation Fuji Building, 2-3-Marunouchi 3-Chome, Chiyoda-ku, Tokyo 100, Japan. *Outlets* Australia: Maxwell Optical Industries Pty Ltd, Unit 5, Level B, 100 Harris Street, Pyrmont 2009, NSW. Austria: Prihoda & Beck GmbH, 1072 Wien Schottenfeldgasse 14, PO Box 104. Belgium & Luxembourg: H. De Beukelaer & Co., Peter Benoitstraat 7-9, 2108 Antwerp. Canada: Nikon Canada Inc., 1366 Aerowood Drive, Mississauga, Ontario, L4W 1C1. France: Nikon France SA, 16 Rue de la Cerisaie, B.P. 33, 94222 Charenton-le-Pont, Cedex. Italy: Konos SPA, Via Ticino 12-14, Osmannoro, Florence. The Netherlands: Nikon Europe BV, Schipolweg 321, 1171 PL Badhoevedorp. UK: Nikon UK Ltd, Nikon House, 380 Richmond Road, Kingston, Surrey

KT2 5PR. USA: Nikon Inc., 623 Stewart Avenue, Garden City, New York, NY 11530.

Nippon Sanso KK (Japan Oxygen Company Limited) 1435 Simonakano, Yoshida City, Nishi-kanbara-gun, Niigata-ken, Japan.

Noto Via Vigevano 8, 20144 Milan, Italy. *Outlets* France: Protis, 77-101 Av. du Vieux Chemin St. Denis, 92230 Gennevilliers. Japan: Ambiente International Inc., Sumitomo Seimei Bldg. 3-1-30, Minamiaoyama, Minato-Ku, Tokyo 107. The Netherlands: Surplus PBVA, Zwarte Zusterstraat 9, 9000 Ghent. Scandinavia: Decasa, Hyskenstraede 3, 2, 1207 Copenhagen, Denmark. Spain: Casimiro Fernandez, Urbanizacion Soto de Llanera Casa Nr. 5, Pruvia, Llanera, Asturias. Switzerland: Schreinerei Anderegg AG, Olensbachstr. 7, 9631 Ulisbach, Toggenburg. UK: Aram Designs Ltd, 3 Kean Street, London WC2B 4AT. USA: Modern Age Galleries Ltd, 795 Broadway, New York, NY 10003. West Germany: Quartett GmbH, Haupsstr. 95, 3004 Isernhagen F.B.

Nunco Co. Ltd 5-6-17 Axis B1 Roppongi, Minato-ku, Tokyo, Japan.

Nuova Vilca Loc. Gracciano, Colle Val D'Elsa, Siena 53034, Italy.

Oakbrook Esser Studios 129 East Wisconsin Avenue, Oconomowoc, Wisconsin 53066, USA.

Magnus Olesen AS Rosleu 7870, Denmark. *Outlets* Belgium: Mobica PIBA, 50 Gosselaan, Groot-Bijgaarden 1720. France: MDM/SEID International, 10 Boulevard des Batignolles, 75017 Paris. Japan: Royal Furniture Collection, Co-op Broadway Center, Room 1003, 5-52-15 Nakano, Nakano-Ku, Tokyo 164. The Netherlands: Bax Meubelagenturen, 45 Fruitenierstaat, 3334 Kazwijndrecht. UK: Scandia Furniture Group, Dorton Park, Dorton, Aylesbury, Bucks. HD18 9NR.

Oluce SPA Via Cavour 52, 20098 San Giuliano Milanese, Italy. *Outlets* France: Horas, 150 Rue Championnet, 75018 Paris. Japan: Arflex Trading, 2-9-8 Higashi Shibuya-Ku, Tokyo 150. The Netherlands: Carlo Wanna, 14 Houtkopersstraat, 3330 AJ Zwijndrecht. Norway: Martens, 18 Nobelsgate, Oslo 2. Sweden: Inside Gallerian, 37 Hamngatan, 10395 Stockholm. UK: London Lighting, 135 Fulham Road, London SW3 6RT. USA: Lighting Associates, 305 East 63rd Street, New York, NY 10021. West Germany: Floetotto Handelsagentur, 38-40 Ringstrasse, 4835 Rietberg.

Omniate Ltd c/o Branson Coates Architecture, 23 Old Street, London EC1V 9HL, UK.

One-Off Ltd 39 Shelton Street, London WC2, UK.

Svend Onø 19 ST TH, Judithsvej, Hellerup 2900, Denmark.

Oun Corporation 7-12-14 Minami-Aoyama Minato-ku, Tokyo 107, Japan.

Owo Chemin du Val, 78490 Montfort L'Amaury, France. *Outlets* Austria: Die

Kommode, Lerchenselderstrasse 12A, 1400 Wien. Belgium & Holland: Espaces et Lignes, Rue Ulenstraat 55, 1210 Brussels. Japan: Idée, 5-4-44 Minamiaoyama, Minatoku, Tokyo 107. Scandinavia: Design Distribution, Dobelnsgatan 38-A-1TR S/11352, Stockholm, Sweden. Spain: BD Ediciones, 291 Mallorca, 08037 Barcelona. UK: Ikon Corporation, BSL Metropolitan Wharf, Wapping Wall, London E1 9SS.

Pallucco SRL Via Salaria 1265, 00138 Rome, Italy. *Outlets* Belgium: Tradix, 104 Avenue Louis Lepoutre, 1060 Brussels. France: Ready Made, 40 Rue Jacob, 75006 Paris. Japan: Arc International Isugarucho, Kamanzadori, Nakagyo-Ku, Kyoto 604. The Netherlands: Hansje Kalff, 8 Puttenstraat, 1118 JE Amstelveen. West Germany: Abitare, 3-5 Auf dem Berlich, 5000 Cologne 1.

Elio Palmisano Edizioni Tessili Via Stra Madonna, PO Box 142, 21047 Saronno, VA, Italy.

Pastoe BV Rotsoord 3, 3523 CL Utrecht, The Netherlands. *Outlet* UK: Royalty Studio, Lancaster Road, London W11.

Perobell Av. Arraona 23, 08205 Sabadell, Barcelona, Spain.

G.B. Plast San Benedetto Val Di Sambro, Bologna, Italy.

Philips NV Building SX, PO Box 218, 5600 MD Eindhoven, The Netherlands. *Outlets* Austria: Österreichische Philips Industrie GmbH, 64 Triester Strasse, 1100 Wien. Belgium: NV Philips, 2 De Brouckëreplein, PO Box 218, 1000 Brussels. Denmark: Philips Elapparat AS, 80 Pragsboulevard, 2300 Copenhagen. East Germany: Philips GmbH, Unternehmensbereich Haustechnik, 19 Kilianstrasse, 8500 Nürnberg. Finland: OY Philips AB, 8 Kaivokatu, Helsinki. France: SA Philips Industrielle et Commerciale, 50 Avenue Montaigne, 75380 Paris. Italy: Philips Italia SA, Piazza IV Novembre 3, 20100 Milan. Japan: Philips Industrial Development and Consultants Co Ltd, Shuwa, Shinagawa Building, 26-33 Takanawa 3-Chome, Minato-Ku, Tokyo 108. Norway: Norsk AS Philips, PO Box 5040, 6 Soerkedaksveien, Oslo 3. Spain: Philips Iberica SAE, 2 Martinez Villergas, Apartado 2065, 28027 Madrid. Sweden: Philips Norden AB, 115 84 Stockholm. UK: Philips Electrical and Associated Industries Ltd, Arundel Great Court, 8 Arundel Street, London WC2 3DT. USA: North American Philips Corporation, 100 East 42nd Street, New York, NY 10017. West Germany: Allgemeine Deutsche Phillips Ind. GmbH, 94 Steindamm, 2000 Hamburg.

Polaroid Corporation 565 Technology Square, Cambridge, MA 02139, USA.

Poltrona Frau SPA SS77 KM 74, 500, 62029 Tolentino, Macerata, Italy. *Outlets* France: Poltrona Frau France SARL, 242 bis Boulevard St. Germain, 75007 Paris. The Netherlands: Poltrona Frau Benelux, 9 Parkstraat, 4818 SJ Breda. Switzerland: Seleform AG, 8 G. Maurerstrasse, 8702 Zollikon. USA: Poltrona Frau USA Corp., 14 East 60th Street, New

York, NY 10022. West Germany: Andreas Jaek, 3 Neuestrasse, 2900 Oldenburg.

Porcelanas del Bidasoa SA Barrio de Ventas, 20300 Irun, Guipuzcoa, Spain. *Outlets* Italy: Cuoma & Censi SPC, Via G. Jan. 2, 20159 Milan. UK: Barbecco Ltd, Goldwell House, Bath Road, Newbury, Berkshire RG13 1JH.

Portfolio The Coach House, Gate Burton, Nr. Gainsborough, Lincolnshire DN21 5AY, UK. *Outlets* UK: Viaduct Furniture Ltd, South Building, Spring House, Spring Place, London NW5. USA: Modern Age, 795 Broadway, New York, NY 10003.

Porzellanfabrik Arzberg Postfach 1241/42, 8594 Arzberg, West Germany. *Outlets* France: Intertrade France Z.I. Mitry Mory, Rue Gay Lussac, 77290 Mitry Mory. Italy: Corrado Corradi, Via Medici del Vascello 8, 20138 Milan. Japan: Hutschenreuther AG/Japan Office, c/o Vaubel & Partners Ltd, Ark Mori Building 22nd Floor, 12-32, Asaka 1-Chome, Minato-Ku, Tokyo 107. The Netherlands: Schott-Zwiesel Glas en Kristall BV, Postbus 83, 2050 AB Overveen. Scandinavia: Hutschenreuther Skandinavien A/S, Bella Center, Center Boulevard 5, 2300 Copenhagen S, Denmark. Spain: Enrique Riera, Vilamari 72, 08016 Barcelona. UK: Barbecco Ltd, Goldwell House, Bath Road, Newbury, Berkshire RG13 1JH. USA: Hutschenreuther Corporation, 41 Madison Avenue, 26th Street, Room 14 C, New York, NY 10010. West Germany: Porzellanfabrik Arzberg, Jakobsburg 1-7, 8594 Arzberg.

Louis Poulsen & Co 11 Nyhavn, Copenhagen 1001K, Sealand, Denmark. *Outlets* France: Louis Poulsen cie SARL, 9 Rue Coypel, 75013 Paris. USA: Louis Poulsen Lighting Inc., 5407 NW 163rd Street, Miami, 33014-6130 Florida.

PP Møbler 30 Toftevej, Allerød 3450, Denmark. *Outlets* The Netherlands: P.A. Hesselman, 284 P.J. Oudstraat, W.J. Papendrecht 2354. Scandinavia: Bennick of Scandinavia, 22B Vallensbakvej, Glostrup 2600, Denmark; Carl Magnus Heigard, 134 Danderydsvägen, Djursholm 18265, Sweden. USA: DSI, PO Box D, Croton on Hudson, New York 15020. West Germany: Peter Biehl, 46 Parkstrasse, 6252 Diez-Lahn.

Product M 500-2 No, Gyôda-shi, Saitama-Ken 361, Japan.

Punt Mobles Islas Baleares, 48 Pol. Ind. Fte. del Jarro, 46980 Paterna, Valencia, Spain. *Outlets* Austria: Otto Dunkelblum, Herrengasse 6/7/3, 1010 Wien. Denmark: Frank Rasmussen, Hummeltoften 49, 2830 Virum. France: Dominique Devoto, 47 Rue Henri Barbusse, 75224 Paris Cedex 05. Italy: C & C Distribuzione, Località Grand Chemin 1, 11020 Saint Christophe, Aosta. The Netherlands: AMDA, Oosternoutlaan 37, 1181 AL Amstelveen. Scandinavia: Sten Bergstroem, Liljekovanjens Wag 9, 13200 Saltsjo-boo, Sweden. Switzerland: Claudia Marlier-Pollo, Rebbergstrasse 40, 8102 Oberengstringen. UK: Maison Design Ltd, 917-19 Fulham Road, London SW6 5HU. USA: Susana Macarron Imports, 934 Grayson

Street, Berkeley, California 94710. West Germany: Traudel Comte, Alfred Drexel Str. 1, 8000 Munich 50.

Reisenthel Program 3 Benzstrasse, Puchheim, 8039 München, West Germany.

Rosenthal AG 18 Casinostrasse, Postfach 1520, 8672 Selb, Bayern, West Germany. *Outlets* Australia: Rosenthal Australia Pty Ltd, 520 Collins Street, 9th Floor, GPO Box 2029S, Melbourne, Victoria 3001. Canada: Rosenthal China (Canada) Ltd, 55 East Beaver Creek Road, Unit 6, Richmond Hill, Ontario L4B 1E5. France: Rosenthal Porcelaines-Cristaux SARL, 50 Rue de Paradis, 75484 Paris Cedex 10. Italy: Rosenthal Studio-Line, Via Rubattino 4, 20134 Milan. Japan: Rosenthal Tokyo Liaison Office, OAG Haus, Room 405, 5-56 Akasaka 7-Chome, Minato-Ku, Tokyo. The Netherlands: Rosenthal Benelux BV, 1 Porcelainstraat, PO Box 1006, Maastricht. Scandinavia: Rosenthal Skandinavien Försäljnings AS, Box 5289, 51 Karlvägen, 10246 Stockholm, Sweden. Spain: Porcelaines-Cristaux, 32 General Person, Planta 25, Madrid 20. Switzerland: Rosenthal Schweiz AC, 734 Badenerstrasse, 8048 Zürich. UK: Rosenthal China (London) Ltd, 3 Abercorn Trading Estate, Bridgewater Road, Alperton, Wembley, Middlesex HA0 1BD. USA: Rosenthal USA Ltd, 6636 Metropolitan Avenue, Middle Village, NY 11379.

Argenteria Sabattini SPA Via Don Capiaghi 2, 22070 Bregnano, Como, Italy. *Outlets* Japan: New Robin Co Ltd, 2-11 2-Chome, Kajimachi, Kokurakita-Ku, 802 Kitakyushushi-Fukuoka. The Netherlands: Mobica PVBA, Gossetlaan 50, 1720 Groot, Bijaard. UK: Objects, 49 Parliament Street, Harrogate, North Yorkshire HG1 2RE. USA: Italarte, 4203 West Alamos 106, Fresno, CA 93711. West Germany: Sabattini Deutschland, 50 Kennedyallee, Frankfurt A/M.

Salviati & Co. Fondamenta Radi 16, 30141 Murano, Venice, Italy. *Outlets* USA: Hampstead, 19772 Macarthur Boulevard Suite 203, Irvine, 92715 California. West Germany: Graf Bethusy, 2 Hans Sachs Strasse, 8033 Krailling.

Santa & Cole Santisima Trinidad Del Monte 10, 08017 Barcelona, Spain. *Outlets* Austria: Ronni Kufferle, 7 Rennagasse, 1010 Vienna. Italy: Roberto Sorba, 29/5 Corso Chieri, Turin 10132. The Netherlands: Binnen, 82 Keizersgracht 82, 1015 CT Amsterdam. West Germany: Susanne Wirth, 168 Herbeusstraat, 6211RH Maastrich.

Sasaki Crystal 41 Madison Avenue, New York, NY 10010, USA.

Sasaki Glass Co. Ltd 2-2-6 Nihonbashi-Bakurocho, Chuo-Ku, Tokyo, Japan.

Sawaya & Moroni Via Manzoni 11, 20121 Milan, Italy.

Scarabat Ctra de Benifasar 11, 43560 La Senia, Tarragona, Spain. *Outlets* Belgium: Tradix SA, Avenue Louis Lepoutre 104, 1060 Brussels. France: France Printemps, 102 Rue de Provence, 75009 Paris. Spain: Galerias Vincon, Paseo de Gracia 96, 08008 Barcelona.

UK: Ikon Corporation, B5L Metropolitan Wharf, Wapping Wall, London E1 9SS. USA: Furniture of The Twentieth Century, 227 West 17th Street, New York, NY 10011; Pacific Design Center, 8687 Melrose Avenue, West Hollywood, CA 90069. West Germany: D-Tec Industriedesign, Telleringstrasse 5, 4000 Düsseldorf.

SCP Ltd 135-39 Curtain Road, London EC2A 3BX, UK. *Outlets* France: Fenêtre sur Cour, 57 Rue de Vaugiraud, 75006 Paris. Italy: Cappellini SPA, 7 Via Cavour, 222060 Carugo. Japan: Kiya Gallery, 19 Frognal, 9 Saragaku-Cho, Shibuya-Ku, Tokyo. The Netherlands: Domani Designs BV, Singel 90, 1015 AD Amsterdam. Scandinavia: Rupert Gardner AB, Slottsvagen 43, Nasey Park 18352 Taby, Sweden. Singapore: Abraxas Designs Pty. Ltd, 300 Orchard Road, 0201 The Promenade, 0923 Singapore. Spain: Pilma, Valencia 1, Diagonal 403, Barcelona. USA: Modern Age, 795 Broadway, New York, NY 10003. West Germany: Naefke & Co., Eppendorfer Landstrasse 60, 2000 Hamburg 20.

Sedie & Co. 24 Via Borgheria, Pesaro 61100, Italy.

Sisal Via Emilia Pavese 107, 29100 Piacenza, Italy.

Skipper SPA 1 Via Serbelloni, 20122 Milan, Italy. *Outlets* Belgium: Skipper Benelux, 78 Avenue Louise, 6069 Brussels. France: Gennaro Dellisanti, 17 Rue des Closeaux, 77240 Vert St. Denis. The Netherlands: Koos Rijkse, Tr. Christinalaan 1, 7437 XZ Bathmen. UK: Atrium Ltd, 22-24 St. Giles High Street, London WC2H 8LN. West Germany: Rohoff Edgar, Reinhard Hoppe Str. 6-8, 6900 Heidelberg 25.

Solar Belysning A/S Industrivej Vest, Vejen 6600, Denmark. *Outlets* Austria: Sonja Kubatsch Modern Lichtelemente, 12 Hickelgasse 1140 Vienna. Finland: SLO Idman OY, PL4, SF-04501 Mäntsälä. The Netherlands: Indoor, 22-24 Paulus Potterstraat, 1071 Amsterdam. Norway: A/S Solar Belysning, 25 Drengsrudbekken Postbox 363, 1371 Asker. Scandinavia: Ljusgruppen AB, Box 9131, 20039 Malmö, Sweden. Switzerland: Regent Beleuchtungskörper, 390 Dornacherstrasse, 4018 Basel. UK: Thorn Lighting, Trinity House, 284 Southbury Road, Enfield, Middlesex EN1 1TJ. West Germany: Concord GTE Licht GmbH, 2 Zeissstrasse, Cologne 2, 5000 Lövenich.

Solid 62 Via Guzzanica, Stezzano 24040, Bergamo, Italy.

Sony Corporation 6-7-35 Kitashinagawa, Shinagawa-Ku, Tokyo 141, Japan.

A/S Stelton PO Box 59, Gl. Vartov vej 1, Hellerup 2900, Denmark. *Outlets* Australia: G. & C. Ventura, GPO Box 1034, Sydney, 2001 NSW. Austria: O. & S. Dunkelblum, Herrengasse 6/7/3, 1010 Wien. Belgium & Luxembourg: Tradix SA, 104 Avenue Louis Lepoutre, 1060 Brussels. Canada: Danesco Inc., 18111 Trans Canada, Kirkland, Montreal, H9J 3K1 Quebec. Finland: Korhonen ØY, Ulvilantie 29/3 K370, 00350 Helsinki. France: Anc. Ets. Martin SA/Melior, 49 Rue Ernest

Renan B.P. 13, 94201 Ivry-sur-Seine. Greece: Agelco SA, 19 Stadiou Str., 10561 Athens. Holland: P. Andriessen BV, Postbus 9, 4286 ZG Almkerk. Hong Kong: Deeko International Ltd, 12/F Min Yip Bldg., Jervois St. 69. Iceland: Kristjan Siggeirson Ltd, PO Box 193, 101 Reykjavik. Israel: Danish Plus, 3 Tuyoat Haretz St., Shikun Dan, 69866 Tel Aviv. Italy: G. Wiedenmann & C.S.A.S., Via delle Stelline 9, 20146 Milan. Japan: J. Osawa & Co. Ltd, Shibaura 4-2-8, Minato-ku, 108 Tokyo. New Zealand: Andrew Hawley Ltd, PO Box 27-121, Wellington. Norway: Royal Copenhagen Norge A/S, Pilestredet 15, 0164 Oslo 1. Singapore: D. Scan Furniture Ltd, 19 Jurong Port Road, Singapore 22. Spain and Andorra: Pasaje Gayola 24 bajos, 08013 Barcelona. Sweden: Royal Copenhagen Svenske AB, Vastra Hamngatan 12, 41117 Göteborg. Switzerland: Leutwiler AG, Buttenenhalde 38, 6006 Lucerne. UK & Ireland: Storrington Trading Ltd, PO Box 32, Chichester, West Sussex PO19 4FD. USA: Stelton USA Inc., 223 East 78 St., New York, NY 10021. West Germany: Drabert Agency, Musterhaus am Messekreisel, Deutz-Mulheimer-Str. 30, 5000 Cologne 21.

Sugahara Glass Corporation 4-33-13, Tachibana, Sumida-ku, Tokyo, Japan.

Sunstar Incorporated 3-1 Asahi-Machi, Takasuki, Osaka 596, Japan.

Swid Powell 213 E 49th Street, New York, NY 10021, USA. *Outlets* France: Au Bain Marie, f10 Rue Boissy D'Anglas, 75008 Paris. Japan: Yojiro Grotori, Index Collection, Suite 2A, 3-8-26 Nishiazabu, Minato-Ku, Tokyo. Spain: BD Ediciones de diseño, Calle Mallorca 291, 08037 Barcelona. West Germany: Restform, Weibelshidestrasse 40, 5760 Arnsberg 1.

Tacu Bolivar 1219, Buenos Aires 1141, Argentina.

Tebong 3 Rue du Maine, 35133 Landean, France. *Outlets* France: Academy, 5 Place de l'Odéon, 75006 Paris. Japan: Wilmotte Japon, Oishi Compound, 2-7-1 Shiroganedai, Minato-Ku, Tokyo 108. UK: Mary Fox Linton Ltd, 249 Fulham Road, London SW3 6HY. USA: Mirak Inc., 3461 West Alabama, Houston, Texas 77027.

Tecta Axel und Werner Bruchhäuser KG, Sohnreystrasse, 3471 Lauenforde, West Germany. *Outlets* France: Nova Distribution San, Cit Tour de Montparnasse, 3 Rue de l'Arrivée, BP 258, Bureau 833, 75749 Paris Cedex 15. Italy: FAI SRL Internazionale, Casella Postale n.70, 20033 Desio MI. Japan: Actus Corp., 2-1-13 Shibuya, Shibuya-Ku, Tokyo 150. The Netherlands: Herrn Ton J. de Geus, Gondel 17/23, 8243 BV Lelystad. Scandinavia: Inside, Box 7689, 10395 Stockholm; P. Thorsen Möbler, H.H. Seedorffs Straede 1-5, 8100 Arhus C, Denmark. Spain: BD Ediciones, c/Mallorca 291, Barcelona 08037. USA: Melodrom Ltd, 525 Broadway 8th Floor, New York, NY 10012. West Germany: Marianne Bruchhäuser, Staustr. 13, 2900 Oldenburg; Alfred Reik, Ulrichstr. 32, 7320 Göppingen.

Gebrüder Thonet GmbH 1 Michael-Thonet-Str., Frankenberg 3558, Hessen, West Germany.

Thonet/Madison PO Box 5900, Statesville, North Carolina 28677, USA.

Tisettanta SPA 96 Via Furlanelli, Giussano 20034, Milan, Italy.

Toshiba Corporation 2-15 Soto-kanda 1-Chome, Chiyoda-ku, Tokyo, Japan.

Toulemonde Bochart Z.I. de Villemilan, 14-16 Boulevard Arago, 91320 Wissous, France.

Toyo Sasshi Co. Ltd 2-2-2 Uchisaiwaicho, Chiyoda-ku, Tokyo, Japan.

Transtam 63 Mariá Cubi, 08006 Barcelona, Spain.

J. Tresserra Design SL 42 calle Freixa, Barcelona 08021, Spain. *Outlets* France: Biobject, 6 Rue Domat, Paris 75005. Japan: Akane International, 5-10-15 Higashinakano, Nakano-Ku, Tokyo. UK: Mary Fox Linton Ltd, 249 Fulham Road, London SW3 6HY.

Ultima Edizione Via Angelini 20, 54100 Massa, Italy.

Up & Up SRL Via Acquale 3, 54100 Massa, Italy. *Outlets* Austria & Germany: Giovanni Marelli, Casella Postale 148, 20036 Meda Milan, Italy. Belgium: Trueno, 78 OL Vrouwstraat, 2800 Mechelen. Canada: Marble Trend, Unit 3, 2050 Steeles Av. W., Dowsview, Ontario. France: Roger von Bary, 18 Rue Lafitte, 75009 Paris; Studio Enea, 2 Place St. Sulpice, 75006 Paris. Germany: Andrea Mazza, Berenger Mark 12, 4300 Essen Bredeney. Japan: Everfast Ltd, Iwoki Bldg 9-6-12 Akasaka, Minato-Ku, Tokyo; Joint Inc., Daikanyama-Parkside-Vill. 207-9-8, Sarugakucho, Shibuya-Ku, Tokyo 150. USA: Inside, 715 5th Street, San Diego, California 92101; Italdesign Center Inc., 8687 Melrose Avenue Suite 547, Los Angeles, California 90069; Design Studio Inter. Inc., 908 Linden Avenue, Winnekta, Illinois 60007; Frederich Williams, 200 Lexington Avenue, New York, NY 10016; Modern Living, 4063 Relwood Avenue, Los Angeles, California 90066.

Vanini Via Rovereto 7, Vimercate, Italy. *Outlets* Austria: Die Kommode, Lerchenfelderstrasse 12, 01080 Wien. Belgium: Sonja Vanhee Agencies, Leffingerstraat 60, 84100 Oostende. Canada East: Angle International, 296 Ouest Rue S. Paul, Montreal, Quebec H2Z 2A3. Canada West: Infor Contract Inc., 200-134 Abbott Street, Vancouver, B.C. V68 2K4. Denmark: Finn Sloth, Heilsmindevej 1, 2920 Charlottenlund. France: Edifice, 27 bis Boulevard Raspail, 75007 Paris. Greece: Maria e Thani Korda, Analipseos 22 Panorama, 55236 Salonica. Hong Kong: Le Cadre Gallery, 8 Sunning Road G/F, Causeway Bay. Italy: Imago SNC, Giovanni XXIII 2, 20057 Vedano al Lambro, Milan; Andrea Balia, Sigmund Freud 40, 80131 Naples; Rolando Malaguti, Lungo Po Antonelli 127, 10153 Turin; Carlo Parlanti, 6 Verdi 8, 51011 Borgo A Buggiano, Pisa; Gianni Bondavalli, Pzza Bertazzolo 4, 46100

Mantova; Andrea Ricco, D. Morelli 53, 95125 Catania. Japan: Casatec Ltd, 2-9-6 Higashi, Shibuya-Ku, Tokyo 150. The Netherlands: Domani Design By, Singel 90, 1015 AD Amsterdam. Scandinavia: Design Distribution, Dobelnsgaten 38/A1, 110352 Stockholm. Singapore: Businessworld Services Pte Ltd, Abraxas Designs, Unit 01-01 Shing Kwan House, 4 Shenton Way, 0106 Singapore. Switzerland: RGM di Gambi Mario Snc, Cesare Battisti 23, 48100 Ravenna, Italy. UK: Maison Designs, 917-19 Fulham Road, London SW6 5HU. USA: Repertoire, 207 South Street, Boston, MA 02111.

Veart SPA 23 Via Moglianese, Venezia Scorze 30037, Italy.

Venini SPA Fondamenta Vetrai, 50, 30141 Murano, Venezia, Italy. *Outlets* France: Jean Gabriel Robin, 36 Allée des Trailles, 69960 Corbas, Lyon. The Netherlands: Kees Biermans, Parkstraat 9, 4818 SJ Breda, Holland. Scandinavia: Erik Rosendhal A/S, Lundtoftevej 1/C, 2800 Lyngby, Copenhagen. Switzerland: Guido Mayer SA, 9 Route du Port Franc, 1003 Lausanne. USA: Hampstead Investments Inc., 19772 MacArthur Blvd., Suite 203, Irvine, CA 92715. West Germany: Graf Bethusy-Huc Vertriebs, Hans Sachs Strasse 1, 8033 Krailling.

Vereinigte Werkstätten 31 Ridlerstrasse, 8000 Munich, West Germany. *Outlets* France: Nova Distribution SARL, CIT Tour de Montparn, Bureau 883, BP 258, 75749 Paris-Cedex 15. The Netherlands: Bob Smit, 52 Jasonstraat, Amsterdam. Scandinavia: Finn Sloth, 1 Heilsmindevej, 2920 Charlottenlund, Denmark. UK: Aram Designs Ltd, 3 Kean Street, London WC2B 4AT.

VIA 10 Place Sainte Opportune, 75001 Paris, France.

Villeroy & Boch 46 Rieffstrasse, 6640 Merzig, West Germany.

Vitra International AG 15 Henric Petri Strasse, Postfach 257, 4010 Basel, Switzerland. *Outlets* France: Vitra SARL, 59 Avenue d'Iena, 75116 Paris. The Netherlands: Vitra Nederland BV, 527 Strawinskylaan, 1077 XX Amsterdam. UK: Vitra Ltd, 13 Grosvenor Street, London W1X 9FB. USA: Vitra Seating Inc., c/o Stendig International Inc., 305 East 63rd Street, New York, NY 10021.

Vorwerk & Co. Teppichwerke KG Kuhlmannstrasse 11, 3250 Hameln 1, West Germany.

Louis Vuitton Malletier 78 bis Avenue Marceau, 75008 Paris. *Outlets* Austria: Kohlmarkt 16, 1010 Wien. Australia: 63 Castlereagh Street, Sydney 2000. Belgium: Avenue Louise 25, 1050 Brussels. Germany: Maximilianstrasse 21, 8000 Munich 2. Hong Kong: Peninsula Hotel, E2-E4 East Arcade, Salisbury Road, Kowloon. Italy: Via Monte Napoleone 14, 20121 Milan. Kuwait: Salhia Commercial Complex, PO Box 21074 Safat, 13071, Safat. Portugal: Rua Augusta 196, 1100 Lisbon. Scandinavia: 3 Ny Ostergade, 100 Copenhagen, Denmark. Spain: Ortega y Gasset 17, 28006 Madrid. Switzerland: 40 Rue du Marché, 1204 Geneva. UK: 149 New Bond Street, London W1Y 9FE. USA: 433 North Rodeo Drive, Beverly Hills, California 90210; 51 East 57th Street, New York, NY 10022.

Franz Wittmann KG 3492 Etsdorf/Kamp, Austria. *Outlets* France: Horas International, 150 Rue Championnet, 75018 Paris. Italy: Wittmann Italia SRL, Via E. Filiberto 10, 45011 Adria, RO. The Netherlands: Art Collection BV, 63 Weijland, 2415 Nieuwerbrug. Scandinavia: Inside Galleria, 37 Hamnagatan, 11147 Stockholm, Sweden. UK: MW United Ltd, 19 Dacre Street, London SW1 0DJ. USA: Stendig International, 410 East 62nd Street, New York, NY 10021. West Germany: Franz Wittmann KG, 20a Königstrasse, 6729 Wörth.

Wogg AG im Grund 16, 5405 Baden-Dättwil, Switzerland. *Outlets* Japan: Nova Oshima, 9-6-

14 Akasaka, Minato-Ku, 107 Tokyo. UK: HNB Systems, Whittington House, 19-30 Alfred Place, London WC1E 7EA. USA: Cumberland Furniture Corp., 36 36th Street, Long Island City, NY 11106.

Woka Lamps Vienna 16 Singerstrasse, 1010 Wien, Austria. *Outlets* France: Altras, Roger von Bary, 18 Rue Lafitte, 75009 Paris. Italy: Marina de Nardo, Via Lincoln 41, Milan. Scandinavia: Ide Individuell, 8 Norra Liden, 41118 Göteborg, Sweden. UK: MW United Ltd, 16 Dacre Street, London SW1H 0DJ. USA: George Kovacs Inc., 24 West 40th Street, New York, NY 10018.

Xo 3 Avenue Charles de Gaulle, 94475 Boissy St. Leger Cedex 5, Paris, France. *Outlets* Austria: Die Kommode, Lerchenfelderstrasse 12, 1080 Wien. Belgium: Espaces et Lignes, Rue Ulens Straat 55, Brussels 1210. Hong Kong: Le Cadre Gallery, 8 Sunning Road, Causeway Bay. Italy: Cappellini International Interiors SNC, Via Cavour 7, 22060 Carugo, Como. Japan: Eternal, 3F Nakajima, 3-17-15 Nishiazabu, Minatoku Tokyo. The Netherlands: Espaces et Lignes, Nassaulaan 2A, 2514 Den Haag. Portugal: Tradingpack, Larg Eng Antonio de Almeida 70, 4100 Porto. Singapore: Abraxas Designs, 4 Shenton Way, 01-01 Shing Kwang House, Singapore 0106. Spain: Disform, Rda. Gral. Mitre. 63. Sweden/Scandinavia: Design Distribution, 2 Dobelnsgatan 38A, 11352 Stockholm. Switzerland: as West Germany. UK: Ikon, B5L Metropolitan Wharf, Wapping Wall, London E1 9SS. West Germany: Leuschel/Leonardt, Beethovenstrasse 2, 6000 Frankfurt A/M.

Xylos 5 Cité de la Roquette, 75011 Paris, France.

Yamada-Heiando 3-10-11 Nihonbashi, Chuo-Ku, Tokyo, Japan.

Yamagiwa Corporation 4-1-1 Sotokanda, Chiyoda-ku 101, Tokyo, Japan.

Zanotta SPA Via Vittorio Veneto 57, 20054 Nova Milanese, Italy. *Outlets* Australia: Arredorama International Pty Ltd, 1 Ross Street, Glebe, NSW 2037. Austria: Prodomo, 35-37 Flachgasse, 1060 Wien. Belgium: Zaira Mis, 35 Boulevard Saint Michel, 1040 Brussels. France: Giuseppe Cerutti, 1 Località Grand Chemin, St Christophe 11020, AO, Italy. Japan: Nova Oshima Co. Ltd, Sakakura Building, Akasaka Minato-Ku 9-6-14, Tokyo. The Netherlands: Hansje Kalff, 8 Puttensestraat, 1181 JE Amstelveen. Denmark: Paustian, 2 Kalkbraendrilbskaj, 2100 Copenhagen. Norway: Bente Holm, 64 Parkveien, Oslo 2. Spain: BD Ediciones de diseño, 291 Mallorca, 08037 Barcelona. Switzerland: Peter Kaufmann, 123 Rychenbergstr, 8400 Winterthur. Sweden: Inside, 37 Hamngatan, 11147 Stockholm. UK: The Architectural Trading Co. Ltd, 219-29 Shaftesbury Avenue, London WC2H 8AR. USA: International Contract Furnishings, 305 East 63rd Street, New York, NY 10021. West Germany: Fulvio Folci, 14 Dahlienweg, 4000 Düsseldorf 30.

Industrie Zanussi SPA 3 Via Giardini Cattaneo, Pordenone 33170, Italy. *Outlets* Austria: Iaz Elektrogeraete GmbH, Markhofgasse, 19, 1034 Wien. Belgium: Electrolux Belgium NV, Bergensesteenweg 719, 1520 Halle, Lembeek. Denmark: Zanussi Danmark A/S, Lino Zanussivej, 6360 Tinglev. France: Iaz International France, 52-56 Rue Emile Zola, Montreuil Cedex 93107. The Netherlands: Zanussi Nederland, 1 Vennootsweg, Alphen A/D Rijn, 2400 AA. Norway: Zanussi A/S, P.Boks 4064, Gulskogen, 3002 Drammen. Spain: Ibelsa, Sociedad Anonima, 25 Augustin de Foxa, 28036 Madrid. Sweden: AB Electrolux, Luxbacken 1, Lilla Essingen, S105 45, Stockholm. UK: Zanussi Ltd, Zanussi House, Hambridge Road, Newbury, Berkshire RG14 5EP. West Germany: Zanussi Elektrogeraete GmbH, 72-74 Rennbahnstrasse, Frankfurt A/M Niederrad 73.

ACQUISITIONS

BY DESIGN COLLECTIONS IN 1988
Dates given in brackets refer to the dates of the designs (from 1960 to the present day).

France

Musée des Arts Décoratifs, Paris

Martine Bedin Salt and pepper pots, manufactured by Algorithme, France.
Alain Begou Vase (1988).
Andrea Branzi Coffee cup and saucer, *Tatzine* (1986). Tea cup and saucer, *Tatzone* (1986).
Jean-Pierre Caillères Table, *Papyrus* (1987). Armchair (1987).
P. Charpin Sugar basin and milk jug, manufactured by Algorithme, France.
Emmanuel Collin Chair, *Arbre tronc* (1983). Water jug and glasses, *Isis* (1988), manufactured by Cristallerie De St Louis, France.
S. Dubuisson Chafing dish, manufactured by Algorithme, France.
Nathalie Du Pasquier Tea pot, manufactured by Algorithme, France.
Vladimir Jelinek Vase (1969).
Nemo Cheese board and knife, manufactured by Algorithme, France.
Nestor Perkal Fruit bowl, manufactured by Algorithme, France.
Christophe Pillet Candlestick, manufactured by Algorithme, France.
Denis Rivière Fabric (1987).
Bruno Rosenweig Serving dish, manufactured by Algorithme, France.
Jaromir Rybak Vase (1988).
George Sowden Vase, manufactured by Algorithme, France.
Roger Tallon Tableware, *3 T* (1970).
Jean-Paul Wilmotte Chair (1986).

Israel

The Israel Museum, Jerusalem

De Pas, D'Urbino and Lomazzi Chair, *Blow* (1967), manufactured by Zanotta, Italy.
Talia Kiriaty and Iris Paz Lamp (1984), manufactured by One to One Design, Tel Aviv, Israel.
Leo Lionni Jewish ceremonial candle holders (1986), manufactured by Gino Cenedese e Figlio, Murano, Italy.
Bruno Munari Table, *Biplano* (1972); *Libreria* (1973); *Vademecum* (1974); sofa, *Divanetta* (1986), all manufactured by Robots, Italy. Screen, *Spiffero* (1988), manufactured by Zanotta, Italy.
David Palterer *Fauno* (1987), manufactured by Zanotta, Italy.
Ettore Sottsass Mirror, *Ultrafragola* (1968), manufactured by Dilmo, Italy. Armchair, *Westside* (1983); table, *Central Park* (1983); table, *Spyder* (1986); chair, *Mandarin* (1986), all manufactured by Knoll International, USA. Sideboard, *Beverly* (1981); room divider, *Carlton* (1981); table lamp, *Tahiti* (1981); sideboard with cupboard, *Malabar* (1982); fruit

bowl, *Murmansk* (1982); vase, *Mizar* (1982); vase, *Alcor* (1983); vase, *Alioth* (1983); vase, *Nilo* (1983); vase, *Euphrates* (1983); *Tartar* (1985); salad plate, *Indivia* (1985); dinner plate, *Lettuce* (1985); dinner plate, *Rucola* (1985); side table, *Ivory* (1985); vase, *Agelada* (1986); vase, *Ananke* (1986); vase, *Clesitera* (1986); fruit bowl, *Fillila* (1986); vase, *Neobule* (1986), all manufactured by Memphis, Italy.
Marianne Stokholm and Gad Zorea Wall telephone, *Kirk Plus* (1987), manufactured by Alcatel Kirk, Denmark.
Oscar Tusquets Blanca Chair, *Gaulino* (1987), manufactured by Carlos Jané, Spain.
Lidia Zavadsky Plant holders (1986).

The Netherlands

Museum Boymans van Beuningen, Rotterdam

Archizoom Associati Chair, *Mies* (1968–70), manufactured by Poltronova, Italy.
Mario Bellini Stereo set, *RR 130* (1971), manufactured by Brionvega, Italy.
Norman Foster Furniture, *Nomos* (1986), manufactured by Tecno, Italy.
Paolo Parigi Drawing table (1972); chair, *Polo Dattilo* (1975); stool, *Brett* (1985), all manufactured by Heron Delta, Italy.
Dieter Rams Tape recorder, *TG60*; pick up, *Audio 2/3*; pick up, *TC20* (1963), all manufactured by Braun, West Germany.
Bořek Šípek Glasses (1983, 1984), manufactured by Anthologie Quartett, West Germany. Glasses (1985, 1986), manufactured by Sussmüth, West Germany.
Jean Pierre Vitrac Toothbrushes, pens, pipes, cutlery (1981–86), by several Japanese manufacturers.

UK

The Victoria and Albert Museum, London

L. Daehlin Teapot (1988), Norway
English Eccentrics Furnishing fabrics, *Gaudi*, *Gaudi-Stripe*, *Gaudi-Crackle*, *Not in Arcadia* (1987).
Lucy Goffin Quilt, *Apertures* (1987).
Vase (1988), manufactured by A. J. Jutrem, Norway.
Karen Klim Dish, *From the Bottom of the Sea* (1987), Norway.
Teapot (1973), manufactured by W. R. Midwinter, UK.
Leif Porsgrund Tea set (1985), Norway.
George Sowden, Nathalie Du Pasquier et al Furnishing fabrics (1980–88); carpets, *Domino*, *Tressel* (1986), all manufactured by Memphis, Italy.
Furnishing fabrics (1987), manufactured by Timney-Fowler, UK.
V & A Collection Historic furnishing fabrics (1988), manufactured by Habitat, UK.
Bjorn Wiinblad Tureen (1972), Denmark.
Eva Zeisel Jug (1984), manufactured by P. Hesz Zsolney.
Vacuum flask, manufactured by Alfi Zitzmann, West Germany.

USA

The Metropolitan Museum of Art, New York

Archizoom Associati Armchair, *Aeo* (1988), manufactured by Cassina, Italy.
Gae Aulenti Lamp, *Patrocio* (1976), manufactured by Artemide, Italy.
Mario Bellini Table lamp, *Area 50* (1976), manufactured by Artemide, Italy. Armchair, *Cab* (1978); armchair, *Break* (1976), both manufactured by Cassina, Italy. Tray (1980), manufactured by Cleto Munari, Italy.
Norbert Berghoff, Michael Landes, Wolfgang Rang Armchair, *Frankfurter Stuhl F III* (1985–86), manufactured by Draenert, West Germany.
Ricardo Bofill Textile, *Venise, Eau de Pluie* (1986), manufactured by Brochier-Soiries.
Mario Botta Armchair, *Seconda* (1982), manufactured by Alias, France. Lamp, *Shogun* (1986), manufactured by Artemide, Italy. Water and wine carafes (1986), manufactured by Cleto Munari, Italy.
Achille Castiglioni Goblets (1983); carafe and five tumblers, *Paro & Ovio* (1983), all manufactured by Danese, Italy.
Livio Castiglioni Lamp (1970), manufactured by Artemide, Italy.
Joe Colombo Armchair, *Model 4801/5* (1965), manufactured by Kartell, Italy.
Michele De Lucchi Carafe (1980), manufactured by Cleto Munari, Italy.
Frank Gehry Lounge chair (1982), manufactured by Easy Ednes, USA.
Ernesto Gismondi Lamp, *Sintesi* (1976), manufactured by Artemide, Italy.
Michael Graves Armchair (1985), manufactured by SunarHauserman. Wristwatch (1987), manufactured by Cleto Munari, Italy.
Gruppo Architetti Urbanistici Città Nuova Lamp, *Nesso* (1967), manufactured by Artemide, Italy.
Hans Hollein Compote (1980); wristwatch (1987), both manufactured by Cleto Munari, Italy.
Arata Isozaki Wrist-watch (1987), manufactured by Cleto Munari, Italy.
Hisatoshi Iwata Vase (1979), manufactured by Iwata Glass Co., Japan.
Toshichi Iwata Vase (1975–76); jar with lid (1970), both manufactured by Iwata Glass Co., Japan.
Henry and Eleanor Kluck Fabrics, *Wanderlust* (1960), *Sargasso* (1962), *Haven* (1963), *Nile Grass* (1964), *Vinery* (1968), *Antigua* (1969), *Woodbine* (1969), *Tide* (1971), *Floriance* (1972), *Exx* (1973), *Pebble Beach* (1974), *Terra Vista* (1976), *Forest* (1977), *Water's Edge* (1978), *Borealis* (1979), all manufactured by Elenbank Designers, USA.
Shiro Kuramata Armchair, *How High the Moon* (1986), manufactured by Vitra International, Switzerland.
Masayuki Kurokawa Wrist-watch, *Rabat* (1985), manufactured by Citizen Watch Co. Table lamp, *Demani* (1976), manufactured by

the Nippon Light Company, Japan. Armchair, *Ingot Batta* (1975).
Pjote Leonow Teacups and saucers (1975), manufactured by Dulevo Factory.
Vico Magistretti Table, *Demetrio* (1988); armchair, *Vicario* (1971), both manufactured by Artemide, Italy.
Sam Maloof Settee (1987).
Enzo Mari Desk set, *Colleoni* (1970); container with spoon (1970); vase (1969); vase, *Trifoglio* (1969); vases, *Bambu* (1969), all manufactured by Danese, Italy.
Bruno Munari Tray (1960), manufactured by Danese, Italy.
V. Perelli Tea kettle (1980–86), manufactured by Dansk International Designs, USA.
Gaetano Pesce Armchair, *Sit Down* (1976), manufactured by Cassina, Italy.
Jens Quistgaard Candleholder, *Spider* (1962); ice bucket (1988); tumblers, *Forum* (1988); cutlery, *Odin* (1988); cutlery, *Tjorn* (1988), all manufactured by Dansk International Designs, USA.
Elsa Rady Vase, *Cold Rolled Steel/Double Triangles* (1987).
Richard Sapper Clock, *Tantalo* (1988); lamp, *Tizio* (1973), both manufactured by Artemide, Italy.
Afra and Tobia Scarpa Chair, *925* (1966), manufactured by Cassina, Italy.
Carlo Scarpa Carafe (1977); compote (1977); cutlery (1977), all manufactured by Cleto Munari, Italy.
Ettore Sottsass Lamp, *Pausania* (1983), manufactured by Artemide, Italy. Wristwatch (1987), manufactured by Cleto Munari, Italy. Chair, *Synthesis 45* (1972); candlestick, *Silvershade* (1986), both manufactured by Swid Powell, USA.
Shigeru Uchida Armchair, *September* (1973), manufactured by Build Co., UK.
Robert Venturi Mirror, *Mirror in the Greek Revival Manner* (1983), manufactured by Formica Corporation, USA. Textile, *Tapestry* (1984), manufactured by Knoll International, USA.
Tassilo Von Grolman Tea pot with stand and tray, *Mono* (1982), manufactured by Mono-Metallwarenfabrik, West Germany.

The Museum of Modern Art, New York

Karin Andersen Cutlery (1979).
Nickie and William Campbell Infant's bottle (1983).
Joe Colombo Stacking side chair (1967).
Johannes Foersom and Peter Hiort-Lorenzen Folding newspaper holder (1981).
Norman Foster Associates Dining table, *Nomos* (1987), manufactured by Tecno, Italy.
Frank Gehry Lounge chair, *Bubbles* (1987).
Enzo Mari Wastepaper baskets, *Chio* (1986).
Ingo Maurer Adjustable lighting system, *Ya Ya Ho* (1983–84).
Gaetano Pesce Chair, *Felt* (1986).
Emma Schweinberger Umbrella stand, *Dedalo* (1966).
Olaf Von Bohr Clothes hooks (1972).

The Philadelphia Museum of Art

Frank Gehry Side chair (1972).
Oskar Kogoj Cutlery (1972), manufactured by Rino Greggio Argenterie, Italy.
Vignelli Designs Side chair, *Handkerchief* (c. 1985), manufactured by Knoll International, USA.

West Germany

Kunstmuseum, Düsseldorf

Alessandro Mendini Armchair, *Poltrona di Proust* (1978); chair, *Sedia redesign Breuer* (1979).
Alessandro Mendini and Studio Alchimia Cupboard, *Vetrina Mobile Infinito* (1981).
Ettore Sottsass Lamp, *Lampada Svincolo* (1979).

Museum für Angewandte Kunst, Cologne

Martine Bedin Lamp, *Super* (1981), manufactured by Memphis, Italy.
Mario Bellini Typewriter, *Divisumma 18* (1973); typewriter, *Logos 68* (1973), both manufactured by Olivetti, Italy.
Norbert Berghoff, Michael Landes, Wolfgang Rang Wardrobes, *Frankfurter*

Schrank I and *II* (1986), manufactured by Draenert, West Germany.
Mario Botta Chairs, *Seconda* (1982) and *Quinta* (1985), manufactured by Alias, Italy.
Achille Castiglioni Oil and vinegar bottles (1980–84), manufactured by Alessi, Italy. Table, *Servomuto* (1974–75), manufactured by Zanotta, Italy.
Achille and Pier Giacomo Castiglioni Ceiling lamp, *Black and White* (1965), manufactured by Flos, Italy.
Joe Colombo Floor and table lamp, *Spider* (1965), manufactured by Oluce, Italy.
Studio Dape Table lamp, *Nefti* (1976), manufactured by Dipa.
Hartmut Esslinger Television, *Wegacolor 3020* (1971), manufactured by Wega-Radio, West Germany.
Gatti, Paolini & Teodoro Chair, *Sacco* (1968–69), manufactured by Zanotta, Italy.
Michael Graves Kettle, *9093* (1985), manufactured by Alessi, Italy.
Perry A. King, Santiago Miranda and G. Arnaldi Table lamp, *Donald* (1979), manufactured by Arteluce, Italy.
Toshiyuki Kita Chair, *Wink* (1980), manufactured by Cassina, Italy.
Willie Landels Chair, *Throw-away* (1965), manufactured by Zanotta, Italy.
Vico Magistretti Table lamp, *Atollo* (1977),

manufactured by Oluce, Italy.
Peter Maly Chair, *Zyklus* (1984), manufactured by Cor.
Più Manzu and P. Hamburger Hanging lamp, *Parentesi* (1970), manufactured by Flos, Italy.
Enzo Mari Doorstop (1962); fruit bowl (1965); ashtray (1967); bowls (1969); desk tidy (1970), all manufactured by Danese, Italy.
Ingo Maurer Table lamp, *Giant Bulb Clear* (1967); ceiling lamp, *Light Structure* (1969–70); table lamp, *Tsching II* (1979); table lamp, *Glatzkopf* (1981), all manufactured by Design M Ingo Maurer, West Germany.
Bruno Munari Bowl (1960), manufactured by Danese, Italy.
Paolo Pallucco and Mireille Rivier Chair, *Hans e Alice* (1986), manufactured by Pallucco, Italy.
Maurizio Peregalli Chairs, *Poltroncino* (1984) and *Savonarola* (1984), manufactured by Zeus, Italy.
Gaetano Pesce Chair, *Sit-down* (1975– 76), manufactured by Cassina, Italy.
Aldo Rossi Espresso machine, *La Conica* (1982–84); kettle, *Il Conico* (1984–86); coffee machine, *Pressofilter* (1986), all manufactured by Alessi, Italy.
Richard Sapper Espresso machine *9090/6* (1979); kettle *9091* (1983), both manufactured by Alessi, Italy. Table lamp, *Tizio* (1971),

manufactured by Artemide, Italy.
Tobia Scarpa Table lamp, *Perpetua* (1981), manufactured by Flos, Italy.
Ettore Sottsass Oil and vinegar set (1978), manufactured by Alessi, Italy. Bookcase, *Carlton* (1981), manufactured by Memphis, Italy. Bookcase, *Cantone* (1981), manufactured by Zanotta, Italy.
Ettore Sottsass and Perry A. King Typewriter, *Valentine* (1969), manufactured by Olivetti, Italy.
Ettore Sottsass and Hans Von Klier Typewriter, *Praxis 48* (1964), manufactured by Olivetti, Italy.
Philippe Starck Light, *Tippy Jackson* (1982); chair, *Costes* (1982), both manufactured by Driade, Italy.
Superstudio Table, *Quaderna* (1970–71), manufactured by Zanotta, Italy.
Wolfgang Tolk Floor lamp (1986–87).
Frans Van Niewenborg and Martin Wegman Wall lamp, *Delight* (1979), manufactured by Design M Ingo Maurer, West Germany.
Hans Wegner Sofa (1965), manufactured by Knoll International, USA.
Stefan Wewerka Chair, *B 1* (1979), manufactured by Tecta, West Germany.
Kasumasa Yamashita Coffee and tea service, *Tea and Coffee Piazza* (1983), manufactured by Alessi, Italy.

DESIGN PUBLICATIONS

Australia

Belle (monthly) Showcase for contemporary Australian architecture and interior design, with a product round-up that includes many imported design influences.
Design World (quarterly) Technical and educational articles covering the design world in the Antipodes.
Interior Design (bi-monthly) Dedicated to decoration, with a mixture of articles on avant-garde designs and traditional interiors.
Vogue Living (ten issues a year) Lively, glossy lifestyle magazine on decoration and design.

Denmark

Arkitekten (bi-monthly) and **Arkitektur** (every six weeks) Edited by the Danish Architectural Press for the professional federations of architects and building contractors.
Bo Bedre (monthly) Translates into English as "Live Better," precisely the editorial policy behind this consumer home-interest magazine.
Design from Scandinavia (annual) For the past 17 years, a useful index of designers and manufacturers against a background of illustrated stories of architectural interest.
Living Architecture (bi-annual) Scandinavia's best-looking glossy magazine on buildings and their interiors, both old and new, by the celebrated photographer and architect Per Nagel. Published with English text.
Rum og Form (annual) "Space and Form," edited by the Danish Association of Furniture Designers and Interior Designers.
Tools (monthly) Tabloid-format magazine in English produced by the Danish Design Council, with lively interpretations of product design worldwide.

Finland

Design in Finland (annual) Published by the Finnish Foreign Trade Association to promote the year's products abroad, with colourful, good-quality presentation of the designs and an index of manufacturers and designers.
Form & Function, Finland (quarterly) As the name suggests, a magazine concerned with mass production and functional design in Finland, aimed at the export market, published by the Finnish Society of Craft and Design.
Space & Place (annual) Contract furniture collections presented by the Furniture Exporters' Association.

France

L'Atelier (monthly) Specializes in objects, gadgets and daring designs.
BAT (monthly) Excellent coverage of design and advertising in fields as diverse as graphic design, video and interiors.
Cent Idées (monthly) DIY fashion and furnishings home-interest magazine with a centre section of cut-out patterns and templates for the ideas featured.
Crée (monthly) Leading professional design magazine with an architectural background.
Décoration Internationale (monthly, but erratic) Eclectic publication in its ninth year, covering houses, objects and painters in exotic locations. Initially directed by the Alchimia group.
Intramuros (monthly) Large-format black-and-white design and interiors magazine with in-depth interviews with people ahead of the pack. Technical information, freshly presented, is aimed at professionals, but the layout makes it generally appealing.
La Maison de Marie-Claire (monthly) *Le style français* in a glossy magazine in which everything from plates to pastries is chic.
Maison Française (monthly) Covers furniture, interiors and architecture with special regional bias and promotional features.
Vogue Décoration (monthly) Weighty and opulent interiors magazine aimed at the Cartier end of the market, with beautiful presentation and in-depth interviews.

Italy

Abitare (monthly) English text published alongside the Italian in a heavily merchandized, up-to-the-minute round-up of new designs. Architects and interior designers look to its photographic stories for an international perspective. Some issues are devoted to a single country.
L'Arca (monthly) Recently launched publication, dedicated to architecture, design and visual communication, with technical monographs.
Casa Vogue (monthly) Definitive listing of new trends-in-the-making around the world in interiors, decoration, houses and furniture. An invaluable talent-spotters' magazine, famous for the inspired art direction of its merchandizing stories.
Design International Review (bi-monthly) The theory and the practice of graphic and industrial design. A magnificent publication produced in Bergamo, it proves that Italy does not begin and end in Milan.
Disegno (quarterly) Technical, covering the tools, instruments and software needed for graphic and industrial design.
Domus (monthly) Giò Ponti founded this authoritative magazine on architecture, interiors, furniture and art; now Mario Bellini is its outspoken, informed editor. More textual than visual, it is consulted by architects and designers who submit schemes.
Eualpino (bi-monthly) Mainly covering architecture, but included here because it is excellently printed on fine paper.
Gap Casa (monthly) Trade figures and commercial marketing strategies sit alongside the product lines in this stylish magazine aimed at retailers.
Gran Bazaar (monthly) Environmental topics and architecture in a fairly specialized formula, with monographs on general and philosophical themes, treated from the point of view of design, image or art. Interesting; a little irregular.
Interni (monthly) More than its name suggests, a round-up of products relating to external, as well as interior, design. Has interesting supplements, catalogues of addresses and international editions.
Modo (monthly) Articles and opinions on design in depth, with a directory of products and producers, created by the omnipresent Alessandro Mendini. Regarded as *the* magazine of the avant garde in Italian design.
Ottagono (quarterly) A review of architecture, interior design, furniture and industrial design worldwide, published in Italian and English editions by eight Italian manufacturers – Arflex, Artemide, Bernini, Boffi, Cassina, Flos, ICF and Tecno. Leading design and architectural writers contribute to this small-format publication.

Japan

Axis (quarterly) A high-quality round-up of furniture and product design from around the world, with special interest in Italy.
Brutus (monthly) A consumer magazine with informed, international coverage of design and interiors.
FP: Fusion Planning (bi-monthly) Surely one of the most complete publications, with the freshest worldwide information and excellent quality of printing. Text in Japanese only.
GA: Global Architecture Definitive photographic essays on high-quality paper, edited by Yukio Futagawa to be the *National Geographic* of architecture.
Icon (monthly) An iconoclastic view of architecture, design, interiors and art.
W.IN.D (quarterly) New Japanese publication dedicated to interesting and evocative interiors – shops, places, restaurants and spaces from around the world, with good coverage of Europe.

Mexico

Magenta (quarterly) Produced by a private foundation to promote design, this is proof of the need for private initiative.

The Netherlands

Avenue (monthly) Stylish photo-reportage of cars, products, travel, lighting and furniture alongside avant-garde fashion.
Industrieel Ontwerpen (bi-monthly) Eminently technical and professional publication covering industrial design and product development.

New Zealand

New Zealand Home Journal (monthly) A home-interest magazine with interior design coverage.

Norway

Hus og Hem (quarterly) A consumer magazine on decoration and interiors.
Skala (monthly) Architecture and design from around the world.

Spain

Ardi (bi-monthly) Brilliantly art-directed publication introduces the best Spanish designers, architects, cartoonists and graphic artists to the world, alongside special reports on the international avant garde.
Artics Multilingual publication on the arts, with strong graphics. The last issue is scheduled for December 1989.
La Casa 16 de Marie Claire (monthly) Quality Spanish edition of the French magazine, edited by Group 16.
Hogares (monthly) "Homes" is published in colour with photographic spreads on Spanish houses and interviews with Spanish designers.
De Diseño (monthly) Brainchild of Quim Larrea and Juli Capella, currently directors of *Ardi*. After a rigorous, risk-taking start, it later changed direction.
Futura (bi-annual) Covers art and design and is excellently printed in northern Spain.
I La Nave Va (fortnightly) Internationally published booklet in which the well-known Valencia group La Nave puts forth its latest multidisciplinary ideas. Private circulation only.
Nuevo Estilo (monthly) Major publication on design and furniture, aimed at a wide public; neither tendentious nor avant-garde, but the editing is exemplary.
ON Diseño (monthly) Pioneer in design, with articles on home-grown talent, with an international round-up of graphics and architecture.

Sweden

Arkitekten (monthly) A small, in-house official publication for the Federation of Architects and allied building trades in Sweden.

Arkitektur (monthly) A round-up of architects' building projects in Sweden, with plans and pictures.

Form (eight issues a year) The professional magazine for interior designers. Text in Swedish and English.

Kontur (monthly) Surveys industrial design with product information for the contract market.

Möbler & Miljö (ten issues a year) This specialist magazine, "Furniture & Environment," is read by the decision-makers who buy and make furnishings for interior designers.

Sköna Hem (six issues a year) Sweden's showcase home-interest magazine with colourful photographic coverage of architecture and interior design.

Switzerland

Werk, Bauen and Wohnen Austere, sober publication on architecture and industrial design.

UK

Architects' Journal (weekly) The professional, opinionated and sometimes controversial magazine for British architects.

Architectural Review (monthly) A well-written and informed magazine which examines projects, with plans, worldwide.

Art and Design (monthly) Art, architecture, design, fashion, music, photography, news.

Blueprint (monthly) Fast-forward into what's being planned, built, assembled, launched or revived. Racy layouts in a large format, mostly black-and-white, with informed, hard-hitting comment.

Creative Review (monthly) Well-presented review of mainly graphic design, whether applied to computers, textiles or advertising.

Design (monthly) The official publication of the British Design Council, parochial and sometimes carpingly critical.

Design Week (weekly) Energetic design publication, highly agile in image and content with news and views on the industry.

Designers' Journal (monthly) The enlightened companion to the *Architects' Journal*, aimed at a predominantly contract market with interviews covering all aspects of design from the theatre to products.

Homes & Gardens (monthly) The home-interest magazine equivalent to the high-street design shop, seen as inspirational by those who buy it.

House & Garden (monthly) Condé Nast's biggest-selling design and decoration magazine in the UK. Although the emphasis of the editorial is on interior decoration, the design and architectural information is strongly merchandized and it sponsors the annual competition, "The New Designers."

World of Interiors (monthly) *The* interiors magazine to be seen in, offering a voyeuristic tour around some of the world's most lavishly decorated homes, with international gallery listings that are wide-ranging and talent-spotting.

USA

Architectural Digest (bi-monthly) An authoritative celebrity round-up of the lavish homes of the rich and famous, presented in a highly successful coffee-table format.

Architectural Record (monthly) A professional and trade architectural magazine.

HG (monthly) Formerly *House and Garden USA*, with ideas on decoration, design and architecture that follow developments in fashion and the arts.

ID: Industrial Design (bi-monthly) The industrial designers' product guide, with some coverage of the design industry, graphics and fashion.

Interiors (monthly) Rigorous and professional coverage of decoration for interior designers.

Metropolis (monthly) The blueprint for *Blueprint* UK, this large-format tabloid with spirited news, views and ideas in the design world is creatively edited with a strong New York bias.

Metropolitan Home (monthly) An energetic trend-spotting magazine for the upwardly mobile, with fashions in furnishings and furniture presented by a young editorial team with a strong sense of direction. Plenty of consumer information.

Progressive Architecture (monthly) One of America's two heavyweight architectural journals, a forum for spirited debate.

West Germany

Ambiente (bi-monthly) A consumer magazine on interior design.

Architektur und Wohnen (monthly) Interviews with the architects and owners of the remarkable homes featured. It links professional and consumer interests, as well as containing exhaustively researched product reports.

Das Haus (monthly) A consumer-oriented, mid-market glossy magazine on interiors.

Häuser (six issues a year) House case-histories, architectural portraits, design product round-ups and extensive floor plans. There is an English-language supplement.

MD Möbel Interior Design (monthly) Modest (black-and-white only), interesting publication on furniture, with bold graphic covers in the Bauhaus tradition.

Schöner Wohnen (monthly) The world of architecture and design in Germany, with reports from correspondents in all other major countries. Popular, informative and technical.

Select (quarterly) A photographic catalogue full of suggestive images, with special issues occasionally dedicated to particular cities.

Wolkenkratzer Art Journal (bi-monthly) Contemporary art, design, image, architecture and music.

INDEX